Childhood and Colonial Modernity in Egypt

Palgrave Studies in the History of Childhood

Series Editors: **George Rousseau**, University of Oxford, **Lawrence Brockliss**, University of Oxford

Palgrave Studies in the History of Childhood is the first series of its kind to historicize childhood in the English-speaking world; at present no historical series on children/childhood exists, despite burgeoning areas within Child Studies. The series aims to act as both a forum for publishing works in the history of childhood and a mechanism for consolidating the identity and attraction of the new discipline.

Editorial Board: **Jo Boyden**, University of Oxford, **Matthew Grenby**, Newcastle University, **Heather Montgomery**, Open University, **Nicholas Orme**, Exeter University, **Lyndal Roper**, University of Oxford, **Sally Shuttleworth**, University of Oxford, **Lindsay Smith**, Sussex University, **Nando Sigona**, Birmingham University

Titles include:

Heather Ellis (*editor*)
JUVENILE DELINQUENCY AND THE LIMITS OF WESTERN INFLUENCE, 1850–2000

Hilary Marland
HEALTH AND GIRLHOOD IN BRITAIN, 1874–1920

Heidi Morrison
CHILDHOOD AND COLONIAL MODERNITY IN EGYPT

George Rousseau
CHILDREN AND SEXUALITY
From the Greeks to the Great War

Lucy Underwood
CHILDHOOD AND RELIGIOUS DISSENT IN POST-REFORMATION ENGLAND

Stephen Wagg and Jane Pilcher (*editors*)
THATCHER'S GRANDCHILDREN
Politics and Childhood in the Twenty-First Century

Palgrave Studies in the History of Childhood
Series Standing Order ISBN 978–1–137–30555–8 (Hardback)
(*outside North America only*)

You can receive future titles in this series as they are published by placing a standing order. Please contact your bookseller or, in case of difficulty, write to us at the address below with your name and address, the title of the series and the ISBNs quoted above.

Customer Services Department, Macmillan Distribution Ltd, Houndmills, Basingstoke, Hampshire RG21 6XS, England

Childhood and Colonial Modernity in Egypt

Heidi Morrison
Assistant Professor, University of Wisconsin, La Crosse, USA

palgrave
macmillan

First published 2015 by
PALGRAVE MACMILLAN

Palgrave Macmillan in the UK is an imprint of Macmillan Publishers Limited,
registered in England, company number 785998, of Houndmills, Basingstoke,
Hampshire RG21 6XS.

Palgrave Macmillan in the US is a division of St Martin's Press LLC,
175 Fifth Avenue, New York, NY 10010.

Palgrave Macmillan is the global academic imprint of the above companies
and has companies and representatives throughout the world.

Palgrave® and Macmillan® are registered trademarks in the United States,
the United Kingdom, Europe and other countries.

ISBN 978–1–137–43277–3

This book is printed on paper suitable for recycling and made from fully
managed and sustained forest sources. Logging, pulping and manufacturing
processes are expected to conform to the environmental regulations of the
country of origin.

A catalogue record for this book is available from the British Library.

A catalog record for this book is available from the Library of Congress.

For my mom and dad

Contents

List of Figures   viii

Acknowledgments   ix

Note on Transliteration and Translation   xii

Introduction   1

1 Reforming Childhood in the Context of Colonialism   23

2 Nation-Building and the Redefinition of the Child   43

3 Child-Rearing and Class   62

4 Girls and the Building of Modern Egypt   85

5 Constructing National Identity through
   Autobiographical Memory of Childhood   99

Conclusion   123

Glossary   128

Notes   129

Bibliography   156

Index   173

Figures

1.1   Studio portrait   23

2.1   Photo spread of a children's contest   43

2.2   Performing first aid on a child at summer camp   52

2.3   "Student working with his friend in the carpentry workshop after school"   55

2.4   "A pupil incites his compatriots to work for the service of the nation"   55

2.5   "Boy in western suit thanking his father in traditional attire"   57

2.6   "Intelligent, nice boy George Harmoush in Arab dress"   58

3.1   *Baba Sadiq* children's magazine *From right to left*: Ahmad Samir, Hanefa Muhammad Fatha, and Nabil Wahabe.   62

3.2   "Boy and his ball with which he plays"   73

3.3   "Children listening to the sound from the speaker"   74

3.4   "A young boy using a typewriter"   75

3.5   "Child having fun driving his car"   75

3.6   "Lecture about proper children's clothing held at the Centre for Childrearing"   82

3.7   Poem, "The Peasant's Anthem"   83

4.1   "A girl reviews her agenda and checks the time on her wristwatch. With his right hand, her brother points to the watch in his left hand"   85

5.1   "All the women are in the great factory [the kitchen]! Oh, dear God, am I in a room or in a tomb? These hard days have put me in a difficult position!"   99

Acknowledgments

This book would not have been possible without the assistance of numerous people. First and foremost, I would like to thank Nancy Gallagher for her unwavering dedication as my mentor. From my earliest days as a graduate student at the University of California, Santa Barbara (UCSB) and until now as a professor, she guides me with integrity, intelligence, and kindness. This book is also due in large part to the faculty at UCSB's Center for Middle East Studies (CMES), notably Stephen Humphreys, Dwight Reynolds, and Juan and Magda Campo. While serving as the Assistant Director of UCSB's CMES and long thereafter, Garay Menicucci assisted me in writing this book with his undying enthusiasm, knowledge, and friendship. I am also very thankful for Richard Falk and Leila Rupp for serving on my dissertation committee.

I benefited from several generous funding sources that allowed me to conduct the research and writing for the dissertation, which serves as the basis of this book. I would like to thank the following funding sources: Foreign Language and Area Studies (FLAS), Center for Arabic Studies Abroad (CASA), CASA II, Fulbright-Hayes, UCSB Department of History travel grant and graduate fee fellowship, UCSB CMES travel grant, UCSB graduate division dissertation grant, and the UCSB Stephen Hay award. The following funding sources at the University of Wisconsin, La Crosse (UWL) contributed to the transformation of my dissertation into a manuscript: UWL Faculty Research Grant, UWL International Development Fund, UWL College of Liberal Studies (CLS) Small Grants Award, and UWL history department travel fund. I would like to thank the organizers of the following conferences for the opportunity to receive valuable feedback on versions of my dissertation and manuscript: Global History of Child Labor (Social History Institute, Amsterdam, the Netherlands), Photographic Proofs (Yale, New Haven, CT), Middle East Studies Association (Boston, Massachusetts and Washington, DC), The Political Child: Children, Education, and the State (University of Helsinki, Finland), European Social

Science History Conference (Ghent, Belgium), Childhood in the Middle East History Workshop (British Institute, Ankara, Turkey), and Children and the British Empire (King's College, London, England).

Along the way, I have amassed a debt to a number of scholars and friends. My warm thanks go to Susan Miller, Kyriaki Papageorgiou, Kaveh Niazi, Laurel Suter, Sylvia Ducharme, Ebtisam Orabi, Harvest Bellante, Noha Elsharkawy, Carmen Vladila, Walid Asfour, Patricia Desmond, Khaled El-Ayat, Ramadan Hassan Abd El-Baset, Omayma Mostafa Aboud, Mohammad Moad, Lisa Pollard, Liat Kozma, and Diane Belle James. This book could not have been written without the invaluable help of Hussein Hammouda who always went above and beyond the call of duty. I am appreciative of all my Arabic professors over the years, as well as my own students who have motivated me along the way. I received critical feedback from the anonymous outside readers of my manuscript as well as the History Authors Working Group (HAWG) at UWL. I thank the members of the UWL History Department for their support, as well as the UWL Dean's office. The Institute of Childhood Studies at Ain Shams University, the Political Science Department at Cairo University, the Arabic Literature Department at Cairo University, and the Arab Image Foundation provided valuable help. Laurence Brockliss and the staff at Palgrave, notably Jenny McCall, believed in this project. I would also like to thank Pam Bruns, Judy Hein, Vicki Riskin, and Bonnie Wallace for planting the seeds of international travel and writing in me at a young age. Without Miranda, none of this would have been possible.

As a high school student, I spent a summer in Egypt with the widow of the esteemed late Middle East historian Malcolm Kerr. During the tumultuous Lebanese civil war of the 1980s, Malcolm was president of the American University of Beirut. Islamic extremists assassinated him in his office, leaving behind his wife Ann and four children. Ann did not let the unjust and untimely loss of her husband blind her to seeing that the killers did not represent the majority of the Middle East. Ann brought high school students to the Middle East to educate about the region, in hopes of building better US–Arab relations. The catastrophic death of Malcolm set me on the path to becoming a professor of modern Middle East history. My hope for this book is to play a small part in continuing the legacy of Ann and

Malcolm's breadth of humanity. This book is, in part, dedicated to the children of Egypt: past, present, and future.

This book came to fruition because of the constant love of my family, most particularly Shannon Morrison, Michael Mulick, Abraham Morrison, Sharon Morrison, and John Morrison. Finally, a special thanks to Danh Nguyen, my loving partner in life.

Note on Transliteration and Translation

For the Arabic transliterations, I have followed the system used by the *International Journal of Middle East Studies*. The Glossary at the end of the book lists some important Arabic words used in this book. The translations are all mine, unless otherwise noted.

Introduction

At the end of the summer of 1920, seven-year-old Egyptian ʿAʾisha returned to her hometown of Dumyat to find her childhood turned upside down. While she and her family had been visiting relatives in the countryside, underwater demons had eaten her girlfriends back home. At least that is what ʿAʾisha initially thought had happened to her playmates when she did not see them one afternoon at their usual meeting place on the bank of the Nile. ʿAʾisha's thinking was in line with Egyptian lore, which attributed much of the unknown to invisible good and bad spirits.[1] Inquiring around the neighborhood, she discovered that the girls were in reality safe and sound, sitting in rows of chairs indoors, wearing uniforms and reading books. Excited to join them in their new endeavor, ʿAʾisha ran home to ask permission from her father. He informed ʿAʾisha that these girls had indeed been consumed by a demon: the new government-run school.

ʿAʾisha's father, a religious scholar, said that no daughter of his would study anywhere except in the home. "The school corrupts," he declared, commenting on the new government-sponsored, secular schools that were popping up in Egypt alongside the longstanding religious schools.[2] He ordered ʿAʾisha to read a verse from the Qurʾan about the Prophet's wives. She wanted to retaliate against her father's conservative interpretation of the Qurʾanic verse, but remained silent out of fear. For the next few months, ʿAʾisha watched longingly through the window of her house as the schoolgirls in her neighborhood passed by every day.

Were it not for ʿAʾisha's mother approaching her own father about the matter, her daughter might never have gone to school. The maternal grandfather, who was also a religious scholar, made a deal with his son-in-law to let ʿAʾisha go to school on condition that she also continued her religious studies at home and that she stopped attending at 13 years of age. ʿAʾisha's father agreed.

When ʿAʾisha reached 13, she wanted to continue her schooling, but there was no high school in her area. Her mother snuck her out of town to take a placement test, and sold her own gold bracelets to buy ʿAʾisha a ticket for a school in Cairo, but ʿAʾisha's father covertly sabotaged the process by making sure there was no spot for his daughter in the school when she arrived there. Eventually, ʿAʾisha returned to Dumyat to appease her father, and studied on her own at home. ʿAʾisha ʿAbd al-Rahman, known today in Egypt as Bint al-Shatiʾ (Girl of the Shore), held various academic posts and wrote on religion and women's rights until her passing in 1999.

One afternoon, at seven years of age, ʿAbd al-Rahman suddenly found herself at the center of different expectations about how she should spend her childhood. ʿAbd al-Rahman's father thought that home, religion, and family could provide the best upbringing for her, whereas government leaders favored the new schools. Within ʿAbd al-Rahman's family, there were also different ideas about her future. The tug of war that ensued was similar to that experienced by many other children, boys and girls, across Egypt at the time. Girls customarily spent their childhood at home doing chores and learning homemaking skills. Daughters of the economic elite or daughters whose fathers were religious clergy (such as ʿAbd al-Rahman) received a basic religious education from a private tutor. Even though government primary schools for girls had operated in a limited number since 1873, the idea was still foreign to most Egyptian families in the early twentieth century. Many boys at the time also found their childhood disrupted by the new prospect of attending government schools: primary schools for them had operated in a limited number since 1837. Parents weighed the options of sending their sons to these schools or continuing the customary routine of attending religious schools and working the land.

The late nineteenth and early twentieth centuries were a pivotal period in Egyptian history. The country was searching for an identity in the face of intensifying western imperialism, the emerging nation-state, changing gender roles, and a rising middle class. In the context of colonialism, Egypt's encounter with these forces of modernity resulted in new experiences for children. Attending secular school was one of these, and also important were changing children's pedagogy, relations with parents, and expectations for the future. The late nineteenth and early twentieth centuries were a time of ferment for childhoods all over the globe owing to the forces of modernization. This book explores how, in the context of colonialism, changes in constructions of childhood occurred in Egypt, thanks to the ongoing modernization process. The existing narrative on Middle Eastern childhood history, which is expressed tentatively in the form of Elizabeth Fernea's multidisciplinary edited volume *Remembering Childhood in the Middle East* (2002), claims that reactions to modernization and colonialism only served to reinforce traditions related to child-rearing, such as the protection of girls.[3] However, this is not the full story. As the example of ʿAbd al-Rahman shows, family dynamics were not static during this period.

The process of modernization in Egypt dates to Napoleon's arrival in the country in 1798, when Egypt became the first province of the Ottoman Empire to be occupied by a western power. Napoleon sought to disrupt British trade with India, as well as to found an empire that revived the ancient Greek world. He capitalized on the power vacuum caused by tensions between Egypt's ruling Mameluke dynasty and the Ottoman sultanate in Istanbul. Easily taking Cairo with the aid of gunpowder, Napoleon presented himself as a friend of the Muslims, coming to deliver Egypt from the Ottomans and the Mamelukes.

Napoleon's adventure in Egypt only lasted until 1801, but it was important in that it led to the emergence of the Muhammad ʿAli dynasty that ruled the country until 1952. Muhammad ʿAli was an Ottoman commander from Albania who took advantage of the turmoil in Egypt to establish a monarchy. He had ambitions to run the entire Ottoman Empire himself, and turned Egypt into a large state-owned farm in which all crops had to be sold to his government at fixed prices. Feeling threatened by ʿAli, the Ottomans asked the British for support in exchange for adopting a free-trade treaty (the Treaty of Balta Limani of 1838) that gave Britain tariff privileges and the right to sell anything in the Ottoman Empire. This treaty would later prove to set the stage for British colonial dominance in the region. ʿAli established the basis of the modern Egyptian state by initiating several agricultural, economic, educational, military, bureaucratic, and social reform projects. His goal was to found a European-style state, and to this end he sent missions of promising Egyptians to Europe to learn the latest innovations and governance methods, while he had the peasantry conscripted into military and labor service.

After ʿAli's death, his grandson ʿAbbas ruled from 1848 to 1854, effectively closing the region off to the West during his rule. ʿAli's fourth son Saʿid ruled from 1854 to 1863, borrowing large sums of money from European banks to finance modernization projects, particularly infrastructure. Saʿid granted a concession to a French engineer to construct the Suez Canal, the terms of which were highly unfavorable for Egypt. When Ismaʿil took to the throne in 1863, he opened the canal with an opulent ceremony. Ismaʿil, who ruled from 1863 to 1879, continued the modernization projects, funding them with loans from the West that ultimately led to a declaration of bankruptcy. The British deposed him, placing his son Tawfiq on the throne in 1879. He assumed full sovereignty in 1882 after defeating the proto-nationalist Urabi Revolt. Egypt technically remained under Ottoman sovereignty and was governed by ʿAli's descendants, but Britain controlled its military, economic, and governmental structures, declaring it an official protectorate in 1914. In 1919, the political leader Saʿd Zaghlul led Egyptians in massive anti-colonial demonstrations against the British. Egypt gained nominal independence in 1922, which resulted in a constitution but also the continuation of Britain's indirect rule through the monarchy. The new prime minister had limited authority and the British retained control of the Suez Canal and Egypt's external defense. The 1936 Anglo-Egyptian Treaty changed the relationship to a 20-year military alliance, although full independence and the end of the ʿAli dynasty did not occur until 1952, when the Free Officers' Movement, led in part by Gamal ʿAbd al-Nasser, took control of the country.

Historians have shown that the process of making modern Egypt was not just one of throwing off the occupiers and awakening as a nation-state. The process required control over many segments of the population: peasants to build the army and cultivate the land (Fahmy 2002; Gasper 2009); mothers to raise future citizens (Pollard 2005); middle-class (*effendi*) men to strengthen national honor (Jacob 2011); and the poor, around whose needs politicians vied for power (Ener 2003). Children were also increasingly controlled and turned into subjects in the modernization process. As part of the increasing state control over the people, ensuring the well-being of children was recast as a responsibility of government and elites. Adults in distant cities began to play a significant role in decisions that affected children, although they were unrelated to them. This was a change from the situation whereby family and community had served as the sole caretakers of children. Tangible manifestations of the professionalization of child-rearing occurred in the establishment of new institutions for children, such as government-run schools, as well as children's literature and health and welfare campaigns. In 1923, a year after Egypt was transformed from a protectorate into a semi-autonomous state, nationalist reformers saw to it that elementary education became compulsory for all Egyptian children, even though very few actually attended school.[4] In 1920, there were 70,000 pupils in the country's 700 elementary schools, whereas by 1948 there were a million attending 5000 such schools.[5] Reformers created new ways to communicate with children, through standardized school curriculums, a children's press, and so on, so that nationalist ideas, class identities, and gender roles that were essential aspects of making Egypt's modernity could be passed on.

Additionally, nationalist reformers relied on representations of childhood to advance their visions for Egypt, to mobilize and emotionally manipulate adults to suit political agendas, and to legitimize nationalist narratives. Photographs in children's magazines, for example, showed children mastering new western technology, such as the telescope, even though in reality most Egyptian children did not even attend school. Representation is a disciplinary act because one person is speaking for another. The photographs embodied the characteristics that reformers wanted Egyptian children, and by extension Egypt, to embody. The fact that the reality of children's lives was usually very different from the representation further illuminates the visionary aspect of the photographs. Representations of childhood also appeared in autobiographies of childhood. Egyptian authors encoded social critiques in a palpable manner by articulating them through the innocent voice of the child. ʿAbd al-Rahman's autobiography, for example, is not just a testimony of her life, but also a contemporary plea to reform girls' education. Controlling representations of the child in Egypt's past was a way of envisioning the country's present and future.

Existing historical narratives about Egypt's encounter with modernity generally do not acknowledge that the encounter created new social knowledge about childhood. From the start of the nineteenth century, however, changes in childhood began to take place. Muhammad ʿAli sent missions to Europe to learn customs and habits (including those relating to offspring, marriage, games, and sports) that could be transmitted to Egyptian domiciles in the hope of modernizing the masses.[6] Changes for children intensified at the turn of the twentieth century owing to Egypt's encounter with western modernity in the context of a British occupation. Egyptian intellectuals, reformers, and nationalists sought to modernize the country and to end the occupation by making Egyptian children competitive with their European counterparts at social, political, and economic levels. As symbols of the next generation, children were a means for social change. The elite reconfigured notions of childhood in order to produce and reproduce new class identities, gender norms, and state apparatus (autonomous from the British). Reconfiguring childhood was a common phenomenon among states throughout the Middle East and the world in the early twentieth century, and the dynamics of this for Egypt are examined here.

Viewing early twentieth-century Egyptian history through the lens of childhood reveals new conceptions of childhood that impacted the country's institutions and family dynamics. It also reveals that modernity cannot be associated with linear progress and development, nor a direct embodiment of western ideals. Discourses about childhood were a microcosm of larger forces underway in Egypt at the time. While new opportunities emerged for some upper-class Egyptian children, most children saw no change at all, created hybrid identities (combining the new and the old), or intentionally evaded change altogether. Furthermore, discourses on childhood unfolded within a primarily religious framework and in a language that embraced Egyptian heritage. Changes for children were often couched in terms of a lineage of *adab* (culture, good manners), a literary genre dating to the ninth century that focused on norms of conduct, such as building children's moral character. A new cultural conception of childhood emerged for some children in Egypt during the first half of the twentieth century. This had a synergistic relationship with the process of modernization. Modernization cannot be separated from the reconceptualization of categories of age.

Approaching the past through children and childhood

Telling the story of childhood is not just about inserting children into the historical narrative. A comparison with the study of gender history is useful. Some of the first historical narratives for Egypt that included gender consisted of bibliographical inserts about important women. Gradually scholars began to discuss how women impact and are impacted by historical forces.[7] Children should not be tagged onto historical narratives as an addendum, but instead discussed in the context of existing questions about the past. Filling this lacuna in Egypt's historical narrative starts with valuing childhood as a category of historical analysis.

In the last few decades, the history of childhood in western societies has blossomed as a field of study. This body of work, combined with a growing number of works on non-western regions, evidences the scope of contributions that childhood can make to historical awareness. French historian Philippe Ariès opened the door to studying the history of childhood in the 1960s. He claimed that the concept of childhood in medieval Europe did not exist because artwork either left children out or depicted them as small-scale adults.[8] He said that western society did not begin to "discover" childhood until the end of the sixteenth century. Scholars continue to debate the ideas in Ariès' book, with many labeling it as a present-centered form of history. Shulamith Shahar argues that Ariès did not see a form of childhood in the past that looked like the one he knew, and so he assumed it was nonexistent.[9] She says that the general absence of children from medieval art meant that conceptions of parental roles and attitudes toward children differed from those prevailing in contemporary western society; and claims that no society can exist without a process of socializing its young, which requires childhood to be viewed as a distinct period in human development separate from adulthood. Valuing a child's special physical and mental needs ensures the group's survival. Colin Heywood notes that Ariès did not see childhood as a social construct: "Most people assume that their ideas and practices concerning childhood are 'natural' and are shocked to discover that other societies diverge from them."[10] Scholars today generally agree that the concept of childhood did exist in the Middle Ages, but that it was radically different than the one which would come to prominence later in the West. James A. Schultz, for example, finds that in the German High Middle Ages adults did not think that their treatment of children affected children's outcome as eventual adults, but that childhood was important because it could reveal to a discerning eye the traits in the child that would remain with him/her as an adult. Although Ariès' ideas are contested, he provoked historians in the 1970s and 1980s to start thinking about the role of childhood in the past, and scholars of various disciplines continue to feel his significance.

The growth in studying the history of childhood over the last few decades relates to many changes in societal attitudes. Postmodernism's emphasis on viewing social phenomena in a matrix of domination led scholars to see not just race, class, and gender as developing in a social context, but age as well. Childhood is more than a chronological marker based on biological maturity. Even though all adults have lived through childhood, making it a universal experience, the particularities of how a person experiences childhood depend on the time and space in which he/she lives. As such, childhood is a cultural system that is historically conditioned. Discourses on childhood reverberate with discourses about mortality, life expectancy, organization of family life, kinship patterns, different ideologies of care, and philosophies of need and dependency.[11] The variations in meanings of childhood reflect the social, political, economic, and cultural priorities of an era. Since adults associate children with the future of society and children are an emotionally resonant site, discourse about them sometimes relates to topics that seem to have little connection with children themselves. Paula Fass finds, for instance, that the excessive attention American twentieth-century media gave to kidnapping reflects larger societal concerns with institutions such as the police.[12] Nara Milanich shows that late nineteenth- and early twentieth-century Chilean state attitudes toward illegitimate children helped reproduce restrictive class distinctions.[13] Children are always in the crossfire of forces that shape history.

The feminist movement also influenced development of the history of childhood. As doors opened to viewing women as active agents in history, conventional historiographical favor for the "great men of history" decreased. Initially youth were much more likely than children to be the focus of historical studies based on age because of their tendency to engage in visible political movements.

With the trend to view history from the bottom up, scholars realized that children's everyday ordinariness wrongly disguises their importance. Despite the economic helplessness that generally places children in a position of subordination to adults, they are active historical agents. For example, in a collection of essays on young women in Europe, the editors of *Secret Gardens, Satanic Mills* argue that including children, particularly girls, in historical narratives on Europe means rethinking our understanding of agency (Maynes, Soland, and Benninghaus 2005). Actors in the margins of power often silently reshape society. Bourgeois girls' consumption and leisure practices are just one instance of how young women were significant in the emergence of European modernity. Further, Jane Humphries looks at over 600 autobiographies of working-class children to argue that without children's participation the industrial revolution might not have unfolded in Britain as it did.[14] The feminist movement helped bring attention to the idea that children are not a trivial matter, but constitute a category worthy of scholarly analysis.

The growth in study of the history of childhood over the last few decades evidences a changing attitude toward the worth of the child in society. There has also been a shift away from a worldview that places the adult at the center of human experience.[15] Chris Jenks claims that the world has generally regarded the adult as mature, rational, and competent while the child in juxtaposition is less than fully human, unfinished, and incomplete.[16] The societal tendency has been to view childhood as a prelude to adulthood, or a period of transition when the being moves from a nobody to a somebody. It has largely been assumed that children are born in a world that traps them into a subordinate position because of their presumed incomplete mental capabilities.

Questioning an adult-centric vision of the world means not viewing adulthood as the sole purpose of being born. It also means considering children as subjects themselves and therefore with their own conscious and awareness.[17] The idea that children can think for themselves and that children matter because they are alive (and not because of the adult they will become) formally dates to the 1989 Convention on the Rights of the Child's (CRC) provision that children are the subject of rights (and not objects of concern). Also relatively recent, and indicative of changing adult attitudes toward the worth of a child, is the CRC's recognition that children can engage in making decisions that impact them. Since 1989, many historians have come to think that children merit a story of their own because they are makers of history in their own right. Catriona Kelly, for instance, looks at mid-twentieth-century Soviet nationalists' efforts to manage society and create new citizens by managing children's reading and the books geared at them.[18] She finds that children's individual reactions to books opposed monopolizing political forces.

The field of the history of childhood is still coming of age, but its infancy is even more pronounced in the Middle East than in the West. There are challenges to writing the history of childhood that are specific to non-western regions of the world. The study area came into being in the 1970s, in the early days of post-colonialism, when historians of many non-western regions were less concerned with seemingly minor actors, such as children, and more with major forces that caused their regions to be "underdeveloped" according to modernization theory. Additionally, the field of the history of childhood developed within a western narrative of modernization.[19] Historians of childhood in the West are traditionally concerned with how childhood appeared within their own modernity, which is not a universal fit for childhoods everywhere. Lastly, stereotypes that only associate non-western childhoods with immediate crises of war, famine, and disease can sidetrack research agendas from exploring dynamic pasts and rich heritages.

There is no existing monograph dedicated solely to childhood in modern Middle East history. Avner Gil'adi's pioneering work (1992) focuses on conceptions of childhood in the early Islamic and medieval periods.[20] However, there is work on the late Ottoman empire and modern era that addresses topics related to children, such as education, orphans, domesticity, and parenting. For example, Benjamin Fortna writes about state-led initiatives to modernize the late Ottoman Empire population by infusing imported western educational systems with moral content appropriate to the Islamic–Ottoman context.[21] Scholars such as Lisa Pollard (2005), Taylor Long (2011), Omnia El Shakry (1998), Kathryn Libal (2002), and Nancy Stockdale (2010) write that controlling parenting practices, reforming households, and teaching domesticity were political acts for missionaries, nationalists, and colonial administrators in such regions as Turkey, Iran, Palestine, Lebanon, and Egypt.[22] Works such as these evidence that children, despite their legacy of illiteracy, are omnipresent in most of the same types of documents, creative works, and material culture that are used for studying any aspect of Middle East history. The crucial point is to notice children, as childhood is a fruitful new vantage point from which to view Middle East history. Additionally, historians of western childhoods are increasingly interested in hearing about global contexts, calling the imbalance "frustrating," for example.[23] Although a focus on the history of Middle Eastern children comes late in the day, it can provide interesting and useful insights into historical processes and transformations.

This book examines late nineteenth- and early twentieth-century Egyptian experiences and representations of childhood by using unexplored Arabic sources such as the children's press and literature; as well as more familiar Arabic sources, such as autobiographies and the writings of Egyptian intellectuals, whose discussion of childhood has so far been untouched. These sources indicate the ways in which the literate classes were thinking about childhood.

Typical childhoods

Before discussing some of the changes in how literate classes thought about childhood in early twentieth-century Egypt, it is important to provide a brief summary of typical Egyptian childhoods in that era. The details are fleshed out later in the book. Typical Egyptian children's experiences with labor are laid out in Chapter 1; play, education, discipline, and decision-making appear in the first half of Chapter 3, with further details about girls in Chapter 4. Chapter 5 explores all these examples, showing that adults' recollections of childhood experiences are a form of selective self-representation. The intent of the summary here is to provide a general point of reference for discerning and gauging the types of change that Egyptian reformers, nationalists, and intellectuals sought to bring to some children. For the purposes of this study, childhood is the period beginning around the age of five and ending around the age of 15. The categories of youth and babyhood fall outside the parameters of the book.

In rural areas, adults largely believed that their sons' futures were in their immediate surroundings, either on the land or in local artisan trades. Boys usually stayed home until the age of five, when they would begin to take the donkeys to the field or the buffalo to the canal, and by the age of seven (when they were circumcised) they usually began part-time religious schooling in a *kuttāb* (traditional Qurʾanic school) and working in the fields. This is the age at which adults believed children developed ʿ*aql*, which is reason, maturity, and the ability to learn. In the *kuttāb*, children learned, to varying degrees, to memorize the Qurʾan and write in Arabic. Adults taught children in school through repetitive rote memorization exercises. The best students might go on to study Islamic law in Cairo's Al-Azhar University, but most had their schooling cut short by parents who needed their labor in the fields or in shops. The single most common feature of most Egyptian childhoods was participation in the cotton economy.[24] Peasants were locked into a life of picking and fieldwork from childhood.

Girls also stayed at home until around the age of five, when they would begin fetching water and helping their mothers with work such as cooking, cleaning, and making fuel cakes. At around the age of eight, some girls might begin work as a maid in a middle-class home; a few began part-time schooling. In 1898, an estimated 91.2 percent of males and 99.4 percent of females were illiterate.[25] People of upper-class families generally hired private tutors to come to their homes to instruct their boys, and sometimes their girls.

Most Egyptian children spent part or all of their childhoods afflicted with illness. In 1913, the Rockefeller Foundation found that 60 percent of the lower and upper Egyptian population was infected with hookworm, bilharzia, nonflaciparum malaria, and other parasitic diseases.[26] By 1940, one Egyptian professor reported that 75 percent of Egyptian people were afflicted with bilharzia, and all suffered from numerous childhood diseases; child mortality had increased 15 percent in the previous 15 years.[27]

Within the family, most children experienced tensions between harshness and love and between restriction and freedom. Adult–child relations were autocratic and adults managed children in the home through orders and obedience.[28] Parents expected children to identify less as an individual and more as a member of the family (but not as a member of the state, with which most Egyptians had relatively little contact). Physical punishment and fear of evil spirits played a key role in the discipline of children. On the other hand, children had tender and loving relationships with their families, particularly their mothers and grandparents. Generally, when children were not working or in school they spent most of their time playing freely with older siblings and mixed-age children's groups. Parents did not organize play for children, nor provide them with toys. Children, including girls up to a certain age, romped around rooftops, fields, and waterways.

Thus, adults did not throw children immediately into the world of adults as soon as they developed ʿaql, but instead gradually introduced them to work, also allocating time for school and play. Education consisted mainly of rote memorization. Obedience to family was important, and non-kin did not play a large role in childhoods. Important gender differences were established in childhood, as adults guided boys and girls into different social milieus and appointed them to different tasks.

Modernizing Egypt, transforming childhood

Similarly to people throughout history and around the globe, Egyptians have always viewed childhood as an important period of life that is different from adulthood.[29] Because childhood is a social construct, it has been in flux in Egypt, evolving with changing times.[30] However, in the late nineteenth and early twentieth centuries, changes came for some children at an accelerated speed. Remaking the category of childhood was a crucial component of Egypt's modernization process. Leading figures, such as feminist Huda Shaʿrawi, testify in their autobiographies to the transformations in conceptions and experiences of childhood during the late nineteenth and early twentieth centuries. Shaʿrawi was born in 1879 and dictated her autobiography to her secretary in the 1940s. She writes about the changes for children that she witnessed: "When I pause in front of the memories of my childhood, it becomes clear to me the big difference between the life and experiences of a child in the past and what has become the methods of upbringing in the present time."[31] The history of modern Egypt is inseparable from the history of changing ideas about childhood. (The same could be argued about other categories of age, such as adolescence, which research by Omnia El Shakry shows developed in part from a fear of youth as political insurgents in the postwar era.[32]) Intellectuals, reformers, nationalists, and elites intently discussed childhood in the late nineteenth and early twentieth centuries to shape the future nation, particularly in light of exposure to western child-rearing norms.

The main aspects of the western model of childhood at the beginning of the twentieth century were the view that children were innocent, were in need of protection from adult society by attending age-graded schools, and were important for the future of the nation. (The idea that children are important in their own right and are subjects of rights, as opposed to objects of concern, evolved later in the twentieth century.) The modern western model also involved extending the years of childhood and decreasing the number of children in families. Children changed from an object of discussion to an object of scientific observation. This model evolved from the eighteenth- and nineteenth-century Enlightenment and Romantic movements in Europe, which introduced the idea that childhood needed to be reserved for school and for the development of creativity and individuality. Enlightenment thinkers said that children were born as blank slates and open to learning. Rousseau's groundbreaking notion of original innocence claimed that the child was born pure, without adult vices, which was an idea in opposition to the traditional Christian notion that children were born sinful. The Romantics said that childhoods needed to be spent carefree, instead of suffocated by industrialization, which transformed children into factory workers. European states embraced these notions about childhood in order to produce a new generation of healthy, skilled children for the state.[33]

Egyptian nationalists, reformers, and intellectuals encountered these ideas about childhood during their travels and studies in Europe. They were attracted by the idea of redefining the country's child-rearing practices in order to strengthen the nation, as this could fuel the movement to obtain independence from British imperial rule: an educated and strong future generation of Egyptians could govern Egypt on its own. Breeding a new generation of children translated into rethinking how some children should spend their childhoods. For instance, Egyptian intellectual Muhammad ʿAbduh (1849–1905) expressed the importance reformers attached to children attending school. He wrote: "The strength of the human spirit is vested in upbringing and edification. This is similar to the earth, which does not produce results without cultivation and special tools. This is also similar to a piece of writing not existing without a pen and God."[34] Egyptian nationalists, reformers, and intellectuals sought to strengthen their country by advocating the state to increase its investment in education. The state started to interfere with the role of parents in raising children: growing up was not just for the sake of the family or home economy any more. Children were supposed to spend their time sitting in rows engaged upon activities that were structured by non-kin experts in order to learn how to be obedient citizens.

Strengthening the nation also meant changing pedagogy to be less memorization-based and more critical thinking-based. Some elites and reformers talked about children as thinking individuals who could make their own demands. For example, the fundamental Egyptian intellectual of the nineteenth century, Rifaʿa Rafiʿ al-Tahtawi (1801–1873), whose work served as a base for early twentieth-century intellectuals, argued that Egyptian children needed to be taught personal independence. This would make them more like children in Europe, Russia, and the USA, whom he said were taught this "by having nannies and being sent to boarding school so that they do not become dependent on their parents."[35]

These ideas about childhood were so new that they created conflicting notions about just how much free rein to grant to children. This conflict is captured in a fictional story published in the 1920s by Ibrahim al-Mazini, a leading figure in modern Arabic literature. The story, "*al-Saghir wa-l-kubar*" ("The Small One and the Great One"), is about a father and son who contemplate writing a book in which their roles are reversed.[36] The imaginary book would show how unfairly parents treat children, with the goal of giving more independence to children. For example, a boy playing the role of a father would not let his son (his father) go to see a movie if he ate too much chocolate. At the end of al-Mazini's story, the father decides not to write this book with his son, fearing that his son will believe the game and hence feel entitled to power. The father's final lack of consent seems to carry the message that adults should have ultimate authority. The story shows that this was a time when adults were considering new ideas about lessening adult domination over children, but that such new ideas were potentially dangerous. In the case of this story, the ideas provoked so much fear that a carnivalesque distortion of reality was required before they could even be contemplated.

In general, reformers argued that the government and trained professionals needed to play a larger role as caregivers of children in order to ensure that children reached their full potential for the nation. By 1882, Egypt was a protectorate of the British, and the urgency to liberate the country intensified elites' engagement with childhood. One children's book written by a member of the Egyptian intelligentsia tells the story of a community of monkeys whose sultan builds schools and hospitals for the smallest members. This has the intention of normalizing the role of the state: through the use of endearing characters that children can relate to, the book helps children become comfortable with the state's parental role.

Turning children into subjects, however, was not a smooth process, and Egypt experienced a convergence of old and new ideas about childhood. Autobiographies of childhood, as will be explored in Chapter 5, reveal that the modernization process was mixed with feelings of fear, humiliation, and love. Some children, for example, sought to evade new systems of control that were placed on them, for example running away in fear when city health inspectors showed up in their villages to vaccinate them. Furthermore, feelings of humiliation were widespread among children, often engendered by the British elite, who disparaged Egyptian culture in front of them. ʿAbd al-Rahman recalls, for example, that when she did not know how to use the knife and fork required in the school cafeteria, the school doctor ordered her to eat separately from the other students until she learned "the modern ways of eating."[37] At the turn of the twentieth century, children were at the point of intersection of many forces of change that were occurring in Egypt.

When children are written into the historical narrative, their vulnerability makes historians come face to face with an era's emotional communities, or "groups in which people adhere to the same norms of emotional expression and value- or devalue- the same or related emotions."[38] Historians have traditionally not taken emotions seriously. As Joanna Bourke explains, "Although fear, hate, joy, and love have always been at the heart of human experience, in the heart of historical scholarship they still tend to be regarded as byproducts."[39] The fearful trembles of small children were an inseparable part of the social historical process that made modern Egypt. As the autobiographies reveal in Chapter 5, many nationalist Egyptian reformers and intellectuals advance their political agendas as adults through memories of childhood feelings. For instance, ʿAbd al-Rahman recollects humiliating experiences with foreigners in childhood as a way of speaking back to the British empire. Further, she uses these experiences to paint a picture of herself as authentically Egyptian, and hence justified in her adulthood calls to reshape Egyptian gender norms. Modernizing Egypt was not a process under scientific control, as post-Enlightenment reasoning might conceive. Egyptian reformers and intellectuals built the Egyptian nation in part on memories of childhood sensibilities. Bourke expresses the idea that historians must take into account the issue of emotion: "Historians love to talk about rationale responses and 'moral economies' and causality – and are less comfortable with irrationality, a characteristic often given to emotions."[40] Robert Darnton says that historians seeking to understand the emotions of a people who lived centuries earlier are no different from anthropologists seeking to understand and interpret the thinking of subjects of an alien culture. "Mental undergrowth can be as impenetrable in the bush as in the library," he writes.[41] On many occasions adults strategically express through the innocent voice of the child emotions they might otherwise hesitate to lay claim to.

The model of childhood that developed in Egypt in the early twentieth century resembled aspects of the western model, but maintained its own unique qualities. Historians of childhood have a tendency to proclaim that all societies around the world have moved in the last few centuries toward the western model of childhood, as manifest in the spread of western-style education and the near unanimous global endorsement of the CRC at the close of the twentieth century. But societies around the world did not all adopt an exact duplicate of the western model.[42] Peter N. Stearns holds that non-western regions of the world developed conceptions of childhood *alongside* the modern western model.[43] Even in the West there was not universal application of this model.[44] The origins of the western model are largely to be found in the Enlightenment, Romanticism, and industrialization. The model of childhood that developed in Egypt had its roots in colonial resistance and Islamic heritage. Intellectuals and reformers grounded their calls for change in Arab, Islamic, Mediterranean, pharaonic, and/or Egyptian heritage. For example, Egyptian intellectual Muhammad ʿAbduh justified his claims for western-style education by saying that western ideas about child-rearing were Eastern in origin as the East used to be the center of the Enlightenment.[45] Egyptian reformer Hasan al-Banna presented the western childhood institution of the Boy Scouts as an institution imbued with the spirit of Islam; that is, the Prophet as the ultimate

Scout.[46] Because reforms for children were often discussed in terms
of an authentic Egyptian heritage, Egyptian reformers often situated
their discussion of childhood in *adab* literature, an indigenous corpus
of instructions on how to raise a child dating back to the Middle Ages.
This literature focused on improving children by providing them
with a moral education. Intellectuals equated the future of Egypt with
personal behavior taught in childhood. They articulated the actualization of the child's self (or, in other words, the fulfillment of the
child's potential) as a rebirth for the whole community, more so than
for the individual.

Rejection of imperialism and building a new state were not the only
factors playing a part in transforming childhood in early twentieth-
century Egypt. The emerging urban middle class (*effendiya*) embraced
new ideas about childhood as part of defining their new identity
vis-à-vis the peasant class. Becoming middle class was a strategy
and performance played out through child-rearing. Instead of spending their time working, *effendi* children were to be engaged in play
and educational activities. Middle-class children's books, poetry, and
magazines sought to outfit children in western-style attire and teach
them western technology. On the one hand, the middle class and
power-holders talked about needing to reform peasant children, but
on the other they perpetuated peasant children's subordinate position by lauding them as the backbone of society. The middle class
tried to change themselves before the peasants, and in order to establish and maintain a position of privilege, they kept peasants working
in the fields.

New roles for children were not just class-based but also gendered.
Reforms for children both liberated girls and further bound them to
the home. Girls were afforded more educational opportunities, the
goal of which was to produce better caregivers for future generations.
Whereas boys were encouraged to learn the principles of popular
sovereignty, girls were encouraged to learn handicrafts, homemaking
skills, religion, and obedience to a future husband for the sake of the
nation. Homemaking skills were class dependent and could range
from cooking to supervising servants. These gendered roles were in
line with the patriarchal structure of the region in that era.

Even though the new educational opportunities offered to girls
were gendered, they were groundbreaking for the era. In the case
of ʿAbd al-Rahman, her childhood was spent negotiating conflicting

conceptions of how she should grow up. On the one hand, she continued to be raised under the authority of her father's traditional expectation that a girl should not venture far from the home, that a child's obligations were to the family and local community, and that the best education for a child came through memorization of religious texts. Yet, on the other hand, for ʿAbd al-Rahman to take advantage of the new government schooling opportunities available to children at the start of the twentieth century, ʿAbd al-Rahman had to enter the public sphere, take exams that tracked children into professions that would serve the state, and become acquainted with unfamiliar ideas and concepts taught in school. The latter happened with the assistance of family members whose opinions on education differed from her father's. Negotiating these two realities meant in practical terms that ʿAbd al-Rahman did not attend government schools but instead had to teach herself the government school curriculum on her own at home, with books she borrowed from a new local government-funded library. When ʿAbd al-Rahman could, she showed up for nationwide placement tests that were offered in larger cities. Many girls created hybrid identities that allowed them to engage with the old and the new.

Egypt's encounter with modernity played out through its children, as reflected in the quandary that ʿAbd al-Rahman found herself in when taking a school exam. Needing to explain how a thermos flask kept water warm, ʿAbd al-Rahman asked the proctor if there was a spelling mistake in the word thermos. The only thermos that ʿAbd al-Rahman had ever known was the pickled one she ate, called *turmus* (lupini beans). When ʿAbd al-Rahman was told there was no mistake, she deduced that since people in her village put apricot seeds in water to clean it, city people put *turmus* around jugs to keep water warm. When ʿAbd al-Rahman's friend later explained to her what a thermos really was, she thought that such an innovation must be a form of magic. The thermos represented modern science, and was becoming a common household item in urban families. ʿAbd al-Rahman's ignorance of it stemmed from her disadvantaged education, and in the exam she hit the limit of her modernity.

Children were at the heart of Egypt's encounter with modernization, in the sense of being impacted by it and impacting it themselves. As a result, a distinctively different form of childhood evolved which included for a few children such characteristics as the addition of government care, encouragement of non-memorization-based learning, decrease in gender differentiation, spread of age-graded schools, more participation in decision-making processes, and protection from the harshness of the adult world of work. These characteristics remain in Egypt today and have shaped the development of the country's institutions. This book focuses on general changes in the literate classes' thinking about childhood, less so than on the concrete, institutional transformations these changes generated.

Chapters

Chapter 1 looks at the role of empire in shaping Egypt's modern model of childhood. Egyptian intellectuals resisted British occupiers' racialized taxonomies of childhood and the homogenization of Egyptian children. They called for reform in their country's child-rearing practices so that the next generation could be as strong as their occupiers, yet remain authentically Egyptian. They wanted primary education for all, the content of which differed for boys and girls. Egyptian intellectuals searched Egypt's pharaonic, Mediterranean, and Islamic heritage for echoes of modern European Enlightenment and Romantic models of childhood. They articulated a modern model of childhood in a basically religious framework. Basing reforms on both western ideas and Islamic concepts of moral character formation, intellectuals articulated a vision of the child's self as an asset for the whole community, more so than for the individual. Coptic Christian intellectuals articulated a similar vision, but in a more secular discourse.

Chapter 2 explores how childhood for some went from primarily a private family affair to a matter of concern for the state. In order to build the Egyptian nation, Egyptian intellectuals claimed that the next generation needed to learn the language, history, and geography of Egypt, as well as proper behavior. This transformation, they said, required trained professionals, such as children's literature writers and new government-run institutions, such as public schools. Building the Egyptian nation meant that the child, like the mother, began to exist less for the family unit and more for the nation. Children's survival and prosperity no longer depended exclusively on kin and local community, but also on unfamiliar persons in the state apparatus. The state built new institutions for children, putting into question the conventional notion that anti-colonial/anti-western movements primarily reinforced traditional family patterns. Similar to many countries all around the world over the last two centuries, Egypt engaged in a process of family reorganization for the supposed good of the nation.

Changes in conceptions of childhood did not stem from colonial resistance and the process of nation-building alone. There was a new class system emerging in Egypt, which is the focus of Chapter 3. The history of childhood is inseparable from the country's rising urban middle class, the *effendiya*. Becoming *effendi* was a strategy and performance for people from lower-class backgrounds who wanted to join the ranks of middle-income families. Advancing in social class meant raising western-clad children who were not educated through the age-old technique of rote memorization. *Effendi* children learned that their peers in the cotton fields were both uncivilized and the backbone of Egyptian society. The new class system created a childhood for some Egyptians that was recognizably different from that of the common child. Social classes emerged by disciplining children into various roles. Some children evaded these systems of control in their own ways.

Chapter 4 is a gendered analysis of intellectual discourse on childhood. Egypt's turn toward modernity cannot be associated with linear progress and development for children. Modern girls did not benefit from the same opportunities and freedoms as their male counterparts. Education of girls was geared at producing managers of the home, whereas education of boys was geared at producing managers of the nation. Despite being formally powerless, girls participated in the nation-building project by challenging patriarchal authority in different ways. They created hybrid identities that allowed them to maintain both family obligations and individual aspirations. Young female ingenuity must not be denied its place in history by gender historians. There is a historiographical tendency to lump mothers and offspring together in the same category (i.e. women and children), hence obfuscating the specificity of women's experiences and children's experiences.

Memory of childhood played a critical role in modernizing Egypt, and this is the subject of Chapter 5. Autobiographies of childhood are not always transparent texts; they are retrospective narratives that are mediated by selective self-representation. Autobiographies speak as much about the historical moment in which they are written as the era that they recall. Prominent Egyptian intellectuals who wrote their memoirs dozens of years after their childhood, namely in the prime or at the end of their careers, use representations of childhood to tell a story about Egypt's past and form visions for its future. Authors use the voice of the child to accentuate their authority as modern-day reformers. Autobiographies reveal that the lives of children played a significant role in shaping diverse forms of Egypt's national identity in the twentieth century. The corpus of autobiographies examined in this book reflects Egypt's diversity in class, regional, gender, and religious upbringings.

Thus, discourses on childhood and experiences of children played an integral role in modernizing Egypt. Studying childhood means studying the voices and experiences of as much as half the Egyptian population at any one particular historical moment. These voices and experiences provide a fresh look at how modernity came of age in Egypt. The changes that happened in conceptions of childhood and experiences of children speak to larger changes occurring in Egypt regarding changing roles of class, gender, and citizenship. Modernization in Egypt was inextricably linked to development and reinvention of categories of age. This book opens the door for further study not just of modernization and childhood but also of modernization and other age categories, from infant to senior.

1
Reforming Childhood in the Context of Colonialism

Figure 1.1 Studio portrait
Source: Alban, Cairo/Egypt, 1945–1950.
Collection AIF/Georges Family Mikaelian
Copyright Arab Image Foundation

A 1940s photo by one of Egypt's most important studio portraitists, Aram Alban, who went by the name of Alban,[1] depicts a father dressed in Egyptian peasant attire sitting steadfast in front of his son dressed in semi-European attire. On their heads are two different symbols: the father wears an *imama* (traditional head wrap) and the son a *tarboosh* (felt, cone-shaped hat worn by the educated upper/middle-class Egyptian elite). The father's eyes look away, the son's look to the camera. The diverted eyes of the father, in comparison to the son's, point to a tension between old and new.

The headgear on the father and son in this photo are both symbols of resistance. The father seems to represent an authentic Egyptian tradition, while the son represents the *effendi* (middle-class) child that will be discussed further in Chapter 2. Fused together father and son embody the nationalist message of early twentieth-century Egypt, a country searching for a national identity after years of British occupation. Resisting imperialism meant becoming a nation as modern as its occupiers, yet grounded in authentic, Egyptian roots. Many Egyptians saw children as a surrogate for the nation and hence represented resistance through them. In Egypt, clothing expressed tensions about European imperialism and the struggle to stay true to oneself while current with modern times.[2]

Europe developed new ideas about childhood during the nineteenth and early twentieth centuries that coincided with its growing global influence. While Europe may have exported some new ideas about childhood to its empires, this did not translate into wholesale adoption in places like Egypt. The chapter refrains from reducing the history of childhood in Egypt to a comparative one that holds the modern western standards of childhood as the model. Modernity was not a force emanating from the West and replicated by Egypt.[3] Egyptians carved out an identity that accepted, rejected, and modified various aspects of modern European ideas.

Egyptian reforms on childhood came in large part from a resistance to imperialism, specifically the colonial gaze. (Other chapters in this book explore how childhood changed, thanks to new ideas about the nation, gender, and class.) The colonial gaze sought to keep Egyptians in subordinate positions to their British rulers by denigrating Egyptian culture and deeming it inferior to western. The colonial gaze embodied aspects of the white man's burden. Ashis Nandy claims that in colonial situations, psychological domination impacts the inner life of the colonized.[4] One impact is that the colonized fight the oppression. Historians of modern Egypt, such as Lisa Pollard, Beth Baron, Omnia El Shakry, Michael Gasper, and Wilson Jacob, have studied how tensions with imperialism manifested in

Egyptian discourses on gender, sexuality, peasants, and the social sciences. However, no scholar has looked at how this tension manifested itself in Egyptian ideas about childhood.

Late nineteenth- and early twentieth-century Egyptian intellectuals' responses to western imperialism changed child-rearing in three ways. First, Egyptian justifications and motivations for reforming childhood in Egypt emerged from resistance to imperialism, which translated into Islamic heritage playing a role in shaping new ideas toward childhood. Second, Egyptian intellectuals' concern in reforming childhood focused on providing a moral education. Intellectuals equated the future of Egypt with personal behavior taught in childhood. Third, intellectuals in Egypt, unlike their contemporaries in Europe, articulated the actualization of the child's self (or, in other words, the fulfillment of the child's potential) as a rebirth for the whole community, more so than the individual.

In order to understand how some Egyptian intellectuals sought to refute the colonial gaze through discourses on child-rearing, this chapter begins by looking at the way many Europeans depicted Egyptian children in the imperial imagination. This depiction is explored through representations of the Egyptian child laborer.

Child labor in Egypt

We cannot discuss how the British imperial gaze manifests itself in ideas about child laborers without first situating that discourse in the economic and institutional framework that kept Egyptian children in exploitative conditions. Muhammad ʿAli, regarded as the founder of modern Egypt, tried decades prior to the British protectorate to turn Egypt into a state-run farm for his profit, leading some peasant families to lose their status as self-sufficient producers. Land passed to large landowners through land seizures, conscription, and heavy taxation.[5] The system of Capitulations, which contained privileges for foreign merchants under the pretext that foreign business in Egypt was in the country's best interest, also helped to ensure that peasant children remained locked in their spot as laborers in the global market. The cotton produced in Egypt fed the factories of the industrial revolution in Europe. Historians of childhood in the West argue that children in Europe reinvigorated modern European economic growth, were the glue that held it together, and should not be overlooked.[6] These historians fall short of acknowledging that in the same era Egyptian children also footed the bill of Europe's industrial wealth. It was not until the 1952 Revolutionary government of Nasser that the structure of the Egyptian economic system changed; that is, redistribution of land and adoption of import-substitution, and the patterns of child labor really began to change.

In Egypt's rental system, the tenant family used their children for labor. If the family did not hire outside labor, then they only paid land usage (which cost between half and four-fifths of the crop). Rented farms were far from lucrative for families, even if they used their own children, and the families were far from being their own masters since the owner retained control of the water and fixed crop rotation and harvesting dates. The large landowners were primarily British and local elites.

Families depended on all members to work, even if it meant sending children off to neighboring villages for seasonal work through the *tarḥīla* system. In this system, the employer usually paid a certain sum to the contractors who distributed the amount earned among the workers. Contractors directed children in cotton and sugar cane harvesting, picking and eliminating insect infestations, ginning factories, digging canals, and repairing roads. At crop processing plants in the Nile Delta and in Middle Egypt, it was common to find up to 300 peasants from nearby villages (half of them children) feeding gins and sorting raw cotton.[7] There are accounts as early as 1932 that refer to the practice in ginning factories whereby girl employees were recruited by an officer who received the total of wages earned and who, in paying them to the girls, frequently retained a portion of their small earnings.[8]

While children in Egypt have always worked in the fields with their families, the pattern of exploiting children to work for the benefit of people not related to them began under Muhammad ʿAli at the start of the nineteenth century. ʿAli transformed the Egyptian economy and army to establish his own hereditary rule independent of the Ottoman Empire. ʿAli's reorganization of the Egyptian economy around long-staple cotton as a cash crop allowed him to secure a monopoly that locked peasant children into working for the state. ʿAli prohibited family migration to the cities, conscripted child laborers, and ordered Egyptian peasant families to cultivate cotton to the exclusion of all other crops, which he bought and then sold to British textile manufactures at a higher price. The successors of ʿAli and the Egyptian landed elite continued his policies.

Child labor also existed because there was little recourse for child laborers through unions. The first trade union organization was set up at the beginning of the twentieth century and by 1911 there were 11 unions with 7000 members. In 1919, the government officially recognized labor unions by setting up a central committee of conciliation, and in 1942 the government recognized freedom of association in trade unions. Despite the legal recognition of trade unions, the laws did not cover agricultural workers, and the minimum age for joining trade unions was 15 years.

There was little protection for child laborers in the law. The earliest protective legislation, enacted in 1909 and prohibiting the employment of children below the age of nine in certain industries, was widely acknowledged to be completely ineffective.[9] Regarding the 1909 legislation, the Labor Research Department in London reported in 1928:

> Its provisions were a dead letter from the first, because there was nobody to see that they were enforced and the penalties were limited to a fine not exceeding L1 for the first offence and for the second imprisonment up to seven days. Child labor continued to be employed and is still employed for very long hours, both in cotton picking and in ginneries.[10]

The first Labor Office was set up in Egypt in 1930, but its main function was formulation of legislation and settlement of disputes in matters relating to the trade union movement, and not to children. After an ILO mission to Egypt in 1932, a law was promulgated in 1933 to regulate the employment of children. The ILO report observes boys and girls under the age of ten being paid low wages in traditional handicraft workshops and factories.[11] The 1933 law established 12 years as the minimum age for employment, but children over nine years of age could work in certain industries (including textiles, carpet weaving, and furniture) upon production of a certificate of physical fitness. This was the first law regulating child work enacted since 1909, but it fell short of necessary protection.[12] The law was largely ignored and inadequately enforced, as the Labor Office employed only three inspectors, two inspectresses, and one clerk to cover all of Egypt.

The explanation for child labor in Egypt's cotton industry relates to the cheapness of their wages, as well as their abundance in supply. Political scientist Ellis Goldberg claims that Egyptian cotton was produced as a labor-intensive good in an economy with abundant labor, as opposed to a capital-intensive good in an economy with abundant capital that could invest in mechanization of production. Britain was the most advanced industrial power, had more cotton spindles, mechanical looms, and capital invested in textile production than any other country in the world. Goldberg writes, "It is thus no wonder that powerful England easily subordinated Egyptian interests to its own and exploited the Nile Valley to provide the Lancashire mills with raw cotton harvested by children."[13] As Peter Stearns says, the Industrial Revolution was a global process, though an uneven one.[14]

The capitalist economic system to which Egypt was tied kept Egyptian children out of school and in the labor force, as did minimal legal protection for children and a lack of financial investment in education. Racialized notions of childhood in the imperial imagination played a significant role as well.

Colonial representations of Egyptian child workers

During the nineteenth century and first half of the twentieth century, Europeans employed Orientalist stereotypes in their discourse on Egyptian race, gender, and sexuality. The stereotypes included representing Egyptians as inferior, degenerate, and feminine and Europe as active, civilized, and virile. Europeans used such stereotypes for various reasons, including justifying imperial rule, selling commercial products, disciplining subjects, and building the field of anthropology. Wilson Jacob argues that England idealized imperial masculinity to cause changes in conceptions of gender in England and maintain a paternalistic attitude toward the colonies.[15] Lisa Pollard argues that England legitimized colonial control in Egypt's public realm because of polygamy, extended families, and bizarre sexual habits.[16]

Egyptian children did not escape the colonial gaze. British depictions of Egyptian children often focused on their supposed biological prowess to work as farmers. This image helped England justify its exploitation of the Egyptian cotton industry, and particularly its child workers. Britain's depiction of Egyptian children as biologically inclined to do peasant labor was in line with other social engineering projects of the era.[17] El Shakry holds that much European social science inquiry in Egypt sought to understand the peasant. Such inquiry was based on Romanticism, that there was an essence of society that could be ascertained, and on Positivism, that the laws that govern a society can be understood through using the scientific method. European social scientists came to the conclusion that Egyptian peasants had a physical aptitude that was different from their European counterparts. For example, they said that an Egyptian woman could carry heavy objects on her head because of her pelvic bone structure and musculature.[18] (The way in which the Egyptian elite viewed peasants is discussed in Chapter 3.)

Europeans created racialized constructions of childhood throughout all the colonies, not just Egypt.[19] For instance, European settlers and officials in colonial Zimbabwe made concerted efforts to direct indigenous children into mining, agricultural, and domestic services because they said that Africans' childhoods should be organized differently from settler childhoods.[20] Likewise, with regard to the indigenous children in Australia, British administrative officials stated that they would eventually become an extinct race and so did not need their childhoods organized around education.[21]

The fact that Britain created hierarchal constructions of childhood for western and non-western children does not mean that there was one uniform construction of childhood in the West. European attitudes about childhood were changing in the late nineteenth and early twentieth century, with childhood being increasingly viewed as a period of carefree dependence (isolated from the adult world of work); however, poverty played a major factor in why many European children did not experience these changes. Male heads of household did not earn enough to maintain their families or were unemployed owing to illness, accident, or service in armed forces.[22] Jane Humphries describes European states as having a "greedy appetite" for the labor of their children, because states were constantly looking for more and more earners to meet the financial demands of fighting national battles.[23] Historian Harry Hendrick writes, "Child labor has always stood in relation to the lives of nonworking middle and upper class children, whose status so often required the exploitation of their social inferiors."[24] The difference between child labor in Egypt and in Europe was that Egyptian children, generally speaking, did not shift at the same rate as European children away from labor toward schooling.[25] Egyptian children became locked in agricultural patterns that still to this day plague the country, as will be discussed in the conclusion of the book.

The single most common feature of Egyptian childhoods during the first half of the twentieth century was participation in the labor force, particularly the cotton industry on which the Egyptian economy was almost exclusively based. Ellis Goldberg finds that in Egypt during the period 1880–1950 child labor contributed significantly to the country's cotton production. Overall, boys accounted for nearly 35 percent of the total labor requirement for the major Egyptian crops, and they were mostly employed in cotton.[26] When children worked, it was either because they were helping their family on a small unit of land rented from a large landowner or it was because they made money for their family by being casual or recruited employees for a landowner (in the *tarḥīla* system, which also employed adults).[27]

The British maintained a lower age of admission to work in Egypt than in Britain, claiming Egyptian children reached the age of puberty earlier than their western European counterparts. As the 1932 ILO report on labor conditions in Egypt states:

> In most European countries and in Japan, the age of admission of children to industry is generally fixed at fourteen, as laid down in the International Convention adopted at Washington in 1919. In India, Palestine, and in most of the French North African Territories, where climatic conditions make for earlier development, the age of employment in factories is fixed at twelve and no exceptions are permitted below this age.[28]

(The British also equated the onset of adolescence with loss in learning ability.[29]) At the 1937 International Cotton Conference, a delegate said that Egyptian children had extraordinary skill in ensuring the quality of cotton. The delegate announced that an exhibit of the way Egyptian children work was at the Royal Agricultural Society Museum. This display showed step by step how Egyptian children were able to: pick from the plants in the field that have the largest number of fully open sound bolls; eliminate any cotton of blackish color; keep the floors clean in the ginning factory to prevent mixture of seeds; hand pick seeds bearing a small amount of fuzz; and sieve out dirt.

To British imperialists, all Egyptian children were racially suitable for farm labor.[30] At the 1927 International Cotton Conference a British delegate said to a committee meeting on the cost of producing cotton, "I would like to say that the Egyptian farmer is the best farmer in the world; you can hardly improve on his methods." The tendency for foreigners to explain Egyptian physical ability through their connection to the land is captured in ethnographer Henry Habib Ayrout's 1938 words, "How can we explain this physical stability, extraordinary sameness in a race of men? The answer is in the soil – just as one might explain the uniformity of Egyptian art which has been inspired by assimilation to the environment."[31] In a 1932 ILO report for the Egyptian Ministry of Interior, the inspector describes the peasant worker's outlook on labor as "medieval" and "still being influenced by new notions."[32] The inspector notes that the Egyptian worker has not yet acquired the professional pride that characterizes European and American factory workers. While the inspector acknowledges the economic and educational factors inhibiting industrialization in Egypt, it also says that the customs of the people must be borne constantly in mind:

> It would, obviously, be impossible to transplant to Egypt the highly developed social and industrial systems which exist in Western Europe ... The lines along which Egypt may be reasonably expected to advance in the immediate future can only be determined by reference to the fundamental features of her present position.[33]

The ILO inspector claims Egyptians are unable to contemplate advanced institutions that come along with industrial labor (such as health insurance and old age pensions), and as such should remain working the land.

In the British imperial imagination, not only did the physical body and culture of the Egyptian peasant child fashion him/her for work, but so too did the notion that the alternative (school) was unpopular among parents. The annual British parliamentary reports equate

Egyptian parents' unwillingness to pay for education with lack of interest in education. The 1899 report on the condition in Egypt states in the section on education: "One of the surest tests of the popularity of education in this country is to inquire how far parents are prepared to pay for tuition of their children."[34] The British did not make education of Egyptian children compulsory. Public schools were not free, as teachers in the schools were not paid by the government but received a small sum from each pupil. Acquiring a job in the government required obtaining a secondary school certificate and the British administrators said they might not be able to employ Egyptians because the parents refused to educate their sons:

> [If] parents are willing to pay for the tuition of their sons, and if the latter take full advantage of the opportunities for instruction now afforded to them, it will be possible to employ Egyptians or the most part in the various Departments of State. On the other hand, should these anticipations unfortunately not be realized, it will be necessary, in the interests of the general body of the Egyptian taxpayers, to fall back on the alternative plan of employing a comparatively greater number of foreign agents.[35]

According to the British, Egyptian indifference to education led mothers to blind their children to keep them from school.[36]

In line with the notion that Egyptian parents did not value knowledge and learning, the British often talked about the education system in Egypt prior to their arrival as being useless. The British claimed to have brought an "intellectual movement" to Egypt.[37] As the report to the Parliament in 1891 states regarding the improvements made in instruction: "Previously pupils were allowed to waste their time and addle their brains by attempting the study of an impossible number of languages. I trust that the time-honored methods adopted in Egypt of loading the memory without exercising the mind have now been finally abandoned."[38] In reality, money invested in Egyptian education by British occupiers did not go toward creating an "intellectual movement." Money was largely directed toward establishing courses to improve the efficiency of the fellaheen (*fallāḥ*, pl. *fallāḥūn*, peasants), particularly after the completion of the Aswan Dam in 1902.[39] For example, students were taught in school the work of cultivating the soil, planting, irrigating, and harvesting. The British invested a lot of money in establishing a School for Agriculture and holding horticultural shows, bringing in the director of the Indian Agricultural College to assist in improving Egypt's education.[40] Thus, British interest in providing education for children focused on skills that would keep them as field workers.

The belief that Egyptian parents preferred to have their children work in fields rather than attend schools is part of the general colonial ideology in which the British portrayed themselves as bearers of civilization. Western images of Egyptian children often stressed the irresponsibility of Egyptian child-rearing practices and conveyed the idea that the ragged conditions of poor Egyptian children were due to moral and cultural decline.[41] For example, a series of commercial slides produced by an American company in Egypt and distributed in the United States and Europe in 1896 shows a group of naked children sitting in the dirt.[42] The caption reads: "Degenerate Egypt – Wretchedness of the People." The photo conveys the message that Egyptian mothers are negligent and bear hordes of children.

The imperial gaze had a strategic role in maintaining Britain's system of colonial domination in Egypt. Colonizing Egypt required not only physical control of the country and its political and economic institutions, but also control of the inner, mental sphere of Egyptians. As Ashis Nandy says, colonialism was produced and driven "by persons and states of mind."[43] British administrators targeted children as messengers through which a new "progressive" and "civilized" nation could be born. Egyptians had to prove that they were grown up and capable of self-governing. Lisa Pollard argues that the most important lesson that Egyptian children learned was that their culture was backward. Wilson Jacob writes, "The nature of colonial occupation was not only a matter of military and economic domination; it was equally and perhaps more insidiously a question of psychological domination."[44] Ashis Nandy gives an example of psychological domination as colonialism encouraging colonizers to "impute to themselves magical feelings of omnipotence and permanence."[45]

Disjuncture with the imperial imagination

Imperialism acted on Egyptians, and Egyptians responded.[46] Ashis Nandy writes, "[C]olonialism colonizes minds in addition to bodies and it releases forces within the colonized societies to alter their cultural priorities once and for all."[47] During the nineteenth and early twentieth centuries, Egyptian reactions to imperialism and the colonial gaze occurred at many levels of society, elite and non-elite.[48] Scholars such as Albert Hourani, Malcolm Kerr, Israel Gershoni, Omnia El Shakry, Michael Gasper, and James Jankowski have written on the elites' intellectual discourse on imperialism; however, they have not looked exclusively at the role of children in this discourse. Egyptian intellectuals sought to free Egypt from the colonial gaze through discourses on gender and sexuality, resulting in changing conceptions of womanhood, motherhood, and *effendi* masculinity.[49] Intellectuals' attempts to free Egypt from the colonial gaze also manifest in discourses on child-rearing practices, resulting in calls for reform.[50] The intellectuals targeted boys and girls alike, the differences of which constitute Chapter 4.

Throughout the nineteenth and early twentieth centuries, European imperialism was an all-pervasive reality in the lives of Middle Easterners. The colonial gaze, though not usually mentioned explicitly, is often a subtext in Egyptian intellectuals' writings on child-rearing. Egyptian intellectual elites rejected the colonial idea that European child-rearing practices should subsume Egyptian. Intellectuals were concerned with the social and economic problems of foreign domination, and they were also concerned with cultural confusion and religious corruption introduced by imperial hierarchies that devalued indigenous methods of rearing children. Two aspects of intellectual discourse on child-rearing practices convey how resistance to the colonial gaze helped change early twentieth-century Egypt.

Authenticity

The majority of Egyptian intellectuals of the nineteenth century and first half of the twentieth-century were equally conversant in western and Arab intellectual traditions. These intellectuals were known as the Salafis. The Salafi movement encompassed numerous intellectuals and grew out of the ideas of Rifa'a Rafi' al-Tahtawi (1801–1873) and Jamal al-Din al-Afghani (1839–1897). Tahtawi was part of a team of Egyptian elites sent to Europe by Muhammad 'Ali to collect information about western science, habits, and customs. Tahtawi's legal, social, moral, economic, and political reforms were geared at strengthening Egypt against foreign invasion. Similar reforms were taking place throughout the Middle East, notably the

Ottoman Tanzimat (1839–1871) and the constitutional and administrative changes advocated in Iran by Malkom Khan (1833–1908). Afghani wrote his books a few years later than Tahtawi, at a time when European powers were no longer seen as possible political allies and sources of new ideas and inventions for those who wished to reform. In the years between 1875 and 1882, Tunisia and Egypt had been occupied by European powers. For Afghani, Egypt was weak not because of an inherent inferiority with Britain, but because Muslim society was decaying from the top down.

One of the main characteristics of Salafis was that they grappled with how to prevent Egyptians from overly consuming western ideas and goods. El Shakry explains that there was a "tension between a commitment to a universal mode of knowledge production and a commitment to the specificity of local difference."[51] Mona Russell finds that there was resistance among intellectuals to Egyptians' blind consumption of western medicine, foods, utensils, clothes, and forms of entertainment.[52] Figure 1.1 at the beginning of this chapter exemplifies how tension relating to social knowledge and consumption manifested itself in ideas on child-rearing. Creeping up on the older generation was a new type of child, who went to secular school and wore European clothing.

Fear of losing cultural authenticity pervaded Egyptian intellectuals' reaction to the colonial gaze on child-rearing. Fear is the acknowledgment of a threat or change or loss to something of value, as defined by Rebecca Kingston in her work on public moods and emotions.[53] Joanna Bourke claims that the nature of fear changes throughout time, depending on the perceived threats of the era. For instance, owing to medical advances, anxiety about being wrongly declared dead (and buried alive) shifted to anxieties about being wrongly obliged to stay alive and not die with dignity. She writes, "Fear could ascend for irrational reasons; it could subside just as impulsively."[54] Fear is not necessarily bad or dysfunctional for a person or society, as it can cause people to act. Fear does not have to be grounded and can be based on something uncertain. For example, Paula S. Fass argues that in twentieth-century America fear of pedophilia and murder of children became front and center in the media less because of the actual number of occurrences, and more because of the American public's grievance with social institutions such as the police and family.

Intellectuals were apprehensive about western paradigms for child-rearing subsuming indigenous identity. As such, intellectuals attempted to articulate an authentically Egyptian form of child-rearing that did not depend on western ideas. Intellectuals, such as Rifaʿa Rafiʿ al-Tahtawi, Jamal al-Din al-Afghani, Muhammad ʿAbduh, Muhammad Rashid Rida, and ʿAbdallah al-Nadim, claimed that European child-rearing practices had precedents in Islamic heritage. For example, ʿAbduh says that western ideas on child-rearing are eastern in origin as the East used to be the center of enlightenment and if it were not for eastern sciences the West would not be what it is today.[55] Other intellectuals, such as Qasim Amin, Muhammad Husayn Haykal, Taha Husayn, Salamah Musa, and ʿAbbas al-ʿAqqad, claimed that the new Egyptian ideas about childhood adopted from Europe derived from a pharaonic, Mediterranean, and Arab past. This past was neither purely secular nor purely Islamic.

When western ideas about child-rearing could not be found in an indigenous past, then intellectuals claimed there was historical precedent for accepting change. This precedent meant that western ideas could be made uniquely Egyptian by an indigenous process of appropriation. For example, ʿAbdallah al-Nadim (1845–1896) states that the Islamic writers who lived during the Golden Age of Islam were great because they came from different types of lands and had different thoughts from one another.[56] Nadim was a social reformer who authored widely circulated articles on education in Egypt. According to Nadim, during the old days, "the feet of the East were firmly established in this method [method of differing in ideas] and their men were educated and made to go to the highest point of erudition."[57] Similarly ʿAbduh writes: "Enlightenment today comes from the West."[58] ʿAbduh justifies his claim that Islamic civilization can be open to western ideas about child-rearing by referencing the days of Granada when tolerance was an important principle. He says that the Islamic sciences no longer employ the books of these moderate scholars from the past. ʿAbduh cites Japan as a non-western country that adopted western models of raising children to become modern. He says that rejection of western ideas based on their not being Islamic is unacceptable.[59] Additionally, ʿAbduh claims that God does not change people unless they change themselves. He gives the example of raising money for schools through beneficial endowments (*waqf*, pl. *awqāf*) to illustrate that making changes for children are in effect religiously sanctioned.[60]

Qasim Amin (1865–1908) harkens to Islamic civilization to support his argument that children require new methods of teaching that cultivate their, and the nation's, embrace of western freedom. Amin defends his position on freedom by saying that concepts expressed through language – just like those expressed through Islam – are subject to human development and hence should not be dismissed just because they are new. He writes sarcastically:

> It appears that the door of ijtihād (independent judgment) is closed in language just as it is locked in tashrī'(legislation). It has been established among us that the Arabic language encompassed and encompasses everything. In order for this assertion to be true, we must ordain that this language is a miracle that appeared complete from the day it came into this world.[61]

Amin states that because he has never even seen the most learned of people read without making a grammatical mistake,[62] this is enough sanction for new words, such as "freedom," to enter the Arabic language.[63]

Taha Husayn (1889–1973) makes clear that his proposed reforms on child-rearing are in line with the Islamic heritage. He refers to God's will to justify his argument because he says that his new approach to the education of children will promote the democratic values that God wishes for humanity.[64] He says that democracy is not paradise, but that it allows people to live a good life without poverty and oppression, which is what he says God intends for people to have on Earth. Husayn writes:

> Democracy guarantees for people that they can sustain themselves and prevents them from hunger. But, it also guarantees for them as well the ability to improve their conditions and to go beyond sustenance to what God has destined them to enjoy, as God permits pleasure and comfort for people in this life.[65]

Egyptian justifications and motivations for reforming childhood in Egypt emerged in large part from a desire to refute the colonial gaze that left no room for indigeneity in Egyptian child-rearing. Egyptian intellectuals were quick to defend new ideas about child-rearing by claiming sanction from Islamic heritage and religion. This translated into Islamic heritage playing a role in shaping ideas on childhood. In contrast, European changing conceptions of childhood developed principally from a reaction to industrialization and new ideas from Romanticism and the Enlightenment.

Morality

As shown above, intellectuals fended off the colonial gaze through rhetorical ploys of authenticity. The content of intellectuals' discourse also reveals resistance to the colonial depiction of Egyptian children as an undifferentiated mass of peasants. The content of the discourse focuses on what steps adults need to take to raise a civilized child. El Shakry says that just as European social sciences made the Egyptians passive objects of observation and classification, the Egyptian intellectual elite saw Egyptians as educable and able to move out of stagnation.[66] "The same amount of efforts expended by the colonists to show racial inferiority was expended by the nationalists on the national subject to improve them for the social welfare of the nation," El Shakry writes.[67]

Decades before Egyptians began cultivating a nationalist sentiment per se, Rifaʿa Rafiʿ al-Tahtawi (1801–1873) established priorities about childhood. He said that the rearing of children symbolized the rearing of the nation. He wrote that the future of a country was connected to the edification of its children, or in his words: "The upbringing of children, an analogy of the conditions of the country and the way of its functioning and rule, is to sculpt in the hearts of children the feelings and foundation of good behavior of the time."[68] He claimed that if the disposition of a country is militaristic, then the upbringing of its children will be in the same fashion, such that boys will be courageous and girls will learn to love heroes. Likewise, if a country is agricultural, trade-oriented, or seafaring, then the country should raise children with such skills.

Egyptian intellectuals adopted Tahtawi's view of children as surrogates of the nation. For example, ʿAbduh claims that the human spirit is like the earth, because if it is not tended to and cultivated when it is tender then it will produce no results.[69] "The child is the father of the man," he writes. In a similar vein, Qasim Amin writes that bad adult behavior is a product of guardians who did not curb it in children. He writes:

> Man is born evil, harmful, cruel and deceitful. The small child knows nothing but himself and loves nothing but himself … These vices grow with the child and stay with him until he is a man and learns how to hide them in order to improve his image. If the child is well-educated (raised) then a branch can be cut off from this bad tree (but it can't be uprooted altogether).[70]

Egyptian intellectuals insisted on instilling proper morals in children. The emphasis intellectuals placed on cultivating personal behavior in children can be understood in the context of the imperial gaze which deemed Egyptian parents as incapable of raising civilized children. The emphasis on personal behavior can also be understood in the context of the Middle Eastern heritage of *adab* literature. Dating from the medieval period as part of a large body of literary sources – including medical and legal writings, collections of Hadith, and consolation treatises for bereaved parents – that shows the importance Muslim thinkers paid to childhood, *adab* literature is a corpus of instructions on how to raise a child to possess appropriate manners, morals, hygiene, and comportment.[71] Muslims in the past were familiar with the concept of childhood as a distinct stage in the human life cycle and developed rules and methods of child-rearing, education, and medical-hygienic treatment to assist children in the gradual process of development.[72]

Tahtawi writes that there are three ways to nourish children: first, feed the body; second, feed morals; and third, feed the mind. If any one of these nutrients is lacking in a child, then the child will be incomplete as an adult. A great mind, he says, is nothing without great morals. (Tahtawi illustrates this point by saying that a person, no matter how great their skills, will not be able to successfully debate another person if he has hubris.) Furthermore, he says that whether or not a child is a genius, morals will help the child in life as we cannot all be geniuses but we can all have good morals. Two examples of good moral behavior, according to Tahtawi, are modesty and hard work. Tahtawi asserts that "the progress and civilization" of Egypt depend on including morals in the education of children.[73] As Tahtawi writes, "Man was created in order to develop the world and this responsibility is completed by propagating man and contin-uing his offspring. This is done by having children... and inciting them to cultivate the legacy of earth beneficially."[74]

Similar to Tahtawi, Afghani says that teaching morals to children is important for the good of society as a whole. By morals, Afghani specifies generosity, humility, justice, tolerance, loyalty, and altruism; and he states, "The science of education aims to protect the virtues of the soul and keep it from deviating."[75] He explains that teaching virtues in childhood will allow for unity in Egypt because people will be less likely later to clash with one another.[76] Afghani supports his claim by claiming that it is what God Himself wants: if people have vices, then colonization can enter a society, but if they have virtues then God will give His support.[77]

Nadim pinpoints teaching children the basic behavior necessary for creating popular sovereignty and justice in Egypt. Cultivating citizens who have respect for each other and for diversity requires, according to Nadim, letting children experience "civil rights" when they are young.[78] In one "Boy's School" column, a young child asks a teacher what civil rights means. The teacher says that civil rights begin by respecting others, which requires not envying oth-ers, not harming others, speaking calmly, being honest, not stealing, accepting apologies, and listening to all opinions before making a decision.[79] These qualities all seem to stress cooperation with others, or as Nadim himself expresses in an article in *al-Ustadh*:

> The East, especially Egypt, is filled with many people of different nationalities moving around for trade and seeking a livelihood. You [the child] must get along with people in a way that shows you know civil rights. You need to preserve national particularities; not bring harm to others; not bring destruction to yourself and your brothers; and not let other people control you.[80]

Musa claims that the emotions cultivated in children at home and the intelligence cultivated in them at school create a society.[81] In order to illustrate the impact that not raising children properly can have on society, he offers this analogy: when people move through each phase of life, they bring with them aspects of the phase before, so if a child has bad eating habits, they will stay with him/her as an adult.[82]

According to Husayn, a society that is able to think, be free, and have peace comes from the proper education of children. The ultimate goal of education is not to obtain a job or to learn reading and math:

> If he [the young boy] grows up weak of mind, corrupt of opinion, malformed of thought, unable to understand and make judgment, ready to be influenced by everything that he encounters, and in compliance with everything that prevails upon him, he is dangerous to himself and his nation because he is dangerous to the social system.[83]

Egyptian intellectuals based much of their reforms on indigenous conceptions of child-rearing that were grounded in the heritage of *adab* literature. This shows that there was a significant difference in how the modern conception of childhood developed in Egypt and the West. Starting from the eighteenth century, liberal European social science ideas about the child's self-actualization were disarticulated from religious instruction and based on the individual as a sovereign and autonomous subject.[84] John Locke and Jean-Jacques Rousseau, whose works on childhood played an important role in shaping European conceptions of childhood in the nineteenth century, called for focusing on the individuality of the child. "The art of child-rearing became one of hearkening to Nature, giving free reign to growth, rather than bending twigs to a desired shape," writes Hugh Cunningham.[85] In the last few centuries, western psychological theory has developed in such a way that it presumes autonomy of the individuated self is the only possible means for a child to achieve maturity.

In Egypt, intellectuals framed the actualization of the child's self as having the purpose of serving the rebirth of the whole community, more so than the individual. Intellectuals argued that this rebirth could happen through teaching children moral values. The vision of the self was less individualistic and more relational. According to Suad Joseph, Arab sociocultural systems have often supported the primacy of the collective, but this does not necessarily assume a lack of distinctive agency and initiative in Arab societies.[86] As we will see in Chapter 4, Egyptian girls often constructed hybrid selves that incorporated at once loyalties to the individual, the family, and the nation.

Conclusion

In discussing children and the imperial gaze, I have put forward several arguments. First, discussions of childhood in Egypt were not derivatives of contemporaneous western discussions of childhood. Egyptian intellectuals discussed childhood in an indigenous framework of moral character formation.[87] Islamic heritage aligns the cultivation of the self with public good and religious values.[88] Furthermore, intellectuals sought to reform child-rearing as a form of resistance to imperialism. Egyptian intellectuals grounded their ideas about child-rearing in the local, which served as a rejection of the racialized taxonomies of childhoods that existed in the European imagination. Elites reappropriated childhood, similar to how they reappropriated aspects of the social sciences that Europeans used to stigmatize and oppress Egyptians.[89]

This chapter did not follow the conventional paradigm of laying out the modern conception of childhood in Europe and then explaining how Egyptians reacted. Using the western model as the point of departure for understanding childhood, and its variations, across the globe is not always useful.[90] Such an approach assumes the western model is the ideal point of comparison for diverse contexts. Egyptians worked out ideas about reforming childhood in the modern era through a context of Islamic heritage. Egyptian intellectuals argued that children should fulfill their potential for the sake of the whole community. Whereas modern, liberal European ideas often prioritized the making of the modern child into a sovereign individual, Egyptian thinkers often sought to make the child a morally grounded individual. The dynamics of constructing childhood self in early twentieth-century Egypt indicate that there are a "multiplicity of culturally legitimate paths to mature selfhood."[91]

Reforms to teach children new behavior based on Islamic, Mediterranean, and pharaonic heritage stemmed, in part, from a perceived threat to a loss in their identity from imperialism. Intellectuals argued that the culture that Europeans deemed as the cause of their backwardness was actually a source of progress. Children could reach their highest potential, as well as Egyptian civilization, through techniques that may appear western but have Islamic roots.

2
Nation-Building and the Redefinition of the Child

Figure 2.1   Photo spread of a children's contest
Source: *al-Musawwar*, 1935.

"Children's Competition on the Beach." So reads the title across the center spread of a 1935 edition of the popular Egyptian magazine, *al-Musawwar* (The Illustrated).[1] Under the title, and continued on the last page, are individual photographs of young boys and girls on the beach in swimsuits, dresses, sun hats, and bath robes, holding parasols, shells, pails, and little sand shovels. A number and the child's name are under each photograph for readers to contribute their votes. The competition spanned several editions, and the winning child received a modern, four-piece child's furniture set in steel.

Beauty contests were a common form of entertainment and class identity among the Egyptian bourgeoisie in the first half of the twentieth century. These contests also served the purpose of symbolically expressing and abetting the development of many aspects of the Egyptian nation-building project. Beautiful body contests for weightlifting men, for instance, were a way to put the strength of Egypt on display, nationally and internationally.[2] Beauty contests for children were an educational venue for teaching new ideas about child-rearing. Reformers concerned with the health of the future Egyptian population assumed the winners would be models for parents to emulate at the popular level.

The idea that people, besides those in the family or village, should play a role in judging and evaluating the well-being of other people's children marks a significant change in the history of childhood in Egypt. During the first half of the twentieth century, expertise in child-rearing began to no longer lie primarily with the mother. Intellectuals and reformers recast the system of child-rearing in Egypt along scientific lines.[3] In lectures, pamphlets, magazines, and manuals, mothers learned from experts the proper diet, nutrition, and sanitation for children.[4] Children's magazines offered structured, scientifically designed play options, no longer leaving play to the whims of children and peer groups.[5]

The professionalization of child-rearing meant that the guardianship of children was recast to be a responsibility of the government and elites. Tangible manifestations of this shift occurred in the establishment of new institutions for children, such as government-run schools, children's literature, and health and welfare campaigns. This change toward non-kin caring for children impacted Egyptian cultural notions of childhood in two specific ways, as will be argued in the second half of this chapter. This chapter goes beyond the usual simplification that the colonial era served only to reinforce traditional extended family patterns (Fernea 1995) as a form of refuge from and objection to western occupation.

Children as tools for nation-building

When scholars such as Benedict Anderson and Partha Chatterjee wrote several decades ago that nation-building was more than a political and economic project, but also an imagined and spiritual one, they opened the door to revising our historical self-awareness. Historians of many regions of the world heeded the call, including those of Egypt. Many historians of Egypt problematized the conventional narrative of how the modern Egyptian nation came into existence in the nineteenth and twentieth centuries. They said that the process was more complex than that of the nation awakening, throwing off the occupier, and becoming independent. The idea of Egypt existing as a cohesive community since the age of the Pharaohs is an invented idea. The process by which Egyptians came to call themselves Egyptian in the last few centuries required coercion of the people by its leaders for their own self-interest (Fahmy, 2002, Mitchell, 2002).

During the nineteenth and early twentieth centuries, segments of the Egyptian population were targets of the hegemonic state-building process: peasants to build the army (Fahmy, 2002); mothers to raise future citizens (Pollard, 2005); middle-class men to strengthen national honor (Jacob, 2011); and the poor, around whose needs politicians vied for power (Ener, 2003). No scholar has looked exclusively at how Egyptian children were brought into the fold of state power. Egyptian intellectual elites made children into objects of state power in calls to reform children for the sake of the nation. According to the reformers, parents and the village were no longer sufficient as the main caregivers of children. Children needed the government and trained professionals. Intellectuals claimed that it was out of moral obligation that the government and elites step into the guardianship role hitherto played by parents, kin, and community.[6] Intellectuals claimed the government and elites needed to step into a guardianship role in order to provide more and better opportunities for the education of children.[7]

Jamal al-Din al-Afghani claims that it is the moral responsibility of teachers to help parents properly raise children. This is what God Himself wants: if people have vices, then colonization can enter a society, but if they have virtues then God will give His support.[8] Afghani compares the role of a teacher to the role of a doctor: just as a doctor brings a patient to equilibrium, so must a teacher do that for a student. If the doctor took money without treating the sick person, then the person would die. If children are not educated in schools, then there will be crime and ignorance in society, and it will become sick and decay.[9]

Similarly, ʿAbdallah al-Nadim maintains that keeping children uneducated will lead to the destruction of the country. He writes in *al-Ustadh*, "Past nations were surrounded by a wall of ignorance and so there was little civilization in them, comfort was impossible, the nation was exposed to internal strife, and trade and industry were falling behind, meeting only the bare necessities."[10] Nadim uses the example of the Kingdom of Prussia to illustrate his argument. He says that this nation forged the way, even before the rest of Europe, in upbringing and education because time and time again it scrutinized its types of education and revised its laws, which in turn improved the strength and preparedness of the country itself.[11] He writes, "The government has never held back in spreading education and urging people in it…since 1540 until now, government decrees pertaining to education have been promulgated and reformatory laws have appeared, in both the cities and villages."[12] Nadim places the responsibility for educating the young generation on the government and the elite:

> What is the responsibility of the wealthy in the East if not to establish benevolent organizations under government auspices and use them to open national schools to teach concepts copying Europe. The government should help the wealthy to sustain their projects and ease the diffusion of the schooling. Also, the government should expand the role of these organizations in several areas.[13]

Nadim's recommendations for classroom-based learning imply a critical change in Egyptian culture. Care for children should begin to include non-kin and people not necessarily a part of one's immediate community.

Qasim Amin places the responsibility of achieving a better system of education on the government and the shaykhs. He says that reforms for the nation must come from the government because if reformers waited on the consent of public opinion then "the world would not change from what it was at the time of Adam and Eve."[14] In order to alleviate ignorance, Amin says that Egyptians must be taught by better educated shaykhs. Amin criticizes the shaykhs who educate Egyptian children with the following anecdote: Once a shaykh was eating a huge meal and carelessly tossing away the bones here and there. A man nearby yelled out, "Ouch, my eye!" That shaykh actually believed that a bone had pierced the man's eye.[15] According to Amin, with better education Egyptians will no longer think like a five-year-old child who says after his father lifts him, "I want to lift you too."[16]

Taha Husayn places a large burden of responsibility for effecting changes in child-rearing on the government. He articulates what the government needs to address, that is to say teaching children the language, history, and geography of Egypt and ensuring development of the children's entire being. Husayn writes, "The state is responsible not only for building the mind and the heart of the child, but also for protecting his body from disease and providing him with steady growth that does not expose him to trouble and immorality."[17] He thus claims that if Egypt provides this type of education for her children, then the country is guaranteed generations of people (that is to say, a nation) healthy in body and mind. Husayn places the responsibility of educating children on the state because he does not think the masses can be relied upon alone to educate the country.[18] Most Egyptians are still completely ignorant, he says, and even the small percentage (20 percent he estimates) of Egyptians who are educated have been educated in either a religious or European fashion.[19] One concrete way in which the government must ensure a proper education system, he explains, is by ensuring that teachers are properly trained and supported.

Intellectuals communicated the idea that the household, extended family, and local religious school were not sufficient to raise the next generation of Egyptians. Intellectuals did not call for an end to the loving bonds within families, but they did call for outsiders (such as the state) to play a larger role in rearing children. (The impact of gender and class on professionalized care for children will be examined in Chapters 3 and 4 of this book.)

New institutions for children

The late nineteenth- and early twentieth-century idea that elites should play a role in raising Egyptian children resulted in the establishment of new institutions for children, such as a children's press and social welfare programs. In the West, the late nineteenth and early twentieth centuries are cited as the period of the most important transition in the history of childhood. Hugh Cunningham says that this is when the ideal of education and special protection for children spread to broad segments of the population. Although Egyptian intellectuals articulated similar ideals, the impact was not so widespread. As historian Timothy Mitchell argues, the introduction of modern institutions in Egypt must not be mistaken for humanist progressive reform.[20] These reforms were essentially about redefining power structures in society. This section provides an overview of three new institutions for children that coalesced, in limited scope, at the turn of the twentieth century to advance nation-building.

A children's press

The initial interest in Egypt in children's literature began with the Egyptian intellectual Rifaʿa Rafiʿ al-Tahtawi, who brought the idea to Egypt from France at the beginning of the nineteenth century. Tahtawi founded the first printing press in Egypt, Bulaq Printing Press, in 1824. Children's literature did not begin until decades later, owing to improvements in technology, advancements in the science of book-making, and the changing concept of childhood: Tahtawi's children's press was founded in 1870, and was geared toward the educated elite. After the 1920s, when the children's press became a truly commercial enterprise, it also began to include more and more translated foreign material. The inclusion of this was motivated not just by what writers and editors sought to teach children and what was cheaper to produce but also what readers wanted to buy. The use of foreign material was often modified to fit local customs. For example, Mickey Mouse came to Egypt in 1936 and the translators appealed to local popular tradition by writing the texts in the form of *zajal*s that rhymed, used dialect, and were not enclosed in speech balloons. Tintin arrived in Egypt in 1948, renamed Humhum and changed to a darker color. But Tintin did not use the *zajal* form; and this marked the beginning of the direct translation of foreign texts without adapting them to local style (other than writing from right to left). Local artists and original work for children were revived at the end of the 1960s.

The leading Egyptian writer of children's books written in Arabic for the first half of the twentieth century was Kamil Kilani (1897–1959), who wrote and translated over 200 books for children.[21]

He was an employee in the Ministry of Awqaf who hosted a literary salon in the neighborhood of Hasan al-Akbar Street near Abdeen Palace. Kilani wrote books for children of all ages, including versions of stories from *The Thousand and One Nights* and translations of Shakespeare, *Robinson Crusoe*, *Gulliver's Travels*, and tales from India. Samples of his work will be discussed in the second half of this chapter.

The beginning of the twentieth century also saw the emergence of children's poets, in particular Ahmad Shawqi (also known as *Amīr al-Shuʿarāʾ*, the Prince of Storytellers), Muhammad al-Harawi (1926–1969), Ibrahim Bek al-ʿArab, and Muhammad ʿUthman Galal. As this chapter will explore, the poems were lyrical, to attract the attention of child readers, and they sought to teach children values and information about the world around them. Sometimes the poems were religious in nature.

The third category of children's literature that developed was children's magazines. The first children's magazine by Tahtawi (published in the 1870s) was called *Rawdat al-Madaris al-Misriyya*, and was produced by the government and distributed freely in schools. It was without illustrations, issued bi-monthly, and consisted of 28–32 pages dedicated to explaining sciences and knowledge that related to the school curriculum in physics, math, botany, literature, Arabic, world history, government, and so on. Sometimes the magazine dealt with current events, and it also published poetry by the readers. The first children's supplement to adult magazines appeared in 1946 with the feminist magazine *Bint al-Nil*; this supplement went on to become *al-Katkut*. After the 1950s, there were many more. It was not until the 1960s that the children's press reached underprivileged children, who were illiterate but could follow the illustrations. In the 1970s, Egyptian children's magazines spread to other Arab countries.[22]

Egyptian children's magazines of the first half of the twentieth century were mostly educational and included songs, articles, poems, discussions, interviews, news, and features that sought to teach children reading skills, love of knowledge, correct behavior, and creativity. The goal was to nation-build through education and the promotion of new middle-class values, the latter being the subject of Chapter 3. Most magazines were published monthly for a few years and stopped because of financial constraints, lack of readership, and/or limited distribution. Unlike Egyptian schoolbooks, which were produced officially by the government, the children's press was outside institutional control during the first half of the twentieth century.[23] Nevertheless, popular Egyptian children's magazines served to promote the new government schools by publishing sample lesson questions taken from different schools around Egypt or by publishing intelligence tests that delineated the material children were expected to have mastered by certain ages (*Waladi*, 24 February 5, 1937; *al-Tarbiya*, 1 June 1905).[24]

Several independent children's magazines that existed at the start of the twentieth century addressed political, social, and cultural themes.[25] One that is representative of the whole body of children's magazines is *Baba Sadiq* (Papa Sadiq), launched in 1934 by Muhammad Sadiq ʿAbd al-Rahman and monopolizing the children's press until its disappearance in 1945. It had normative objectives and was almost entirely written in simple classical Arabic. It was published every two weeks and ran to 20 pages, with photographs but few illustrations and no color. Each issue highlighted traveling animals; for example, Chuchu the Rabbit who discovered many parts of the world. The magazine also had moralizing texts, a poetry page, and contests, as well as a page dedicated to girls. Portrait photographs of young readers often decorated the front page, and the last page was dedicated to movie actors or singers (for example, ʿAbd al-Wahhab was featured in the first issue of 1936). The magazine also ran advertisements for certain books, and shops in Cairo and Alexandria. There were several pages dedicated to the King, especially after the death of King Fuad and the coronation of Faruq. The restrictions of World War II brought the magazine to a close.

Other children's magazines that are representative of the larger body are *al-Awlad* (Children), *Samir al-Tilmidh* (Samir the Student), and *Waladi* (My Boy). *Al-Awlad* was first published in 1923: this was a historical event because it was the first time that an Egyptian magazine had been published independently by a publishing house and not under the patronage of an educational institution. It was the first magazine published specifically for children aged 6-13. Published weekly, on Thursdays, it contained humor, entertainment, and contests. (Naguib Mahfouz read this magazine as a child.) It published photographs of child readers (in a section called "Our young friends"), a practice which would be taken up by all the Egyptian children's press later. Publicity for consumer products was given space in the magazine, while there were also ads for other publications by the same publishing house (Dar al-Lata'if), so as to assure a future readership for their adult publications.

Samir al-Tilmidh existed from 1933 to 1937. It was the last monthly national magazine of a pedagogical character. Its 28 pages were entirely voweled, and in order to compete it published photographs after 1935. After this magazine shut, the scholastic press came from the schools themselves.

A few months after *al-Atfal*, the first magazine to introduce Mickey Mouse to Egypt, ceased publication, editor Ahmad ʿAtiyat-Allah undertook to publish another magazine for children in a different style. Named *Waladi*, the first issue was dated February 1937, and published historical accounts and general information. The magazine opened with a letter to readers from the editor, and this was followed by a science page, trivia, customs from around the world, facts from around the world, stories, and games. The magazine only lasted one month owing to a lack of funding.

Welfare projects

New social welfare projects were another way in which outsiders became involved in the lives of children. Throughout Islamic history private groups and endowments ensured some kind of care for the poor. However, the social work undertaken during the last decades of the nineteenth century through the first decades of the twentieth was different, in that its goal was to build the Egyptian nation. Children appeared center stage in discourses on social assistance, public health, and public safety.[26] In 1935, the Egyptian Congress created a program calling for the creation of village health and educational facilities, and in 1936 Congress upgraded the Department of Public Health to the Ministry of Health; but few programs were executed for political and financial reasons.[27] Community networks were being replaced by state agencies that dealt with issues such as premarital defloration and child marriage.[28]

One illustration of the government social welfare programs for children is a camp that began in 1933 and annually brought poor children and orphans to summer camps set up in Alexandria, Port Said, and Ras el-Barr. The program reached a mere 2000 children per year. The targeted group of children was those aged 8–12 who lived in regions far away from the coast and never had the opportunity

Figure 2.2   Performing first aid on a child at summer camp
Source: Governorate du Caire, Rapport détaillé sur les colonies de vacances de 1933 (Cairo [Bulaq]: Imprimerie Nationale, 1934), p. 3.

to take advantage of fresh sea air. In an annual report on the camps, the organizing committee states that Egyptian children would experience clean, safe, modern modes of living "that they are not used to," such as electricity, running water, and toilets.[29] Additionally, the camp would allow the average child to gain five kilos. The annual report includes photographs of the children playing in the sea, alongside photographs that display the health care provided at the camp: an example is reproduced as Figure 2.2, which shows a healthcare worker putting a Band-Aid on a child's finger.

The children on display in this annual report on the camp are a means through which the government expressed the modernization of the country, pointing to the conception of childhood as a conduit for the nation.

Implications of the professionalization of childcare on cultural conceptions of childhood

Intellectual elites' and nationalist reformers' ideas about building the Egyptian state did not create a conception of childhood in Egyptian culture. Motivated by a desire to make Egypt competitive in a world of imperial hierarchies, reformers' ideas helped to create new expectations and meanings of what childhood entailed.[30] The topic of proper upbringing played an important role in Egyptian nationalist discourse at the end of the nineteenth/beginning of the twentieth century. This discourse translated into a new cultural conception of childhood in Egypt: that the child cannot exist without the nation and the nation cannot exist without the child. The value of children shifted away from exclusively lying in land inheritance, care of parents, and reproduction of the hereditary line. Children's worth began to lie in what the child could provide for a nation.

The child cannot exist without the nation

Children's literature sent the message to children that they could not exist and prosper without the nation. Perhaps this is most explicitly articulated in the words of one advice manual: "You must love this country as you love your father, mother, brothers, and sisters."[31] This message can be found throughout the bulk of children's literature, from the cover of the February 1934 issue of *Samir al-Tilmidh*, which features a picture of the Prince with an announcement of birthday wishes on behalf of all readers, to Kamil Kilani's introduction to his translation of a children's story about the Russian leader Boutros (Peter) the Great, which tells readers that the story will provoke in them love of the nation.[32] It is almost as if the king is presented to children as their father and the prince as their brother.

Literature expressed the idea to children that the family (nation) to which they belonged was thousands of years old. In the children's press there are several references to the golden age of pharaonic times and Egypt's roots in ancient civilization. Muhammad al-Harawi, for example, tells his young readers that they are "children of the pyramids."[33] He writes poems about Giza, the Sphinx, pharaonic holidays, and the collection of antiquities held at the Egyptian Museum in the Qasr al-Nil district. He describes the pyramids as the tombs of the old kings of Egypt, and lauds them for their indestructibility through time, which is said to indicate that Egypt is the mother of work and science.

A children's story by Kamil Kilani entitled "Abu Kharbush" epitomizes this new notion that children's survival depends upon a newly defined family that extends way beyond the immediate kinship network. In this story, a monkey named Abu Kharbush, the sultan of a community of monkeys, builds a school after he is cured by medicine brought to him from a land far away. In this school, the monkeys receive food supplied by the sultan and learn math, music, ironing, carpentry, aviation, reading, art, sports, and medicine. The story concludes that Abu Kharbush is the best sultan ever because he teaches and helps the people. Thus, in the utopia described in Kilani's book, government attends to the well-being, that is the health and education, of children.

The nation cannot exist without the child

The intellectual elite not only expressed the new idea that children could not live without the nation, but that the future of the nation depended upon them. Children could perform essential roles for the nation in creating a future workforce, a shared national identity, a society of stewards, and a population skilled in modern technology and customs. The contribution of girls to the nation was not always the same as that of boys.

Children's poet Muhammad al-Harawi produced several collections of poetry that taught children their importance to the nation as future workers and professionals. One of his collections, entitled *The New Child*, is dedicated to teaching children the value of hard work. The poem "Love of Work" treats all types of work, from manual labor to academic toil, with respect. The poem reads: "In the morning I am a student. I have a pen and notebook. Being learned is noble. The ʿulamāʾ have status. In the afternoon I am a carpenter with a chisel and saw. There is no shame in what I make. Being skilled is appreciated."[34] In conveying that the work of the ʿulamāʾ (religious scholars) is just as worthy as the work of carpenters, the poem is also teaching children that each person has a domain in society to which they can contribute.

Harawi's children's poems about carpenters and scholars seem to show that he equates teaching children the importance of hard work with the production of a future society in which all citizens contribute to its functioning and well-being.[35] The photographs accompanying the poems show children acting out the profession under consideration, as if they are small adults. Whether they are at a surgery table surrounded by assistants or toiling in the fields, children are dressed in the attire of the job they are demonstrating and placed in the adult-scale environment of the job. Consider the two photographs of a carpenter and an orator published in 1924 alongside Harawi's poems on the respective professions (reproduced as Figures 2.3 and 2.4):

المهن الحـرّة

تلميذ يشتغل مع زميل له في النجارة بعد الدرس

Figure 2.3 "Student working with his friend in the carpentry workshop after school"
Source: Samir al-atfal, 1924.

سمير الأطفال للبنين ١٠

الخطــابة

نوع من التعلــيم

تلميذ يحث إخوانه على العمل في خدمة الوطن

Figure 2.4 "A pupil incites his compatriots to work for the service of the nation"
Source: Samir al-atfal, 1924.

Work has always been a characteristic feature of the adult world, and by placing children in the workspace these photographs are sending the message that children are valuable for their future contribution to the economy of the country. (These photographs bear little resemblance to the realities of working children's lives. The class dimensions of these photographs are discussed in Chapter 3.)

Not only were children valued for how they could professionally serve Egypt in the future, but also for how they could hold the nation together by having a shared identity. A commonly staged scene in the photography of children's magazines was of a boy wearing a suit and *tarboosh* next to his father in traditional garb.[36] These photographs seem to convey the sense that the boy must not forget the peasant-stock to which he belongs and owes his progress. One image, for example, reproduced here as Figure 2.5, depicts a peasant father bestowing a western gift (a pocket wallet) on his son, who puts his hand to his chest in gratitude. The title reads: "The kindness of fathers and the gratitude of sons."

Even though Egyptian children were often photographed as westernized and modern, Egyptians also wanted to teach the children the sense that they belonged to, and sprang forth from, the nation as a whole. Childhood is thus conveyed as valuable for its ability to serve as a conduit for national cohesion.

Underplaying sectarian differences in order to teach children a shared Egyptian identity was a common theme in photographs of children published in children's magazines.[37] Sometimes this idea was conveyed literally, such as when parents sent in a portrait of their children dressed in Egyptian military uniforms. On other occasions, the idea was conveyed indirectly, such as when children were dressed in traditional cultural attire, even if they were not of a class or religion that usually wore such clothing. Take, for example, the clearly staged portrait of a boy in *Baba Sadiq* magazine's regular column that featured photographs of its readers, reproduced as Figure 2.6. George Harmoush is outfitted in what the caption describes as "Arab dress." Trying to replicate the attire of a Bedouin (a desert nomad), George sits angled before the camera, barefoot in a long gown (*gallābīya*) with a headdress on and camel whip in his hand. His name is Christian, indicating probable Lebanese or Syrian lineage. Christians were not Bedouin. By obscuring sectarian differences, this photograph creates the idea that there is an authentic Egyptian, and that

٢٠

عَطْف الآباء، وشُكر الأبناء

الوالد يمنَح ابنه محفظة جَيب، والولد يِشكرأباه،
وأخته تنتظر دورها

Figure 2.5 "Boy in western suit thanking his father in traditional attire"
Source: *Samir al-atfal*, 1924.

the child portrayed belongs to a coherent national block rather than
a minority.[38]

A common motif of this era was to picture members of the Egyptian
elite in western dress next to antiquities or geographical symbols of
the nation. Likewise, they were sometimes photographed in a car in
the middle of a vast desert. Such costuming and photographs sought
to show that the elite were not only western and powerful but a part
of the nation from which they came.

Another way in which children's literature conveyed to readers the
sense that the value of childhood came from what it could offer the
future of Egypt, was through a common theme of teaching children

Figure 2.6   "Intelligent, nice boy George Harmoush in Arab dress"
Source: *Baba Sadiq*, November 1935.

the importance of serving society. Acclaimed children's book writer Kamil Kilani often wrote stories in which the characters made sacrifices for the good of the community. The story "al-Amir Mishmish" provides an example. In this story three brothers unknowingly face a similar situation in which their willingness to help others is put to the test. The story, in short, is as follows: Two rich brothers named Hamiz and Amiz lived a long time ago. They were greedy. Their brother, Ramiz, told them one day that because they all live in a bountiful oasis that provides more than they need for themselves, they should be thankful to God and give to the poor. Instead, Hamiz and Amiz took their blocks of gold and sold them. One night a storm hit and destroyed the two brothers' living quarters and Ramiz invited them to live with him, melting a block of gold for money to help them. The gold turned into a person named Mishmish, who thanked Ramiz for freeing him. Mishmish tells Ramiz to climb a mountain and put three drops of water on a fire. Hamiz and Amiz tell Ramiz that he is too young to go, and instead they go racing to the top, both wanting to get there first. Hamiz and Amiz got very tired on the way and did not give any of their water to a thirsty dog they encountered. Ramiz, who was weak of body but strong of will, climbed the mountain and gave the dog water, because, he said, the dog is an animal with a spirit and animals have rights in life like humans. When Ramiz reached the top and put the drops of water on the fire, he was rewarded with a huge harvest and lots of land back home. This story conveys to the reader that someone who helps those around him will be rewarded. Generosity has a social meaning in this story: all people feel its implications.

Another story by Kilani illustrates this notion that childhood is important for what it can offer the larger society. Entitled "Narada," it is about a young boy named Narada who, after his warrior father's untimely death, saved the nation by killing a bear that two witches had sent to steal the land. Narada goes on to kill the two witches, marry the woman who appeared tied up in the place of the two dead witches, and become leader of the army. Narada's heroism is accentuated by the description of him as small and not very handsome, gaining his strength from courage and dedication to the nation. Kilani seems to be teaching children in this story that little boys are potential warriors. Thus, for the author, childhood is a valuable time of life because it is when one learns the importance of protecting one's nation from enemies.

Approaching nation-building through the lens of age

Although children were targets of the hegemonic process of building the nation, they were not passively subsumed by the state. Children sometimes resisted the change toward non-kin interference in their private lives. The impact of and experience with nation-building varies in a population with age. Recent scholarship on the history of childhood in the West, for example, shows how children resisted the process by which the state assumed tutelage of child-rearing. Hugh Cunningham writes that in Europe children looked for ways of subverting or escaping from school when it became mandatory.[39] In some cases, parents resisted the first laws about compulsory schooling, claiming that schools were repressive and similar to prisons.[40]

An example from Sayyid Qutb's memoir, *A Child from the Village*, illustrates how the impact of nation-building in Egypt varied by age. He describes the appearance of the state doctor in the village for vaccinations as if it were felt by the children to be a sort of invasion. The villagers referred to the vaccines the doctor administered as "surgery," and as soon as his arrival was announced "everyone would shake and tremble and mothers would go out into the streets wailing and terrified, gathering their children from everywhere in fear and haste, and then shut themselves in their houses and go up to the roofs, ready to leap from one roof to another."[41] Qutb goes on to say that sometimes members of the government medical mission would break down doors and force the "surgery" on whoever was inside. Nonetheless, some children resisted being identified and rounded up, even if they were told their names had already been given to the doctor from the school rolls.

Subject formation is not a smooth process. Historian Khalid Fahmy provides a historical parallel. Under the rule of Muhammad ʿAli, a century earlier, peasants and city-folk fled doctors, forged certificates, and hid their sons so that their sons' names would not be recorded for conscription.[42] Egypt did not have a system of conscription in place in the late nineteenth and early twentieth centuries, but, in similar manner to their brethren a century earlier, children experienced state health campaigns as an interruption in their lives.

Although at times parents and children shared a similar experience of nation-building, on many occasions the experiences differed. This can be seen in how reactions to new government-run schools varied by generation. Parents generally felt that a secular education (i.e. not based on memorizing the Qurʾan) risked the government stealing their religion from them and obliterating the Qurʾan. Qutb remembers that parents in his village initially sent their children to the *madrasa* (government school) because it was run by a shaykh, but once the government had enough trained teachers to replace the shaykh, parents withdrew their children and put them in the *kuttāb* (a traditional Qurʾanic school).[43]

Children often resisted their parents' decision because they preferred the government schools, which were in new buildings and had more supplies for learning.

The unfolding of modern Egypt required new relationships between the individual and the state. There was not one type of new relationship. Relationships varied by gender, class, and religion. Age has generally been ignored by scholars as a category of analysis in writing the history of Egyptian nation-building. While state authorities attempted to control children through health and welfare programs, some children attempted to evade the tight system of control.

Conclusion

The nation-building project played a role in altering the cultural conception of childhood in Egypt at the turn of the twentieth century. New ideas included the following: that the child existed less for the family and more for the nation, and that children's survival and prosperity no longer depended primarily on family and community, but on persons in the state apparatus whom children did not even know.

The variations in the ways in which people experienced health care campaigns and schooling indicate that the process by which the cultural conception of childhood changed in Egypt was not homogeneous.[44] These variations will be explored in greater detail in Chapters 3 and 4, on class and gender respectively. The history of childhood in Egypt must not be written as one of linear progress toward an enlightened present, an easy error to make when writing the first narratives about childhood in the past. The history of childhood in the Middle East is still in its infancy. A teleological version of this history would mistakenly present a horrific past giving way to progress for all.

3
Child-Rearing and Class

Figure 3.1   Baba Sadiq children's magazine *From right to left*: Ahmad Samir, Hanefa Muhammad Fatha, and Nabil Wahabe.
Source: *Baba Sadiq*, November 1935.

Before the publication of the November 1935 edition of the children's magazine *Baba Sadiq*, Ahmad Samir, Hanefa Muhammad Fatha, and Nabil Wahabe – three children who sent in their photographs with a short biography for inclusion on the magazine's regular page of featured readers – may never before have looked so squarely into their own faces in the printed press, nor have introduced themselves to a community of children.[1] The individualization of the child and the creation of a children's culture were two new phenomena at the turn of the last century. Individualization means allowing a space in society for the child to express his/her own identity, as distinct from being lumped together with all other children, without recognition that each child has his/her own needs, wants, desires, and modes of expression. The creation of a children's culture means acknowledging that children form a unique group among the many stakeholders in society, as distinct from being nameless, faceless, and at the mercy of what adults decide for them.

The significance of this new way in which children could interact with themselves and others is that it embodies aspects of the conception of childhood that was developing among the new middle class in Egypt as the twentieth century began. Rearing children to be individuals and to partake in childhood media culture were part of the defining features of middle-class identity. Changing cultural conceptions of childhood in early twentieth-century Egypt cannot be reduced to stemming from only the process of nation-building or resistance to the imperial gaze. There was a new class system emerging, and the history of childhood is inseparable from the rising middle class. This new class system created a childhood for some that was recognizably different from that of the typical Egyptian child. This chapter starts with an ethnography of typical early twentieth-century adult conceptions of childhood and then juxtaposes those conceptions with the new ways in which the rising middle class sought to raise their children. Discourse on the child embodied the emerging public definition in Egypt of what it meant to be middle class, as well as what it meant to be of peasant class.

By typical, I am referring to those children who were not part of the middle and upper classes.[2] The percentage of Egyptians who belonged to these categories was extremely minimal. Historian Jacques Berque writes that society was "a pyramid" with a base in bondage on the Nile and a powerful, exclusive group at the top, concerned with profit-making and modernity. Berque finds that in 1930, 726,000 of the capital's million inhabitants were illiterate.[3] Winifred Blackman, one of the first to gather ethnographic data in Egypt, found that the fellaheen (peasantry) made up the bulk of the population of Egypt in 1927.[4] In Magda Baraka's work on the upper class in Egypt from 1919 to 1952, she finds that upper-class families in Egypt in 1952 made up 5.6 percent of the population, which was a 72 percent increase from 1918.[5]

Ethnography

Generally, when children were not working or in school they spent most of their time with older siblings and in mixed-age children's groups. Parents did not organize play for children, nor provide them with toys. Adult–child relations were autocratic and adults managed children in the home through orders and obedience.[6] Adults taught children in school through repetitive, rote memorization exercises. Physical punishment and fear of evil spirits played a key role in discipline of children. Children had close and loving relationships with their families, and parents expected children to identify less as an individual and more as a member of the family (but not as a member of the state, with which most Egyptians had relatively little contact). Important gender differences were established in childhood, as adults guided boys and girls into different social milieus and appointed them to different tasks.

Play

When not working or at school, children played. An Egyptian proverb and a Hadith speak to the long-standing importance of training the child's body through structured diversions: "*Al-ʿaql al-salīm fī al-jism al-salīm*" (sound mind in a sound body) and "ʿ*Allimu awlādkum al-sibāḥa wa-l-rimāya wa-rukūb al-khail*" (teach your children swimming, archery, and horseback riding). In reality structured activities like this rarely, if at all, existed in the daily lives of most Egyptian children.

Typically, lower-class boys' play during the first half of the twentieth century was left in the hands of the boys themselves. Boys would often wander past houses calling out the names of their friends until a group formed for play. In villages they used the land and canals as their playground, and in cities they used rooftops and neighbor-hoods. During the day, when children were not working or in school, the whole village belonged to them for play. In his autobiography, Qutb remembers with nostalgia running and jumping happily in the fields on Fridays with friends; and also sneaking out of school during flood season to play in the water. His childhood friends even included a cow in the field, with which he says he had a firm bond.

For urban boys, unstructured running and jumping was symbolic of childhood, yet instead of occurring in and amongst mint and basil patches, such frolics took place around suqs, bathhouses, mosques, coffee shops, and, sometimes, trash. Ahmad Amin, who grew up in the heart of old Cairo, writes that his world as a child did not expand beyond the area between his house and Al-Azhar. Boys were allowed to run freely in their neighborhoods without adult supervision, and only once in a while left the area to visit relatives. For boys from very poor families, such as Amin, their neighborhood streets were littered with trash, such as used sugar cane stalks and dirty water thrown from windows. Such dirty conditions for play, writes Amin, did not bring joy. Although city boys were limited to their neighborhood for play, they found ways to interact with nature, such as playing with animals on their rooftops.[7]

During the first half of the twentieth century, participating in adult leisure activities figured heavily in children's idle time. Children spent large amounts of time listening alongside adults to commun-ity storytellers, musicians, and poets. Mahmud Rabiʿi describes in his autobiography how in each season the village gathered night and day for stories. In winter, for example, villagers sat around the fire at night or in a sunny corner out of the wind during the day. Rabiʿi says that no matter where or when the village gathered, all people were included (whether or not this extended to women is not known since the text uses the plural masculine, which may or may not include women). He describes the circle of people around the storytellers as a "stewpot of rich, poor, old, and young."[8] Ahmad Amin describes in his autobiography a similar phenomenon, in which people of all ages gathered in the cafe each Friday around the village shaykh after prayer.[9]

Teaching methods and styles

Most children attended for a couple of hours out of the day a tradi-tional Qurʾanic school called the *kuttāb*. The *kuttāb* provided children with a religious education, and parents could pay for it through barter if they could not afford the tuition fees. The *kuttāb* was run by a shaykh who knew the families of pupils from the neighborhood or village. These schools taught through the method of memorization. Ahmad Amin insists that this was widespread, writing in his autobiography that the teaching methods were the same in every *kuttāb*. The only difference between the schools was "the size of the rooms."[10]

Discipline

In general, adults believed that children could be motivated to avoid wrongdoing by fear, which these adults usually instilled in them through verbal threats about *'afārīt* (evil spirits, sing. *'ifrīt*), a subdivision of *jinn* (demons), which can be both good spirits (such as angels) and evil. *'Afārīt* were superstitious figures present in the mind and on the tongue of both Muslims and Christians, and exist in popular culture throughout the Middle East today. In the face of evil spirits, Muslims would evoke the name of God and Christians the name of the Virgin Mary and Jesus Christ. Examples of manifestations of these evil spirits are diverse in range, including, but not limited to, the following: an identical twin of each human who lives underground; a mule that takes a person on her back up to the sky and then drops the person down; a man with a skinless leg; and a human-eating monster.[11] Sometimes adults invented new spirits to fit particular situations. Salamah Musa, for example, writes in his autobiography that after a little boy drowned in the canal in his village, the adults told children that the spirit of this boy would return if they misbehaved.[12]

Children internalized the fear of *'afārīt* to such an extent that they appeared in dreams or the imagination even when their parents were not present. One of the most descriptive examples of this comes in the first few pages of Taha Husayn's autobiography, which opens with a memory of him as a child awakening in the middle of the night to cover his face and extremities with the blanket so as to not be "at the mercy of one of the numerous evil spirits which inhabited every part of the house, filling every nook and cranny."[13] These spirits were said to fill the air when the sun went down, and Husayn says that as a child he often lay awake at night in terror listening hard to distinguish between crowing cockerels and the voices of evil spirits that were taking their shapes.

Decision-making

Adults usually did not view children as autonomous subjects who should be consulted or granted choice with regard to decisions about their futures. This usually meant that parents and relatives chose boys' career path, and girls' marriage age and partner. Naguib Mahfouz says that his father was flexible and democratic, but this was not the norm: "Democratic discussions between fathers and children in that era were a strange affair because the father had the power to settle any problem with one word, ending it immediately."[14] For most families, the father dictated the decisions and the mood of the house. As Latifa Zayyat writes about her father, "[his] utter silence dictates silence to all who are in the house."[15]

Ahmad Amin recalls that in his house, his father lived on the highest floor and the children could only go see him if they wanted to practice reading. Neither the mother nor the children could leave the house without the permission of the father, who hit the children as a means of discipline even once they had grown up. Huda Sha'rawi's uncle filled the role of her deceased father, and as the man of the house he clapped to announce his entrance into a room.[16] Taha Husayn remembers that as soon as his father got out of bed he called for his morning jug of water. All children in the house stopped running around and sat hushed until their father had completed his ablutions, said his prayers, read a portion of the Qur'an, drunk his coffee and gone to work.[17] The image of children falling silent in the presence of their father almost creates the image of the father as a king who enters and leaves the house. In Henry Habib Ayrout's book about Egyptian peasant life, written in 1938, he notes that adults considered children well behaved and well mannered if they rose and kissed the hand of their father upon his entry in the room, as well as serving him and being attentive to his wants.[18] Edward Lane's observations of the Egyptians from 1833 to 1835 describes similar children's behavior, and he remarks that disobedience to parents is considered by the Muslims to be one of the six greatest sins.[19]

Sha'rawi makes clear in her autobiography that adults did not pay attention to children's feelings and desires in all sorts of situations, not just marriage. For example, she writes that if children did not like the clothing that adults selected for them to wear on holidays, they had no right to refuse to wear it or say they did not like it. "Silence was the basis of cooperation between adults and children ... The child was not allowed to rebel or make an opinion known. It was necessary for the child to ... accept all that was said about an issue without discussion or rebellion."[20]

The home and village rarely afforded the child his/her own space. Sometimes children had their own place to eat apart from adults, as was the case in Qutb's house. Children sometimes found ways to have autonomous space, such as stealing a moment to sit alone on the bank of the Nile or float in the river, listening to its sounds.[21] But the idea that children merited separation from the world of adults, or a designated place of their own in the house or village, was not usually a part of childhood space. Ahmad Amin illustrates this phenomenon when he tells the reader that there were no beds in his house, but mats that were folded up and stored in the corner during the day.[22] Bint al-Shati' conveys the idea of being firmly implanted in a collective community when she writes that her family lived with her grandparents in an old home that had its stone foundation "under the Nile."

It could be argued that the lack of individual choice and space granted to children applied to all people, regardless of age, at the time. Many autobiographies depict in Egyptian culture a sort of collective thinking undertaken by family, village, or neighborhood.[23] One aspect of this was that everyone knew the latest news about each other. As Ahmad Amin states, "The people of our quarter were all neighbors and each knew the business of others, their names, and their professions. They went to each other when they were sick, and they consoled each other in death and shared together in weddings."[24] Another aspect of this collectivity can be found in writers' references to people thinking, acting, and feeling as one person or family. For example, Mahmud Rabi'i refers to the village he grew up in as "our village."[25] Qutb makes similar use of pronouns to emphasize collectivity, such as "the imagination of the village," "the village woke up afraid," and "the village wants."[26]

At the turn of the twentieth century there existed in Egyptian society a conception of childhood as a distinct period in human development separate from adulthood. Adults did not throw children immediately into the adult world as soon as they developed 'aql (reason), but instead gradually introduced them to work, allocating time as well for school and play. Adults provided children with guidance in the form of both harsh discipline and warm care. Children were generally not encouraged to question adult authority, nor develop an identity independent of their family. Adults did not generally encourage curiosity in children, as the use of rote memorization in educating indicates. Kin served as the primary caretakers of children.

Emerging in certain milieus alongside this cultural conception of childhood was a new and different approach to dealing with children. This approach, advocated as the modern and correct way to raise children in middle-class circles, involved the adoption of western clothing and technology, the encouragement of independence, and the use of pedagogical techniques that did not rely on rote memorization. The Egyptian middle class fostered a new form of child-rearing.

The *effendi* child and claiming class identity

At the turn of the twentieth century, Egypt was in the process of developing a new social group called the *effendiya*, often referred to as the urban middle class. The term *effendi* (pl. *effendiya*) was "closely related to status, and was defined by culture, often the result of formal (western) education, and often but not necessarily, by position in the state bureaucracy."[27] There are three main reasons why members of the *effendiya* increased in number during the early part of the twentieth century. First, they were a direct result of nation-building efforts that created increased opportunities for education, and hence mid-level government professions such as teachers, lawyers, and journalists. There was a synergistic relationship between these new professions and Egyptian nationalism. Those who became upwardly mobile through education were engaged in professions such as journalism, which helped produce new ideas for the nation.[28] As Lucie Ryzova writes, "A state-building project based on liberal ideology and institutions needs a middle class."[29]

Second, the growth of the *effendiya* arose out of a reaction to European attitudes about Egyptian inferiority. Imagining oneself as comparable to a European was equated with joining the ranks of the middle class. Being middle class was equated with being modern, or partaking in urban life, capitalism, new modes of communication and transportation, and new ideas about gender and the individual.

Keith David Watenpaugh writes that "being modern and being middle class became intertwined, if not one and the same thing, in the consciousness and praxis of members of emergent middle classes."[30] The civilized Egyptian was supposed to be conversant in the intricacies of middle-class finance (such as mortgages) and know how to act in courtrooms and banks.[31] Many Egyptians believed that European advancement lay in European institutions closely linked to middle-class lifestyle, particularly those relating to their unique system of education.[32] Becoming middle class was not a consequence of European imperialism, but was a historical process that Egyptians negotiated for themselves.[33]

Third, the *effendiya* emerged out of, and were facilitated by, consumption of material culture. Advertisers linked class distinctions, more efficient homes, and more fulfilling marriages to furnishing the home in the right way and dressing in the latest fashion. Consuming new modes of cosmetics and transportation is illustrated in the example of the appearance of creams for men that could keep their hair from becoming disarrayed while riding a bicycle.[34] The structure of consumerism was not new to Egypt, but the link between the consumption of western goods and joining the middle class was new. The consumption of these goods was not a top-down phenomenon, as the agency and resistance of Egyptians to this cross-cultural consumption was complex and shaped the scope of the impact.[35]

The members of the Egyptian middle class never gained the kind of political preeminence and numbers as in the West, but they still altered the society they were in.[36] Becoming *effendi*, or "effendification," was a strategy and performance for people from lower-class urban and rural backgrounds who wanted to join the ranks of the middle-income families. Changing social class was associated with displaying changes in one's ideas about women, the domicile, the individual, and masculinity. For example, Egyptian women of the middle and upper classes challenged old definitions of womanhood through shopping. As Mona Russell writes,

> The shopping experience, whether in the home, in specialized departments for women, or in stores without gender segregation, allowed women to experiment and challenge old forms of identity as well as to confront the British occupation through their consumption (or non-consumption) of goods.[37]

Through education for the burgeoning *effendiya*, the state promoted novel visions of domestic hygiene and architecture that were
seen as fundamental for obtaining independence from the British.[38]
Strengthening male bodies and building young men's courage for
future national service were crucial factors in the attempts to establish an Egyptian Scouting organization at the beginning of the
twentieth century.[39]

Being a part of the *effendiya* meant asserting new fashion tastes and
ideas on gender, and it meant asserting new ideas about childhood.
One of Egypt's leading children's authors, Muhammad al-Harawi,
published a collection of poetry for the literate urban middle class
in 1924 entitled *The New Egyptian Child*. Egypt's version of modern childhood was a product of Egypt's emerging middle class. This
phenomenon happened in many parts of the world in the early twentieth century. In Japan, rearing children became a defining emblem
of middle-class identity, such that by the 1930s elite children pos-
sessed rooms of their own, did daily homework, and read children's
literature.[40] In early twentieth-century Southern Rhodesia, children
who learned English, literacy, and European skills grew up to occupy
new niches in administration. Historian Carol Summers writes,
"In the early twentieth century, Africans' definitions of useful knowledge and schooling changed."[41] The types of adults who remade
childhood in such places as Egypt included child psychologists,
family reformers, pediatricians, department store executives, intellectuals, state bureaucrats, children's literature authors, schoolteachers,
and parents. These institutions, groups, and individuals were, to borrow a term from a historian of childhood in Japan, Mark A. Jones,
"architects of childhood."[42]

Egyptian middle-class ideas of childhood were conveyed in children's literature.[43] Children in Egypt had always been exposed to
stories, but during the first half of the twentieth century classics,
translations of foreign material, and new stories became more accessi-
ble to children through the creation of a children's press and through
the encouragement of reading. Many stories published for children
during the first half of the twentieth century were similar to traditional Egyptian stories, such as those of *The Thousand and One Nights*
and *Kalila wa Dimna*. They were different in that they were written by
one person and reflect a single author's point of view. Furthermore,
the stories in written form are produced by members of the dominant
class and so do not necessarily reflect popular culture.

Outfitting the *effendi* child

To be middle class in Egypt meant having new aspirations for your child, one of which was to make them appear comfortable in western clothing and conversant in western technology. The majority of children in photographs published in the Egyptian children's press are dressed in European clothing: boys wear suits and girls wear dresses or skirts with a button-up blouse. This is the case for photographs printed in magazines to accompany stories and poems as well as those sent in by readers for magazine sections that showcased readers to one another. In full-length or waist-length portraits of boys, a common motif is for the posing boy to put one or both of his hands partially in his jacket pocket, rather than letting them dangle or fidget as one might expect of a child. The boy in a blazer eloquently positioning his hands suggests his sense of ease in western clothes.

Children appear in European-style clothing in just about every situation a child could find him- or herself in, from going to school to playing. The image reproduced as Figure 3.2 shows a small boy holding a ball while dressed in a perfectly ironed white suit; the original caption read "boy and his ball with which he plays" and the text on the opposite page described the game of soccer. The impression is given that the child is so accustomed to a white western suit that he can even withstand its being soiled in a soccer match.

A childhood adorned in western attire also included possession of the most up-to-date western technology. The early twentieth-century Egyptian children's press contains photographs of children posed next to typewriters, automobiles, clocks, cameras, bicycles, telescopes, movies, and record players. What is most striking in all these photos is the way in which the set-up of the scene by the photographer focuses the viewer on the apparatus and not the child. It is as if the child is there only to show off his possession of or mastery over modern western technology. Whether the photo be of a record player on a table in the center of a room, with children's backs pushed up against encircling chairs, or a motionless boy staring at a typewriter, the photographs seem to say that the child is defined less by his/her relationship with the apparatus than the presence of the apparatus itself. The captions say nothing of the

؛

أنشودة لكرة القدم

الألعـاب الرياضيـة

كُرَّةُ الْقَـدَمِ ۰ تَجْـلَـى الْهِـمَمْ

تُنْمِى الْجِسْـمَا ۰ تُذْكِى الْفَهَـمَا

مَا أَسْـمَاهَـا ۰ فِى مَرْمَاهَـا

فِرَقُ الصَّحْبِ ۰ عِنْـدَ اللَّعِبْ

كَالْفُرْسَانِ ۰ فِى الْمَيْـدَانْ

كُلٌّ يَعْدُو ۰ وَلَـهُ نِـدّ

ذَا يَقْـذِفُهَـا ۰ ذَا يَلْقَفُهَـا

وَأخُو الشَّرَفِ ۰ رَامِى الْهَـدَفْ

صبى وكرته التى يلعب بها

Figure 3.2 "Boy and his ball with which he plays"
Source: *Samir al-atfal*, 1924.

children's feelings, but highlight their usage of technology. This in turn conveys the message that childhood is valued not so much for the child him/herself but for what the child represents (see Figures 3.3 and 3.4).

In all these images, the child appears as a statue posed next to his/her piece of modern western technology. Even a photograph of a child "amusing himself" (as the caption reads) in a toy car remains unexpressive in his gaze (see Figure 3.5). The boy cranes his neck sideways to look straight into the camera with what appears almost to be a frown. The car, its aerodynamic shape conveying a sense of motion, sits stationary in front of an anonymous white backdrop that leaves no room for the viewer's imagination even to consider the action for which the child yearns. Although the context in which the photograph was taken is unknown, it is likely that adults placed the child in the car, setting up his pose.

It was not just through photographs that the children's press expressed the new Egyptian middle-class identity; the written

أطفال يستمعون صوت الحاكي

Figure 3.3   "Children listening to the sound from the speaker"
Source: *Samir al-atfal*, 1924.

contents served this purpose as well. There was a large emphasis on science in articles, stories, and poems. The children's magazine *Samir al-Tilmidh*, for example, chose an animal each month for which an encyclopedia-type article was included. The magazine also included long articles on topics such as the movement of the sun and the history of the coal train, postal system, and camera. *Samir al-Tilmidh* published several articles on geography, such as the forests of Congo and winter in Denmark.[44] *Waladi* also emphasized geography, running a regular column called "Around the World" about transportation, food, water, and natural resources in different regions.[45]

As a symbol of middle-class identity, the children's press in Egypt emulated European bourgeois class identity in clothes, technology, and science.

Figure 3.4 "A young boy using a typewriter"
Source: *Samir al-atfal*, 1924.

الرياضة العملية

طفل يسوق سيارته ويتنزه بها

Figure 3.5 "Child having fun driving his car"
Source: *Samir al-atfal*, 1924.

Fostering independent thinking

Claiming a stake to middle-class identity also meant entrusting children with more of an ability to think for themselves and participation in decisions affecting them. The contents of the children's press promoted individuality, particularly through do-it-yourself activities and stories of heroic individuals making choices. The emergence of an industry of books and magazines for children facilitated reading, which itself facilitated the idea of children spending time on their own.[46] A reoccurring theme in children's magazines and poetry was the importance of reading. Children's poet Muhammad al-Harawi wrote a poem called "The Book" in which a young boy says that books are his friend, as the knowledge he acquires from them comes off the page and into his heart. The poem reads:

> I am a sophisticated boy who reads the best books. When my friends are absent, my friend is the book. I ask it [the book] and it answers about everything that interests me. How many very nice stories it told me! It recites poetry and select literature to me. Knowledge in the lines runs into the soul.[47]

Moreover, mothers were taught in women's periodicals to encourage their children to read.[48]

The children's press included many activities that fostered children's articulation of their personal preferences and desires, including writing letters to the editor and engaging in individual projects. Magazines became a forum in which children could assert their unique identity, be it through photographs or written submissions. For example, magazines often announced that they were collecting photographs of readers for publication. Likewise, the magazines often conducted contests in which children could submit entries for publication, with the names of the winners being published.

Children wrote letters to the magazines, with their names being published for all readers to see. There were also forums in which children could ask questions about or discuss matters that were important to them, even such seemingly banal occurrences as the sadness a child felt after his brother cut up his last edition of the magazine. The response reassures the child that he will be sent a free reprint.[49] In another letter, a child worries that he is not as smart as the other children in his class, because he has trouble with memorization. The response claims that there is no connection between intelligence and memory.[50] On another occasion, a child asks for help in stopping his older brother from hitting his sister, the servant, and himself.[51] The response praises the child for his concern, and tells him that there will be a story about a mean child in the next edition. Letters to Mickey Mouse appeared for the first time in the 14 May 1936 issue of *al-Atfal*.[52] One child's letter requested the inclusion of more jokes and funny stories in the magazine; another child asked why one week's edition had not been published.[53] Letters provide a space in which children can talk with each other about their personal wants and concerns.

Children's literature contained several hands-on activities that allowed children to cultivate their individual tastes. Magazines often presented instructions for art projects that children could undertake without adult supervision and with materials that were easy to find in the house. For example, *Samir al-Tilmidh*'s February 1934 edition ran an illustrated section called "On the Table" in which children were taught how to make animal figures out of various pieces of fruit.[54] In addition to art projects, children were frequently presented with mind games that they could play on their own.[55] Examples include mazes, crossword puzzles, retelling a story from the magazine in one's own words, magic tricks, thinking of city names that begin with the same letter, locating hidden objects within drawings, or making sentences out of a given list of words. In the magazine *al-Atfal*, such games appeared in a section called "Competition," where readers were asked questions such as "can you do this?" The "competition," against no one but oneself, creates a private space in which each child can work, play, and develop at his/her own pace and to his/her own particular liking. This is made explicit in one exercise, where a story is written without a title (there are three question marks in its place) and children are challenged to invent one. The readers are told, "We have no doubt that you will rely on yourself in this and refuse help from anyone else."[56]

Children's literature encouraged children to develop their independent thinking skills not only through activities, but also through stories that glorified individuals who were strong and made choices on their own. Children's storybook writer Kamil Kilani epitomizes this idea in a story in his book *al-ʿUlba al-mashur* (The Magic Box). It is about a young coward named Sadak who was so weak that he did not even have the strength to tell people who mocked his short stature that it was not his fault that he was born small. Sadak endured teasing from everyone, including his own servant. One day, he was sitting on the bank of the Nile thinking about leaving this world when he felt a hand on his shoulder. It was a shaykh, who gave him a tin box and said he must wait a whole year before opening it. When Sadak held the box in his right hand, he felt strength in his veins as if he were a new person. Subsequently, he performed many acts of courage while holding the box, such as standing up to his servant and to his co-workers, when they left a dead mouse on his desk. Over time, Sadak's confidence in himself grew, and when the last day of the year came and he was about to open the box as the shaykh had instructed, he caught two thieves and took them to the police station. When Sadak finally opened the box, he found a picture of an eagle and the words "There is no magic in here, the magic is in you." One of the messages of this story is that an individual can and should take care of himself without depending on outside forces.[57]

The middle-class idea of teaching children independence resonated with the reforms of various intellectuals who sought to modernize the country as a form of nation-building. Rifaʿa Rafiʿ al-Tahtawi argues that Egyptian children need to be taught personal independence, like children in Europe, Russia, and the USA, whom he says are taught this "by having nannies and being sent to boarding school so that they do not become dependent on their parents."[58] In advocating independence in childhood, Tahtawi does not necessarily mean that childhood must be exactly like that in the West, as he says that the notion of independence is embodied in the form of "courage" in Islamic heritage.[59] Similarly, Salamah Musa describes the new way in which he believes children should be raised: "Children do not have any freedom and are not allowed to play without permission ... Children should have a room or a parlor where they can play freely. Every child or young person should have a weekly or monthly (not daily) allowance so that he takes responsibility for accounting."[60]

New ways of learning

Part of the process of recognizing the individual needs and tastes of the child included recognizing children's education as a field of specialization and revising the way in which children were taught. The very first children's magazines to appear in Egypt were all about having readers memorize scientific, mathematical, and historical facts, and they did not include much in the way of entertainment, humor, or illustrations. Gradually, children's literature began to employ pedagogical techniques that were different from the traditional method of memorization. Stories and poems conveyed informational messages to children through their imaginations, a method of communication that has the effect of stirring up passion in children. For example, instead of telling children directly that they should not eat unripe fruit, a story entitled "Green Guava" recounts the tale of a little girl named Zaynab who defied her father's warnings to climb a tree to eat a guava that was not ripe. The story concludes by saying that Zaynab got a stomach ache and from then on no longer ate unripe guavas.[61] Similarly, a series of poems about animals by Harawi describes the attributes of different pets, conveying indirectly to children ideas about friendship, loyalty, and obedience.[62] Children were also taught new vocabulary through games that appeared in some magazines, such as a mix and match exercise for placing the heads of animals on the correct body in a science lesson.[63]

The new style of pedagogy in children's magazines echoed the educational reforms espoused by Egyptian intellectuals who were seeking to change the child for the sake of the nation. For example, Tahtawi believed in the use of curriculum to advance new models of citizenship.[64] He advocates the teaching of mathematics, medical science, philosophy, and applied art (such as textiles and pottery) in schools, instead of rote memorization of the Qur'an. The shaykh is not all-knowing, Tahtawi says, and people must use what they acquire in other branches of learning to think about religion itself. Teaching students how to think and debate, and not just memorize the Qur'an, "is the best education so that seeds of faith can grow in the young boy and can become in him a deep-rooted tree reaching into the sky ... "[65] He says, for example, that children must not be told to love God, but instead helped to acquire an independent relationship with God.[66] Furthermore, he writes that math should not only be taught in order to know the numbers and times of prayer. Math enters all aspects of life, not just religion.[67] Moreover, he says it is unacceptable to let a child pray but still be illiterate.[68] Tahtawi praises the pedagogical methods of the ancient Greeks, because after two years in school Greek children sat with elders and had conversations with them in which they expressed their opinions.[69] Tahtawi justifies his argument for teaching children through reason by saying the Prophet himself said "reason and using the mind" were what God gave humans.[70]

Jamal al-Din al-Afghani also claims that a religious education is very important for teaching a child basic virtues, but that this should not be the only model for education, as children should also learn languages and modern sciences. Education, he explains, must seek to bring the child's brain to its highest maturity. "It is not enough for a Muslim to see his son learn the basics of reading and writing and then think that his son has achieved a complete education. Such children are ignorant."[71] Afghani claims that Egyptian society is corrupt because of an education system that relies only on teaching the basics and on the teaching of religion by religious scholars who are ignorant. Afghani says that those religious scholars who teach children often take money and gifts from the families and do not teach any real knowledge. "They [religious scholars] are actually teaching heresy (*bidʿa*)."[72]

Qasim Amin is against children memorizing the Qurʾan in a monotonous way, because children do not understand what they are memorizing and hence will not be able to learn how to be broad-minded people and embrace freedom.[73] In his words:

> Our poets and writers and *ʿulamāʾ* express their ideas in what they write, however, their minds are a like a repository, memorizing what goes into it from what they read and hear and storing the ideas of others. They trade in this merchandise that does not belong to them and they themselves add nothing to it. Everything they have been taught is restricted to repeating the ideas of others that they memorized like children memorize the Qurʾan. When the public hears them or reads their words they clap and scream!! Who is greater than this?!! There is nobody in the world like him!![74]

The peasant child

No single ideal of a child circulated in early twentieth-century Egypt. At the same time that the middle class developed the *effendi* childhood, the middle class articulated a very different type of childhood for children of the peasant class (the fellaheen). The *effendi* portrayal of peasant children must be understood in the larger context of the peasant question. For the urban intelligentsia, the village was a microcosm of Egypt.[75] Egyptian intellectuals vied with European colonialists to control the mass of peasants, and this competition expressed itself in representations of the peasantry. Egyptian nationalists saw the peasants both as a group to reform and as a group to romanticize. Peasants were the "repository of national cultural values" and also a "sphere of backwardness to be uplifted and modernized."[76] Representing the peasants as the true sons of Egypt was a way to keep them from being alienated from the urban classes; yet representing them as uncivilized and as a threat to society increased the validity of the *effendiya* as a civilized group, and secured their predominant place in society.[77]

Peasant children were not exempt from the urban intelligentsia's dichotomous representation of peasants. On the one hand, nationalist associations presented peasant Egyptian children as an issue for wealthy countrymen to take up in order to save the country. For example, associations presented before and after photos of impoverished rural and urban children for fundraising campaigns. Children had potential in terms of their productive contribution to Egypt.[78] Much of the reform of peasant children was targeted at their mothers. Clinics, centers, pamphlets, and manuals for teaching mothers how to care properly for their children were widespread.[79] For example, beginning in 1926 with just three establishments in Cairo, the Centre for Childrearing was, less than ten years later, carrying its message about proper children's dress, hygiene, and schooling to parents across Egypt through 31 centers. Egyptian peasant mothers received lessons from government representatives about modern children's attire, hearing lectures about the utility of objects such as bibs, which were tacked to display boards (see Figure 3.6) in their villages.

The information communicated to Egyptian parents reflected the science and psychology of the modern western conception of childhood. The Centre for Childrearing justified the teaching of these new methods with Qur'anic verses that stated that children were a blessing from God. The intervention of state-trained specialists in the child-rearing practices of the peasantry and lower classes was premised on the idea that healthier children would benefit society.

On the other hand, the urban elite presented positive images of Egyptian peasant children as the backbone and strength of Egyptian society. Children's poet Muhammad al-Harawi conveys this idea in a poem called "The Peasant's Anthem," in which a peasant child

Figure 3.6 "Lecture about proper children's clothing held at the Centre for Childrearing"
Source: *Kull shaiˀ wa-l-dunya* women's magazine, Cairo (March 1934).

describes the beauty of the land he cultivates, concluding with the statement that his father passed the land on to him and he will pass it on to his own son. The poem and its accompanying photo of a child wielding a hoe in front of a map of Egypt (see Figure 3.7) convey to the reader that without the toil of the peasants in the fields, Egypt would not have grapes, sugar, and cotton.[80] Essentially, Harawi claims the country would not function, but instead would turn to dust. The poem reads:

I am a peasant in Egypt.
I turn dust into gold.
My hands are not empty.
From my palms you have dates.
From my vineyard you have grapes.
From my field you have sugar.
My cotton makes riches.
And from my sheep you have wool, and from my cow you have butter.
There are no other birds like mine. I run my farm with beasts of burden and not machines.
I increase the strength of unions and make a renaissance.
I preserve the land of Egypt, the legacy of my father and grandfather.
I give to my children this land that is strong and dominant.

(*Samir al-atfal*, 1924)

رجل مصر فلاحها

فلاح صغير يعمل فى الأرض بفأسه

Figure 3.7 Poem, "The Peasant's Anthem"
Source: *Samir al-atfal*, 1924.

In pages preceding and following "The Peasant's Anthem," Harawi includes poems and photos depicting *effendi* children as surgeons, teachers, and orators.

Marilyn Booth writes that there was no single nationalist or feminist answer to the question of women's places, but rather a multiplicity of ideological offerings.[81] The same can be said about reforms for children. There were multiple ways in which writers deployed discourse on children, sometimes internally contradictory. This section has looked at how the urban elite represented peasant children for themselves. Considering Ziad Fahmy's assertion that nationalist discourse was not confined to the literate – through hearing and sound mass media reached the peasantry,[82] there is a need for research on how peasant children experienced the early twentieth-century changing conceptions of childhood.[83]

Conclusion

Childhood is not a natural phenomenon and as such it can never be entirely divorced from social issues of analysis such as class.[84] In early twentieth-century Egypt, a variety of childhoods emerged contemporaneously. Elites defined themselves by representing childhood, and those representations depended on the economic class to which a child belonged. Middle-class children became increasing associated with mastery of western technology, assertion of personal independence, and articulation of personal preferences and desires. Instead of spending their childhoods working, middle-class children were engaged in creative reading and play activities. Peasant children, on the other hand, were associated with toil, and perpetuation of the backbone of Egyptian society. Elites paid lip service to the impoverished conditions of the peasantry, yet kept them submissive in order to maintain their own privileged place in society.[85]

Building on the ideas of Partha Chatterjee, Michael Gasper argues that early twentieth-century representation of Egyptian peasants was "a disciplinary act."[86] Elites and powerholders spoke for others (women, poor, social outcasts, and minorities) so that the others could not speak for themselves and put forth potentially dissonant voices. Early twentieth-century powerholders sought to represent children in order to establish a modern Egyptian class structure. Egyptian children of early twentieth-century Egypt were among the silenced subaltern voices of the era.

Modern Egypt evolved on the backs of children being told what to do and how to act. Whether the children were lower class or upper/middle class, they were part of the same structure of domination.[87] The lives of peasant children must not be understood as simply a variation on the lives of *effendi* children. The discipline children faced went beyond the social hierarchy of age that customarily subordinates children to adults. This discipline came as a byproduct of nation-building and it came through a code language of class identity. Twentieth-century Egyptian conceptions of childhood emerged out of wealth disparity. To this day, hierarchies in childhoods remain in Egypt, as will be discussed further in this book's conclusion.

4
Girls and the Building of Modern Egypt

الوقت من ذهب

الطفلة تُراجع جدول أعمالها، وتنظر الوقت فى ساعة يدها .
وأخوها يُشير بيمينه إلى الساعة فى يساره

Figure 4.1 "A girl reviews her agenda and checks the time on her wrist-watch. With his right hand, her brother points to the watch in his left hand"
Source: Samir al-atfal, 1924.

85

Muhammad al-Harawi's collection of children's poems about modern technology includes photographs of children, mostly boys, next to such items as typewriters, cars, cameras, and telescopes. In one photo, a girl dressed in western attire sits at a desk reviewing her agenda while consulting a wristwatch.[1] Her brother stands near her, also holding a watch. On one level, the photograph speaks about the early twentieth-century class issues that were discussed in Chapter 3 of this book. The photograph illustrates the new Egyptian *effendi* identity that sought to emulate European bourgeois identity through picturing Egyptian children in western-style clothing and owning modern technology. The image suggests to the viewer that no Egyptian middle- or upper-class child goes without a watch, as they are all constantly keeping time. On another level, the photograph speaks about gender issues of the era. The role of a female student was a relatively new one at this time. The image suggests that studying and knowing how to keep time are important skills for girls. The book targets Egypt's next generation, enhancing the significance of such a photograph.

Placed in the context of the rest of the book, the picture reveals a complex message about gender and the new Egyptian child. The book's numerous photographs of technologically savvy children only contain a handful of girls. Other images show girls putting money in a piggy bank or holding books in their hands behind rows of schoolboys.[2] Harawi's book breaks new ground by including girls, but at the same time establishes restrictive gender distinctions and hierarchies. Learning the home economics of frugality and resourcefulness is important for girls; knowing how to use a telescope is not, however.

This chapter uses the discourse of reformers and the autobiographies of prominent female activists to explore the gendered dimensions of creating the new Egyptian child. Three observations emerge. First, a gendered analysis of the discourse on childhood reveals that Egypt's turn toward modernity cannot be associated with linear progress and development for children. Modern girls had different opportunities and freedoms than their male counterparts. Second, age and gender work together to shape women's lives. Many known Egyptian feminists began their activism (or some form of it) in their childhoods. Girls demanded parental permission to attend newly opening schools. They often succeeded by constructing hybrid identities that incorporated both loyalties to their families and to themselves. Egyptian girls were actors in history. Third, when viewed through the lens of childhood, conventional narratives on Egyptian gender history seem to fall short of granting real conceptual autonomy to women. The historiography of Egypt shows a tendency to discuss mothers and offspring in the same category, denying the specificity of women's and children's experiences.

Commonly practiced gender roles

Before exploring the gendered dimensions of child-rearing reforms in Egypt, this chapter looks at commonly practiced children's gender roles. Many of these customs were widespread among Muslim, Christian, and Jewish Egyptians, as well as across other Middle Eastern and Southern Mediterranean societies at the end of the nineteenth and beginning of the twentieth centuries.[3] Girls in rural and bourgeois settings were generally expected to follow traditional patriarchal roles, which were an important component in how society functioned.

Late nineteenth- and early twentieth-century Egyptian society generally viewed children as vulnerable and dependent beings who develop in gradual stages. Children reached the age of discernment (*tamyīz*) around seven years of age. This was the period when the child could distinguish between good and evil and therefore begin education and the performance of religious duties. Education, in the form of religious instruction and reading and writing, was theoretically open to boys and girls, but it remained "the prerogative of those who had the time, the money, and the ability to pursue it."[4] Most children received a paltry education. Parents felt that boys' socialization into expected gender roles should come primarily from fathers and girls' from mothers. This meant that girls stayed in the house more than boys. The gendering of childhood continued with the onset of puberty (*bulūgh*), or the first menstruation for girls and the first nocturnal emission for boys. After this stage, children were no longer sexually innocent and casual interactions became more restrictive.[5] Girls terminated their childhood when they were biologically capable of tolerating sexual intercourse and reproducing. The transition occurred when her "primary relationship with a man shifted from that with her father to that with a husband."[6] Adults pegged boys' transition to adulthood on changing mental capacities. Sexuality and relations with the opposite sex were nearly absent from discussions of boys' maturity.[7]

Egyptian autobiographies of childhood reveal concrete examples of these gender roles in the late nineteenth and early twentieth centuries. Women recall that adults limited their outdoor play. Bint al-Shati', born in 1913 and raised in Dumyat, remembers visiting her paternal grandfather in the countryside and longing to run in the fields like the boys. On one occasion her grandfather allowed her to leave the house to check the ripeness of the peaches in a nearby orchard. Bint al-Shati' describes her reaction: "I broke out running and I could hardly believe I was free."[8] She even forgot to look at the peaches before returning home. Similarly, Huda Sha'rawi, who grew up in an elite late nineteenth-century Cairene household, remembers gendered limits to play. Sha'rawi's mother restricted her from participating in certain physical recreational activities because they were not deemed suitable for girls. Sha'rawi's brother learned to ride a horse, while she received piano lessons. Leila Ahmed, growing up in a middle-class 1940s home, remembers an abrupt end to her childhood when her mother learned of a boy's inappropriate touch. Her mother yelled at her, hit her on her thighs, and took her to the doctor to be examined between the legs.[9] The doctor said there was no ground for concern, but Leila's mother thereafter prohibited outdoor play, even with her best girlfriend.

The restriction on girls' mobility continued due to the tradition of early marriage. Parents would move their pubescent daughter from the confines of the natal house to the confines of her husband's house, without the girl's consent.[10] Doria Shafik, born in 1908 in Tanta, had an unsettling arranged engagement in her childhood. Her fiancé was a nephew she had seen only once from a distance at a wedding, chosen by her mother because his wealth guaranteed security. Shafik was 12 years old at the time of the engagement and she recalls her feelings: "A ring was put on my finger and with it was the collapse of all my dreams of a free future! A door had been slammed on the unknown and its unsuspected riches. Distressed, I felt marriage was nothing but a mere expedient undertaken in dreadful circumstances."[11] Shafik painfully resigned herself to what she saw as an impoverished future decided by her mother.

Taha Husayn also includes a section in his autobiography about how adults married off girls without their consent. He describes the loneliness and boredom of the wife of one of his teachers, whom he would see sitting in the house when he went for his lessons. The wife was still a child, not yet 16 years old, and took advantage of any opportunity she could to play "young people's games" with him.[12]

The act of sending a girl directly from the family home to the husband's home chimes with an Egyptian colloquial phrase still heard today: *Al-bint mā lahāsh ghair bait-hā*. This literally means that a girl has nothing but her home, referring to the new home she establishes with her husband and children in order to become a woman. When the husband replaces the father as guardian, the girl becomes a guest in her childhood home.

Reform for girls

In the context described above, some strikingly different, yet similar, gender roles emerged to create the new Egyptian child as a result of nationalist reforms. The new child was a prerequisite for the progress of the nation. As discussed in Chapter 3, this new child was supposed to learn to be modern in thought, dress, and manners. The movement to create a new Egyptian child had unique implications for girls because of a contemporaneous movement to create the new Egyptian woman. Qasim Amin heralded the arrival of the new woman on the Egyptian cultural scene in 1900 with the publication of his book *The New Woman*. She was supposed to be educated, and to advance the nation by advancing the moral and material level of the house.[13]

Reforms that affected children and women liberated middle- and upper-class girls from their homes, yet further bound them. This liberation came in the form of new educational opportunities, but the goal of educating girls was primarily to produce better domestic caregivers for future Egyptian generations.[14] Girls were generally not sanctioned to fulfill their potential beyond the limits of being a mother or wife. If a girl strayed from this, she risked denying her femininity. A column entitled "Which education is more influential: education in the home or in the school," published in 1905 in *al-Tarbiya*, a magazine for teachers, illustrates this point. The article reads: "The family is the first school that is responsible for the youth's education at the outset ... Children who deviate and take the wrong path were raised by ignorant, uneducated mothers and it will be impossible to uproot this malignity later [in school]."[15] The simultaneous liberation and limitation afforded to girls makes clear that the evolution of cultural conceptions of girlhood in Egypt was not linear, and did not translate into progressive betterment for all.

Girls' schools

The beginning of state schooling for girls accompanied Muhammad ʿAli's efforts to create loyal civil servants trained in European ways.[16] For boys, Muhammad ʿAli's efforts took the form of schools to train officers, engineers, and doctors. For girls, he established a School of Midwifery in 1832 to train them as doctors. ʿAli's grandson, Khedive Ismaʿil, continued the efforts to bring education under control of the state, reestablishing the Ministry of Education in 1863 and the School of Languages and Administration in 1868. In order to standardize Egyptian education, Ismaʿil's government brought the *kuttāb* (religious school) under its authority.[17] In 1873, he opened Egypt's first primary school for girls, Al-Suyufiyya, in an effort to educate girls without their having to mix with boys. When Egypt fell under British control in 1883, Lord Cromer proclaimed that Egypt's underdevelopment related to the masses of uneducated women. The British administrators believed that Egyptian women were not suitable role models for their children, because they only knew "sex, dancing, singing, smoking and telling stories."[18] The purpose of female education under the British was to teach practical home economics. Public expenditure on education, however, was dismally low, and access for girls was limited because it was not free. In 1898, British parliamentary reports estimated that 91.2 percent of men and 99.4 percent of women were illiterate. In 1910, about 3.4 percent of the state budget was spent on public education, and 90 percent of the pupils in elementary schools were boys.[19]

In 1923, a year after Egypt transformed from a British protectorate to a (semi-)autonomous state, the Egyptian government made elementary schooling compulsory for everyone. In 1920, 70,000 students attended the 700 elementary schools, whereas by 1948 1,000,000 students attended 5000 such schools.[20] While these numbers testify to the increasing role of school in daily life, the reality was that very few children, upper-class boys apart, actually attended.

The country lacked resources and teachers to implement the plan of mass education for girls and boys.[21] Most Egyptian schoolchildren only attended school for two to three years, and the sessions they attended were half a day only, so they were still available for work.[22] By 1955, the percentage of the total child population in schools was a mere 9 percent.[23]

A girl's education: Learning new forms of patriarchy

The intellectual debate over girls' education in late nineteenth- and early twentieth-century Egypt was not over whether girls should receive an education, but what kind of learning they should receive. Within these debates, girls were never completely liberated from traditional patriarchal roles. They received an education to be home-makers, and were blocked from fields such as law and science.[24] The following examples illustrate how old and new gender ideas existed simultaneously, and varied by class.

Debates about girls' education revolved largely around the level of education a girl should be allowed to reach. Girls' engagement in social, cultural, and economic realms was defined as much by class as by gender.[25] For example, the type of education offered to an upper/middle-class girl in a state school was different from that for a lower-class girl. The class-based curriculum meant that upper/middle-class girls had additional opportunities to learn language, art, dance, and piano. The reason for teaching upper/middle-class girls these additional skills was so that they could be appropriate wives for the new *effendi* family, as discussed in Chapter 3. Children of the *effendi* class needed mothers who could stimulate them. *Effendi* husbands needed engaging wives. As a result, reformers sometimes claimed that producing good mothers and wives required more than mastery of homemaking skills; that a home economics education was unstimulating and did not foster intellectual and emotional maturity. For example, Rifaʿa Rafiʿ al-Tahtawi who began the discussion about girls' education in the early nineteenth century, says that girls who are only taught sewing will be interested only in nonsense, such as food and clothes. A girl must learn how to be beautiful on the inside and out.[26] Similarly, Salamah Musa writes almost a century later that teaching girls "cooking, cleaning, and reproduction" will not develop their personality.[27] For these intellectuals, the manager of an *effendi* house was supposed to provide a certain amount of intellectual vigor for her children and husband. Egypt's increasing number of cultured men needed skilled partners.[28]

Some reformers were against offering upper/middle-class girls an enriching curriculum, for reasons that related to the patriarchal norms of women serving the family. A woman with multiple skills could set a path toward scandal and divorce.[29] Hanan Kholoussy's study of early twentieth-century Egyptian marriage finds that some people connected the alleged bachelorhood of too many Egyptian men to female education: a woman educated in more than just the household might not be a subservient and nurturing wife.[30] A 1892 edition of Nadim's magazine *al-Ustadh*, for example, included a discussion between a liberal, elite girl, named Nafisa, and a conservative, rural girl, named Zakia, in which the latter explains to the former that traveling and learning languages have no value to a girl. A girl needs instead to learn how to sew clothes for her future husband and children.[31] The elite girl also needs to learn how to manage domestic service.[32]

The debate over what type of education an upper/middle-class girl should receive played out in children's literature. As discussed in Chapter 3, such literature was part of the new *effendi* class identity. Literature was ostensibly available for all literate girls and boys. Although this new mode of learning was available for girls, its overarching theme was the transformation of women into home managers. In Kamil Kilani's 200-plus stories for children, women are usually portrayed in domestic roles and men as warriors and leaders.[33] There are no female heroines, and women are rarely the main character.[34] The female characters are usually presented as prizes/rewards for the male hero, thus sending the message that the man is guardian of the woman. Take, for example, the story "Bisat al-rih" (The Magic Carpet), in which three brothers want to marry the same girl cousin. During a heated discussion among them about who deserves the marriage, they all stop and say to their father, "In any case the choice is yours [father], you are the judge."[35] The girl's choice is not taken into consideration. Thus, the very existence of literature for children embodied the combination of old and new gender roles. Reading was a new role for girls, but in doing so they were encouraged to follow traditional patriarchal roles. Considering the importance of patriarchy in this era, the continuation of some traditional roles is not unexpected.

In 1936, the children's magazine *al-Atfal* ran an episodic story called "Daria and the Magic Mirror," which provides a quintessential example. A little girl named Daria sits sewing next to a cat that is playing with a ball of yarn. Suddenly, she looks into a mirror and sees a house that she wants to enter. She explores the pictures on its wall, its hearth, and its garden. The story portrays Daria as an adventurer, yet she never actually leaves the confines of her own home. The place she explores in the mirror is really just a reflection of the home in which she lives.

Reformers targeted girls of all classes in the late nineteenth and early twentieth centuries with various forms of education. However, new aspects of these gender roles embodied old forms of oppression, domination, and patriarchy. Examples include educating girls to be housewives, or allowing girls to learn arts but not sciences. A gendered analysis of late nineteenth-century and early twentieth-century child-rearing reforms reveals that modern Egypt did not witness a uniform march toward better and progressive childhoods for all. Changes for girls cannot be reduced to stemming from a difference between traditional girlhood and modern girlhood. As Mona Russell makes clear, there is no baseline standard from which the New Woman emerged.[36] Likewise, old and new ideas about girls existed simultaneously.[37]

Girls act out their own gender roles

The debate over educational reform for girls must not be understood at the level of intellectual discourse alone. The success or failure of educational reforms depended in large part on the girls themselves. Some girls found unique ways to seize new educational opportunities in the face of parental and societal resistance. They often created hybrid identities that allowed them to be loyal to their individual wishes for education, while at the same time appeasing parental demands to follow established gender roles. Historians have generally ignored the role that girls played in building the modern Egyptian state.[38] In order to take advantage of new educational opportunities, girls often manipulated their surroundings and endured taunting. The contribution that these girls made to the nation-building project must not be overlooked. While elite nationalists and intellectuals debated the interworkings of the new Egyptian child and woman, some girls participated in their own version of reform. Girls forced change within patriarchal norms, and experimented with new models of girlhood of their own.

Within this familial hierarchy, fathers generally favored their boys over their girls. For instance, Nawal al-Sa'dawi, who grew up in a small village in the 1930s, remembers her father saying that a girl had half the worth of a boy. She also recalls her father looking only at her brother during story times; while he made eye contact with his daughter when he wanted her to fetch him a glass of water.[39] al-Sa'dawi felt stifled by the dolls her father bought her because they could not move and make noise like her brother's toy planes, boats, and guns.[40] The father gave her brother twice as much pocket money, even when he did not pass his school exams and she did.[41] As a child, al-Sa'dawi often broke down in tears and prayed for God to change her into a boy.[42]

Girls were not passive about the kin structures they encountered in their childhoods. Within patriarchies, girls often made decisions about what to accept and what not to accept from the male. Born in 1886, Nabawiya Musa, for example, took the matter of education into her own hands. In Musa's village milieu, people viewed educated urban girls as disrespectful and without morals.[43] Musa's parents only allowed her to memorize the Qur'an. They refused her request to attend school, deeming it culturally improper.[44] She registered for school by forging her mother's signature (illiterate people used rings to stamp their signature, and Musa stole her mother's ring). When the administrators saw a child's handwriting on the registration forms, they considered rejecting her, but they conceded because she said she would pay tuition, even though the school was free. Musa sold her gold jewelry to raise the funds.

Girls who attended school fought off their peers' taunts. In Sayyid Qutb's autobiographical account of Egyptian village life in the 1910s, he recalls that when the village school finally opened its doors to girls, only seven fathers enrolled their daughters. Since the system of dividing the school day between boys and girls had not yet been devised for villages, the presence of girls evoked both fascination and fear in the boys. Many boys teased them with distasteful words, playful gestures, and inappropriate sounds.[45] In her autobiography, Nawal al-Sa'dawi recalls the taunts she received when she crossed the gender divide by riding a bicycle. Boys ran behind her and shouted, "Look at the girl riding a bike!".[46]

As these examples show, girls practiced individual agency to obtain education in a patriarchal system. Girls filled out paperwork and fended off taunts. In many cases, however, their agency was as much individual as relational: this means they acted for themselves and for others at the same time.[47] Girls cleverly fulfilled their educational aspirations while also fulfilling parental expectations for gender roles. Shaʿrawi's childhood serves as an example. After a large celebration in honor of her memorization of the Qurʾan, Shaʿrawi felt disappointed by the limits of her knowledge. She voiced a desire to learn Arabic grammar, but the adults refused on the grounds that girls did not become judges. Furthermore, they said it was taboo for a male Al-Azhari teacher to enter the house to provide lessons. Shaʿrawi found a solution to the problem. She began studying on her own, putting her efforts into a somewhat more socially acceptable endeavor: studying multiple languages. At times, Shaʿrawi snuck into her father's library while her girlfriends stood watch. She also learned about literature by sitting with a lady poet who sometimes visited the house, and listening attentively when this poet engaged in dialogue with men, a rare occurrence in that era.

ʿAʾisha Taymuriyya's life story provides another useful illustration of how girls balanced multiple identities to achieve an education. From an early age, she was interested in news about other nations, but her mother wanted her to be interested in sewing and other handicrafts. Taymuriyya's insistence on receiving an education compelled her father to make a deal with his wife: Taymuriyya would learn to read and write and her sister would learn handicrafts.[48] Her father took her to his office, gave her pen and paper, got her two teachers, and watched her do her lessons every night. She loved writing so much that she often sat alone listening to the sound of the ink making contact with the paper. Her education was cut short because girls were not allowed to enter the *maglis al-ʿulamāʾ* (lit. college of the learned), where boys pursued higher studies in law and Islamic sciences. "My tent-like clothes prevented me from winning in this matter," Taymuriyya recalls.[49] She says she was kept in "a prison of ignorance" and that there was no place for her to pursue deeper, larger knowledge, which was as far away "as the light of the moon." She writes: "I felt a fire in my chest ... and behind my eyelids were tears."[50] Marriage officially ended Taymuriyya's challenge to patriarchal dictates.[51] The significance of the education Taymuriyya managed to obtain before then was manifold. Her father was not a liberal feminist and he did not act as a supporter of new gender roles.[52] By threatening a serious rebellion, Taymuriyya forced her father to find a solution that met her independent needs and also maintained the status quo (her sister learned handicrafts in her place).

Girls faced additional challenges when it came to gaining an education if a mother supported education but a father did not. In such cases, girls had to find a way to meet their and their father's emotional needs, but also ensure the protection of their mother. Mothers were dependent on husbands, and husbands could easily take punitive measures against their wives. Such was the case in Bint al-Shatiʾ's family. Al-Shatiʾ's mother did not want to keep her daughter ignorant, but she did not want to anger her husband for the sake of the seven other children. Al-Shatiʾ sympathized with her mother, and so she turned down an opportunity to study in a boarding school. Instead, she borrowed books from friends, studied at home, and convinced school directors to let her take the necessary exams for teaching college.[53] She found ways in which to balance her individualism against her feelings for others.

As these examples illustrate, the discomfort and frustration girls experienced because of gender inequality often developed into action at a very early age. Girls went so far as to cheat and lie in order to forge a place for themselves in schools. Girls also maneuvered patriarchy by simultaneously rejecting and accepting aspects of it. Girls participated proactively in state formation, all the while showing ambivalence about the modern and the traditional.

The actions of these girls demonstrate that nation-building in Egypt was not just about leaders building new institutions and reformulating social knowledge. Nation-building was also about individual people, children included, negotiating a day-to-day existence. Beth Baron writes that nationalist narratives are often "neater than the actual events."[54] When historians unearth the narratives of children, lower classes, minorities, and women, counter-narratives emerge that give events "a different twist."[55]

Decoupling of women and children

In academic literature on women, motherhood, and gender in late nineteenth- and early twentieth-century Egypt, there are many references to children and childhood. However, none of this literature separates children from women as a distinct category of analysis. The following examples illustrate this. In *Women in Nineteenth-Century Egypt*,[56] Judith Tucker mentions cases involving child abandonment and child custody when looking at how economic and social changes between 1800 and 1914 reinforced predominant family structures. Beth Baron writes in *The Women's Awakening in Egypt*[57] that female intellectuals in nineteenth-century Egypt did not focus on improving the working conditions of wage-earning women, but instead on improving the domestic environment and reshaping the family. As a result, the mother, and not the father, began to be seen as the central figure in shaping the child. Omnia El Shakry looks at the public narrative of motherhood in turn-of-the-century Egypt in her work "Schooled Mothers and Structured Play: Child-Rearing in Turn-of-the-century Egypt," in *Remaking Women*. She writes that efforts to teach mothers how to tend to the child's health, hygiene, and discipline were similar to the Islamic tradition of the cultivation of body, mind, and self. Thus, in scholarship of modern Egypt, children often appear as appendages to women.

This chapter has shown that the experiences of children were sometimes closely linked to the experiences of women, but they were nonetheless different. Girls sought to obtain new opportunities in the context of an age hierarchy that marginalized children. Sometimes there was tension between mothers and daughters over changing gender norms; and girls were powerless vis-à-vis adults and patriarchy. Scholarship must consider the ways in which expected gender roles vary by age in different historical spaces. In the late nineteenth century, for instance, older women could attend religious and language courses at Al-Azhar, when younger women such as ʿAʾisha Taymurriya and Huda Shaʿrawi could not.[58] Within the sexually segregated system of the time, age had a defeminizing effect that allowed some women to enter male spheres.[59] The vulnerability of women in early twentieth-century Egypt was contingent not just upon their sex, but also their age.

It is well accepted that aspects of oppression are part of the same system. Sex, class, and race are inseparable, for example. Women face multiple forms of oppression at the same time, which makes each woman's experience unique: there is not one universal truth. Historians of Egypt must view the woman as a full being, defined as much by her age as her gender. Doing otherwise denies women and children conceptual autonomy. Additionally, it infantilizes womanhood and devalues childhood.

Conclusion

The making of the new Egyptian child had different implications for girls and boys. Education of girls was based around homemaking, whereas the education of boys was based around more formal politics. Furthermore, there was no single reformist answer to the question of how to educate girls. Reformers put forward a multiplicity of ideological offerings that were sometimes internally contradictory. A girl's education depended on her class, and reforms for all girls embodied aspects of traditional gender roles. The process of creating the new Egyptian child was not one of linear betterment for all.

Despite being formally powerless, girls resisted patriarchal authority and contributed to the nation-building project. Some girls rejected roles intended for them by their families and community; others contested the limitations of their gender and age by assuming hybrid loyalties to themselves and to others. Through transgressive acts, girls tried on new models of girlhood. They cannot be lumped together with mothers in history, as they had their own unique experiences. It is clear that scholars often incorrectly deny girls their place in the genealogy of Egyptian history.

5
Constructing National Identity through Autobiographical Memory of Childhood

كل الإناث فى دار المنتج الأعظم!
أفى غرفة يارب أم أنا فى لحد ؟   ألاَ شَدٌّ ما أنّى من الزمن الوغد ؟

Figure 5.1 "All the women are in the great factory [the kitchen]! Oh, dear God, am I in a room or in a tomb? These hard days have put me in a difficult position!"

Source: Bint al-Shati', *Qadiyat al-fallah* (Cairo: Maktabat al-Nahda al-Misriyya, 1939), p. 70.

A 1939 illustrated book about Egyptian peasants by scholar 'A'isha 'Abd al-Rahman equates corpses to girls doing domestic chores. Another image in the same book depicts an exhausted girl squatting by the side of a box of freshly picked onions. The caption reads: "Young Misery." 'Abd al-Rahman's book was a foray into the then popular genre of peasant studies,[1] and also into the growing feminist press, the latter concerning us here. The book came out in the midst of a vibrant feminist press and movement in Egypt, the junior branch of the Egyptian Feminist Union (EFU) being formed a few years earlier. The photographs and captions reflect a clear condemnation of girls' relegation to the domestic sphere in contemporary Egyptian villages. ʿAbd al-Rahman published this book in the same year in which she overcame decades of gendered barriers to receive an undergraduate degree. After the book's publication, she went on to obtain a PhD and become a professor of Arabic literature, and she was one of the first modern Arab women to undertake Qurʾanic exegesis. ʿAbd al-Rahman lived until 1989, and published many short stories and academic works about early Muslim women. At the peak of her career in the late 1960s, she temporarily expressed feminist themes in a more personal format: the autobiography.

The choice any author makes about writing in the first person rather than the third person at a particular historic moment is significant.[2] ʿAbd al-Rahman's autobiography centers on her childhood struggle to obtain an education in the face of patriarchy, and was written ten years after Egyptian women won the right to vote and run for parliament. She had an agenda in publishing her personal life story. It was a symbolic break with the tradition that women were confined to the private sphere. As Marilyn Booth points out in her book on biography and gender in Egypt, writing narratives that center around women trespasses upon and violates male turf.[3] By asserting authorship as a woman, ʿAbd al-Rahman was asserting that women had potential beyond reproduction. This was particularly important in the 1960s when women were demanding a place in the newly independent state for which they had fought. As with her academic writing and illustrated book on peasants, ʿAbd al-Rahman used her autobiography as a tool to reform society.

Autobiographies are windows into the past as well as into the present. They are personal narratives about the self as told through memory. The autobiographical "I" works within a context that shapes memory, which is not a passive depository of fact but an active process of creating meanings (Portelli, 2000). David Lowenthal in his book, *The Past is a Foreign Country*, argues that we use the past to enrich and also to impoverish us. We change what has come down to us and remold the past for reasons that mirror current benefits. These benefits are often linked to patriotic zeal and private interests. "Memory is a battlefield," writes oral historian Alistair Thomson.

This chapter concentrates on Egyptian autobiographies of childhood written by well-known public intellectuals primarily between the 1930s and 1960s,[4] a period in which Egypt was closing in on its struggle for independence and forming the new Republic's identity. Prominent Egyptian intellectuals and reformers who wrote their life stories decades after their childhood, namely in the prime or at the end of their careers, use memories of childhood to tell a story about the contemporary society in which they live and to form visions for its future. Autobiographies reveal that childhood matters in the process of nation-building for three reasons. First, authors use the voice of the child to accentuate their authority as modern-day reformers and intellectuals. For instance, authors sometimes encode social critiques in a palpable manner by articulating them in the innocent voice of the child. Second, autobiographies of childhood are personal and highly emotive sites of expression. The decisions that reformers and intellectuals make in the present come out of childhood experiences with emotions such as fear, humiliation, loyalty, and love. Autobiographies of childhood poke holes in the post-Enlightenment view of nation-building as a process under rational, scientific control. Third, controlling representations of the child is a way of controlling the present.

A brief encapsulation of some central themes in these autobiographies follows. Feminist and nationalist Huda Shaʿrawi remembers her upper-class urban childhood as dotted with patriarchal oppression. Another feminist, Nabawiya Musa, portrays herself as a child who stood up to the British occupation that invaded her daily life. Journalist Ahmad Amin recalls a middle-class urban childhood filled with class divisions and patriarchy. Salamah Musa was a journalist, writer, and reformer whose memories of childhood strongly emphasize the humiliation he felt at the hands of British colonialists. Journalist and politician Muhammad Husayn Haykal writes about a childhood surrounded by demoralized and complacent peers. Taha Husayn was an author and scholar who remembers a rural childhood colored by poverty and ignorance. Recording traditional village life and arts is a focus in the author and Islamist theorist Sayyid Qutb's autobiography of childhood. He remembers his rural childhood as a time of moral formation. ʿAʾisha ʿAbd al-Rahman associates her rural childhood with a journey for education. All these autobiographers use their childhood as a portal into the past in order to vocalize commentary about the society in which they live at the time of publication. Their autobiographies will be discussed in order of their date of publication.

Muhammad Husayn Haykal

Journalist and politician Muhammad Husayn Haykal (1888–1956) was born into a landowning family in rural Egypt. He was educated at Cairo University School of Law and the University of Paris and is known for many accomplishments, including founding an influential weekly edition of the newspaper *al-Siyasa* in 1922, serving as a minister in seven Egyptian cabinets, and in 1921 establishing with other educated Egyptians the Constitutional Liberal Party, which called for parliamentary democracy. Throughout his life, Haykal struggled with reconciling the democratic principles of his party with the belief that Egypt's most educated citizens should govern the country,[5] and he also grappled with how to rid the country of its British occupiers. These were crucial debates that faced all intellectuals of the era. In his autobiographical writings,[6] originally published in about 1925, Haykal uses memories of childhood to take a stance on these debates.

Intellectuals' frustration with mass ignorance manifested itself in discussions about peasants. Intellectuals of Haykal's era often lauded peasants for being the backbone of Egyptian society, but they also harshly criticized their supposed "backwards" ways that blocked societal progress. (Some middle-class intellectuals carved out their new bourgeois identity by distinguishing themselves from the peasant class, as discussed in Chapter 3.) Intellectuals also chastised peasants for complacency and conformity. In his memories of childhood, Haykal uses descriptions of his childhood peers in the village where he grew up to call attention to the lack of individuality among peasants and the collective nature of village life. He recalls how the children in his school formed groups that were based on peer pressure, and that his classmates teased him without thinking about the difference between right and wrong. Haykal labels this the "spirit of the masses," and writes that the phenomenon still exists at the time he is writing.[7] As an adult, Haykal felt strongly that natural environment was closely linked to human temperament.[8] He believed the peasants of the Nile Valley were tranquil because the river "broke the harshness of the desert and blunted the cruelty and roughness of what would otherwise be wilderness."[9] In other words, the peasants were submissive because of the placidity of their environment. They had no desire to change and accepted the habits passed on to them by their ancestors, as well as any regime. It was not uncommon for Egyptian intellectuals of the first half of the twentieth century to link "Egyptianness" to the country's geography in this way.[10] For Haykal and others, peasant complacency played a role in preventing Egypt's democratization, and his choice to express a stance on this debate through childhood memory is political. Children are presumably untainted by the world and report as unbiased witnesses; therefore Haykal's childhood observation of peasant backwardness increases the authenticity of his adult criticism. Furthermore, showing that the sheep-like mentality of the masses had the effect of victimizing an innocent child increases the urgency of his critique.

In the struggle for independence from the British, Haykal's autobiographical writings also show a strategic use of childhood. The author depicts himself as a child who suffered at the hands of the British. He recalls fear overtaking his elementary school classroom every time a foreign inspector visited. The students stood to attention, saluted, sat on command, then put out their hands for an evaluation of their cleanliness. Haykal writes, "Our legs trembled and violent fear seized us."[11] The Egyptian school director followed behind the inspector, hanging his head. Each time the inspector found dirty hands, he shot the director "a disdainful look as if he were despicable."[12]

Haykal's depiction of the emotional implications of living under the colonial system was an expression of nationalism. Showing the British to be emotionally harmful to children was a form of resistance. Childhood is expected to be idyllic, so memories of harsh realities are particularly striking. Childhood memories of school, for example, are supposed to be filled with positive and productive interactions, yet Haykal's autobiographical writings are replete with the fear and demoralization that the British imposed upon Egyptian children, thus intensifying his nationalist call for self-governance. In 1924, one year before he wrote his autobiographical essays, Haykal wrote in an academic publication that Egyptians should rule themselves by themselves.[13]

Haykal's willingness to divulge his boyhood fears in his autobiographical writings was facilitated by a changing political landscape. In the decade prior to the publication of his autobiographical writings, it would have been uncommon for an Egyptian male author to write about his personal feelings. Such restraint helped to preserve male dignity and a strong manly appearance.[14] Not long before publishing his childhood memoirs, Haykal published a novel called *Zaynab*, using a pen name for self-protection. Fiction was not considered to be serious literature, and it might have damaged his career.[15] (Furthermore, the book mocked the Egyptian elite for ruling in tandem with foreign rulers.[16]) However, by the mid-1920s there was increased freedom of expression, which caused new literary arenas to open up to writers. This was a consequence of the Revolution of 1919 that resulted in quasi-independence and the popularly elected Saʿd Zaghlul assuming office in 1924.[17] Intellectuals sought through various forms of writing to define a new and exclusively Egyptian national identity, changing the focus of their attention from "the narrowly political issues that had preoccupied them since 1919 to the broader issues of the meaning and the elaboration of the Egyptian nationalist outlook that had apparently triumphed in the political sphere."[18] Haykal used the emotional aspects of growing up under the British to contribute to the collective efforts to create a unique Egyptian identity, independent of the British.[19]

Taha Husayn

Taha Husayn's (1889–1973) purpose in writing his autobiography was for social reform. He was born into a lower-class rural family and became blind at an early age owing to a lack of proper medical treatment. He went on to study in France and become a leading writer and intellectual of the twentieth century. In 1926, he published a controversial book on the sacrilegious topic of pre-Islamic literature, which led to his dismissal from Cairo University.[20] In 1950, he was appointed Minister of Education and helped to promote education in line with his life motto: "Education is like the air we breathe and the water we drink." Husayn was a proponent of a strand of nationalism that was based on pharaonism, claiming that the roots of Egypt's unique identity were its Mediterranean heritage. Pharaonism proposed a secular national identity.

Husayn's reflections on the past launch debates and project a roadmap for national progress. Sidonie Smith and Julia Watson explain that this is a common characteristic in the genre of autobiography: "The personal story of a remembered past is always in a dialogue with emergent cultural formations."[21] The social ills of the countryside and villages are the focus of Husayn's writing about his childhood. He ties most of these ills to the religious establishment. Husayn writes extensively about the pressure his father and teachers put on him at a young age to memorize the Qur'an, a significant moment in his life occurring when, at barely nine years of age, he learnt the Qur'an by heart and began to be called "shaykh" by his parents and teacher. His teacher called him "shaykh" as a reward when he was pleased with him, otherwise addressing him as "kid," while his parents attached "shaykh" to his name out of pride. Husayn recalls that he did not have the size, dignity, demeanor, or desire to carry this exalted epithet.[22]

Husayn's critique of religious education had to do not only with the pressure it placed on children, but also its exclusion of other types of learning, particularly science. He remembers the day when his village received word from the city that a star with a tail (a comet) would appear at precisely 2 pm.[23] The village religious leaders became terrified, saying that it was the coming of the day of resurrection in which the Messiah would appear and the land would burn. Discussions among scholars and students occurred for many hours, and when the predicted catastrophe did not take place more discussions ensued, with religious scholars arguing that angels had taken away the sins of the people and told God to stop the disaster. Husayn remembers that the scholars did not listen to scientific reports from the city, which explained that the comet was a result of interactions between planets, ash, and winds.

In these examples Husayn is speaking less about his childhood than about the world in which he lives. His critical memories about religious scholars reflect the reforms he advocated in both religion and education as an adult. He published his autobiography in 1932, and in the late 1930s he wrote that the ideal education for a child was free-thinking and "a compromise between completely religious and completely civil."[24] Husayn rebuffs the idea that Al-Azhar (the oldest Islamic university in Cairo) is the model for education: "Al-Azhar, in its historical and traditional authority and religious duties, is a conservative environment representing the old era and old thinking more than the new era and new thinking."[25] He calls for schools that teach Arabic language, national history, Egyptian geography, and

moderate religious education. This is in line with his nationalist philosophy of pharaonism, which was in opposition to religious-based
national identity.

Husayn's choice to express these ideas through the genre of autobiography was strategic. Expressing new, secular ways of organizing
society through examples taken from childhood experiences was
innovative, particularly at a time when questioning the sanctity of
the shaykhs was risky. This is illustrated by the climax of Husayn's
battle with Al-Azhar in the 1920s, when the publication of his book
Fi al-shiʿr al-jahili (On pre-Islamic poetry), in which he cast doubt
on the authenticity of traditional Arabic poetry and hinted that the
Qurʾan should not be taken as a source of history, led to his prosecu-
tion and his book being temporarily banned. There are many ways in
which Husayn uses childhood to give himself authority as a reformer.
First, he presents himself as a precocious child who questions societal
norms, yet at the same is similar to others in the rural population.
By describing his strong childhood connections to the land, through
depictions of gathering apples, mint, and basil, frolicking in orchards,
running in vast fields, and waking up to roosters, crows, and chick-
ens, Husayn firmly embeds himself in the rural milieu. He critiques
religion not as an elite intellectual, but as a member of the masses.
Second, he makes it clear that he is a product of Egyptian heritage.
Husayn memorized parts of the Qurʾan by hearing his grandfather
recite collects and prayers at dawn and nightfall,[26] while his mother
taught him songs, lamentations, stories, and poems from Egyptian
folklore. Storytellers in the streets filled his ears nightly.[27] Religion
was an essential source of knowledge in the countryside, as well as
a component of stories and popular epics. Husayn paints himself as
having an authentically Egyptian base, not a westernized one. Third,
vulnerability is a characteristic of his childhood persona. Religion
victimized him on many fronts and created a tragic childhood: folk
medicine blinded him; shaykhs filled his head with false knowledge;
he spent nights in bed scared and unhappy from fear of evil spirits;
and shaykhs betrayed his trust when he witnessed one of them steal
from an orphan.[28] Childhood abuse by religion validates Husayn's
critique of it. Fourth, the childhood voice through which he vocal-
izes his critiques comes from a place of honesty. He admits he lied as a
child (but only once). When he cannot remember exact facts from his
childhood he tells the reader. He makes a contract between himself

and the reader that he is setting down the most important parts of his history as accurately as possible. Using "he" and "our friend" to talk about himself, Husayn writes for his audience as someone outside the world of the book, thereby creating distance and objectivity. He is reporting as an adult what the child saw, and his respect for the truth legitimizes the child's observations.

In Fedwa Malti-Douglas's analysis of blindness in Husayn's autobiography, she argues that this feature acts as a conduit for matters of tradition versus modernity.[29] Childhood acts in a similar manner. Husayn wants to encourage a new method of learning based on Cartesian doubt so that Egyptians can learn to distinguish ideas that are not true from those that are false. He wants to create a new generation that thinks, instead of blindly memorizing. Husayn criticizes people who treat religious leaders as if they were made of "a pure clay," distinct from that from which all other people were created.[30] He uses childhood as a license to witness the constraints of traditional religion. Although he states that he is writing his autobiography for his daughter, it is actually for a wider audience; one that will work to reform society for his daughter's generation. (He discloses later that his daughter is not yet old enough to understand the social critiques explored in his story.[31]) In a similar manner to Haykal, Husayn uses childhood to create a sense of authority as a reformer.

Nabawiya Musa

Nabawiya Musa (1886–1951) grew up in a middle-class Alexandrian family and became one of the most prominent feminists of the twentieth century. As a pioneer of women's education in Egypt, she was the first Egyptian girl to have a high school education, in 1907, and was the first headmistress. Before Musa, Egyptian women working in education were only allowed to teach, while foreigners held the administrative roles. She considered education, particularly for girls, to be the most pressing national issue, and advocated this through lectures and in newspaper and magazine articles.[32] In her later years, Musa expressed her desire for social reform in poetry and writings that drew upon her personal experiences. She wrote her memoirs in the mid-1940s in a serialized form, and they later came to be known as her autobiography, *Tarikhi bi-qalami* (My history by my pen).[33]

The desire to return to one's past through autobiography is less about highlighting one's life as spectacular and more about declaring ownership of the past, and therefore ownership of the present. Gillian Whitlock argues that "in the ruins of colonialism" autobiographies are a way of "sifting through the debris" to articulate a collective cultural memory.[34] The imperial narrative justifies past domination by alleging passivity on the part of the indigenous people; in other words, Europeans woke up the slumbering native. Autobiographies can be an empowering route by which to stand up to this narrative, because they allow authors to depict agency. Musa, for instance, paints into the historical narrative how colonial subjects such as herself stood up to abuse. She documents the insults she endured from European teachers during her schooldays, while also claiming that she never kept quiet in the face of demoralizing authority.[35] During an oral English language exam, for example, the Minister of Information, a British man named Paul Carpenter, told Musa that Egyptians were not productive people. He said that Egyptians needed to care more about developing the country's industrial sector than the educational sector. In her characteristically rebellious manner, Musa retorted that a country cannot develop its industries before its schools, and furthermore, told Mr. Carpenter that it must be shameful to be the child of a carpenter.[36]

Musa wrote her autobiography a few years before Egypt obtained total independence from the British. Showing how she stood up to the British authorities rewrote the imperial narrative that justified domination on the grounds of indigenous people's passivity. It also argued that the blame for injustices suffered by the colonized should not fall on the people themselves. Writing her life story was an existential liberation for all Egyptians from the status of imperial subject. Expressing resistance through the actions of a child added to Musa's message. Society often views the child as disempowered and helpless, but Musa turned this assumption on its head, thus magnifying the intensity of the resistance.

Expressing resistance through a girl's educational experience relates to Musa's lifelong feminist activism. Musa sought to liberate education from colonial rule as much as she sought to unify curricula for boys and girls. The schoolgirl in Musa's autobiography demands educational investment for the benefit of the entire country. This contains the message that educating all children, boys and girls, is a tool for development. When Musa wrote the serialized form of her autobiography, socialist feminists were facing a clamp down by the government and the religious establishment. The government feared a communist threat, and ordered the closure of Musa's schools for girls after she criticized government support of British wartime needs.[37] As the Egyptian Revolution of 1952 grew nearer, the religious establishment condemned Egyptian feminists for their "disruptive effects" on Egyptian society.[38] In her autobiography, Musa drew upon the past to define the present. Her memories articulate an identity for Egypt as independent from the British and a provider of equal opportunities for girls and boys.

Sayyid Qutb

Sayyid Qutb (1909–1966) published his autobiography in 1946, at a time when some intellectuals were arguing that eastern identity conflicted with western identity. A central objective of his writing was to reform Egyptian society to be in line with an eastern identity that was based on Islam. His autobiography could be read as an invitation to Islam for those already in the religion. He grew up in a landowning family in an Upper Egyptian village and went on to study in Cairo and the USA. Qutb was an author, Islamist theorist, and, toward the end of this life, a leading member of the Muslim Brotherhood.

Qutb writes his autobiography in an anthropological manner. The book reads as if it is written by a researcher documenting the ways of the village through the life of a child. Chapter titles refer to particular village topics such as "The Local Doctor" and "The Harvest." References to the child are in the third person, just as a scholar would talk about a subject. The book does not just preserve customs, history, and arts, but is also a portal to reform. Couched in the child's experiences are references to Qutb's vision for Egypt as an adult. The child is an effective vehicle for expressing reform because he is "a site for an experience that 'everyone' shares regardless of their differences – age, region, occupation, class, and so forth."[39] In other words, readers might be receptive to new ideas because they can all relate to childhood. Qutb's anthropological style of writing gives way to sharing universal details of the child's life, such as how he plays, whom he fears, and what he wears. He depicts the child as a person with whom the reader can identify. At one moment Qutb even switches from using "he" to the pronoun "we," as if to bring the reader into dialogue with the child.[40] Furthermore, in a similar manner to Husayn, Qutb embeds the child in the heart of the masses. The child in his auto-biography is a patriotic child, the spirit of patriotism having entered him at ten years of age when he heard the principal at his school make fiery speeches about revolutionary duties. Everyone in the vil-lage trusted the child Qutb. Once he had gone to school and "solved the mysteries of handwriting," he became the personal secretary for migrant workers in the village, writing letters for them to their home-towns and reading letters sent to them. Qutb depicts the child as fully integrated into the village. To convey the sense that the village acted as a unit, he personifies it with phrases such as "the village wants," "the imagination of the village," and "the village woke up afraid."[41] Readers of Qutb's autobiography can connect to its central figure, and the child is a symbol through which the author conveys reforms.

A recurrent theme in Qutb's documentation of village life is that adults taught children to believe in superstition. The child observes numerous instances of peasants relying on folk religion for treatment of medical ailments. Popular notions attributed childhood illnesses to the jinn, the evil eye, or the *ʿafārīt* (evil spirits), and based treatment on charms, amulets, spells, ceremonies, and potions. Adults taught children that at night their souls left their bodies and roamed around in the form of cats. Anything that happened to the body of a cat at night had a direct effect on the body of the child during the day. Qutb writes:

> If this cat were confined for any reason, the child whose soul it was remained asleep and never woke. And if the cat were beaten, the child became sick and sensed pain in the area of the body corresponding to where the cat was struck. Ultimately, he died if the soul-bearing cat was killed.[42]

Adults also spoke about the transmission of tetanus to babies. Each time a woman gave birth, her *qarīna* (jinn-like companion) gave birth to a child of the opposite sex. On the sixth night after birth, if the *qarīna* was jealous of the woman's child, she would strangle the woman's baby, which foamed at the mouth and had suffocating fits.

The scientific truth was that if the midwife used an unsterile knife in delivery, and tetanus was passed on, the tetanus microbe underwent an incubation period of six days.[43]

Folk religion took control of children's minds. Qutb gives numerous examples of children shaping their behavior around superstition. Boys in the village convinced other boys to play with them by saying that if they didn't then evil spirits would make them suffer. One taunting song was as follows: "Whoever does not come out and play the snake will bite and the scorpion sting. Even the snake charmer can't charm, even the healer can't heal the harm. The tooth of a mouse, near the herbalist's house, he beats the drum, oh how charming!"[44] Qutb recalls that at ten years of age he could not walk at night without lighting matches to expose the *ʿafārīt* dwelling in dark places. He discarded his belief in superstition after interactions with a teacher from the city, who taught him the scientific method. The teacher exposed Qutb to the idea that the *ʿafārīt* were a superstition fabricated or imagined for an ulterior purpose and based on ignorance. The teacher, he remembers, "purified their minds of it [superstition]" by doing experiments to prove the non-existence of evil spirits.[45]

Qutb's criticism of children's indoctrination into folk religion related to his vision for Egypt's future. Prior to the 1930s and 1940s, the reigning ideology was a reconciliation of the East and West as they were assumed to be compatible or of similar origin (Husayn's pharaonism is an example of this). Qutb was among the intellectuals who played a leading role in disseminating the idea that there could be a uniquely eastern form of progress and modernity in Egypt.[46] He rejected as a form of progress Turkey's attempt to westernize and secularize. He believed Egypt could borrow material goods from the West but that it had to maintain its own spiritual authenticity. Qutb distinguished between "culture" (*thaqāfa*) and "civilization" (*madanīiya*) as the categories that separated unacceptable and acceptable borrowing (from the West).[47] Culture included religion and morals and had to be kept intact, whereas civilization included science and could be shaped by outsiders. Folk religion was one manifestation of cultural deviation. Qutb's attack on this can be viewed as an appeal to strengthen Egyptian culture (i.e. purifying religion by removing superstition) in the fight against western political and economic imperialism.[48] The juxtaposition of Qutb's attachment to his village and his mockery of its ignorant ways was a way in which reform, particularly of deviant religious ideas, could be motivated.

Not long after publication of his autobiography, Qutb became an active member of the Muslim Brotherhood. When it was founded in the 1920s, the Brotherhood held that British rule and economic imperialism were caused by individuals' deviation from the true practices of Islam. The child in Qutb's autobiography is a symbolic representation of the changes that he sought in society. The child borrowed from western civilization without losing cultural authenticity. Qutb depicted the child as entrenched in village life in order to build a broad-based coalition with the masses to support his Islamist imaginings of Egypt.[49]

Salamah Musa

Egyptian journalist, writer, and reformer Salamah Musa (1887–1958) was born into a wealthy, land-owning Coptic family that was from the Nile Delta region. He pursued higher learning in Cairo and France, where he became an advocate of secularism and socialism. His ideas about what an Egyptian identity independent of the British should look like changed throughout his life, and his autobiography speaks to these changes. In the 1920s and 1930s, Musa, like Husayn was a strong proponent of a type of nationalism that advocated a non-eastern identity for Egypt. It held that ancient Egyptian civilization sent the first waves of progress out into the world, ultimately culminating in western civilization. Musa was from the Coptic Christian minority group and believed that Copts were the first Egyptians; and by extension the originators of western civilization. By the 1940s, Musa still wanted Egypt to become a westernized and secular society, but he became less attached to finding parallels between Egypt and Europe, and joined forces with advocates of Arabism, or a shared Arab identity for the Egyptian people. In his autobiography, published in 1947, Musa admits to having fallen prey in his younger years to European propaganda that pushed him toward identifying with the superiority of European culture.[50] His autobiography provides a window into some of the emotional turmoil he experienced as a child, which led to his wanting to identify with western culture.

Musa's childhood experiences with colonialism are in juxtaposition to the official narrative of Empire, which holds that colonialism was primarily an institutional arrangement that mattered for its political economy.[51] Ashis Nandy says there is a consensus to under-acknowledge the emotional impact of the white man's burden on people who lived in contact zones. Musa uses his childhood to show a nuanced picture of Empire, depicting the British as instilling a sense of inferiority and fear in subjects to maintain control. He recalls the typical way in which one of his foreign teachers interacted with the students in his school,

> The students did not know the name of the British teacher who always showed his self-importance by starting his speech with a moment of silence. He was quick to punish the pupil who made the slightest indication of disobedience. The typical punishment was to deprive the student of lunch and give him a piece of bread to eat standing up while his classmates sat around him at tables. I do not think that by this punishment he meant anything other than spreading humiliation and shame among us.[52]

Musa remembers that clear divisions were made in his school between those who were British and those who were Egyptian. There were racist underpinnings that made this divide more than a typical teacher–student hierarchy. He writes: "The British teachers enjoyed torturing us. The relationships between us lacked any human feeling..."[53] The British teacher inscribed a sense of inferiority in the child's body by making him feel physical hunger pains. As this occurred in the setting of school, the child's daily surroundings became associated with humiliation.

Even when he left the school building and walked around on Egyptian land, the child could not escape messages about his inferiority to the British. One of the most prominent memories from Musa's childhood was a visit with his cousin to a pharaonic village called Basta that the British had pillaged. Musa writes that the British did not respect the great history that dotted the Egyptian landscape. As a child he saw the occupiers take stone blocks from ancient structures to build their own houses.[54] He also observed how Britain's cotton farming in Egypt made the water impure, thereby affecting the health and strength of the peasants.[55] Musa received lessons from the

British that stated Egyptian land was only suitable for agriculture and not for industry.[56] Colonizers inscribed a sense of inferiority on children's minds, bodies, and space. Musa testifies to growing up under the imperial gaze, which assumes the white western subject as central and trivializes and infantilizes the Other.

As mentioned earlier, autobiography theorists Smith and Watson claim that "The personal story of a remembered past is always in a dialogue with emergent cultural formations."[57] Musa's depiction of childhood feelings of inferiority is connected to his nationalist aspirations at the time of publication. Musa published his autobiography five years before the Egyptian Revolution that would establish a republic and completely end the British occupation. In the 1940s he had shifted away from campaigning for a Europeanized Egyptian identity toward an authentically Arab identity. His desire in his autobiography was to point out the humiliation he suffered as a child by the British in order to set the record straight about how he stood on colonialism. He shows that colonialism has a perverse impact on the subjects' sense of self; for example, the British disparaged Egyptian culture and land in front of children. After the 1952 Revolution, Musa went on to become an integral part of the Nasserist regime, having fully given up on his desire for Egypt to break off and become part of Europe. The feeling of humiliation that colored Musa's childhood shaped his political career.

Huda Shaʿrawi

Egyptian feminist and nationalist Huda Shaʿrawi (1879–1947) was raised in a cosmopolitan aristocratic household and spent her childhood in the confines of the household's harem. She was an advocate, writer, and philanthropist for Egyptian women until the last days of her life. In 1919 she helped lead the first women's street demonstration for national independence, and in 1923 she founded and was the first president of the Egyptian Feminist Union. Shaʿrawi is famous for being the first Egyptian woman to take off her veil in a staged public event in 1923. She campaigned in her adult life for women's education, ending personal status laws and restrictions on women's dress and movement. All these issues are addressed in her autobiographical depictions of childhood, compiled from her memoirs and stories after her death. Multiple voices speak in her autobiography. Through the "autobiographical pact,"[58] the reader understands these voices are all essentially the voice of Shaʿrawi. One of them is her male secretary, to whom she dictated her memoirs before death: Shaʿrawi was unable to write in Arabic, despite her demands as a child to receive an education equal to that of her brother. Another voice is that of the editor who adds details and notes to the book. Many of Shaʿrawi's stories of childhood can also be read as a defense of her father, whose opposition to the Urabi Revolt made him a problematic figure for many Egyptians. Her autobiography also has a feminist message, and she focuses primarily on the 40 years of seclusion she experienced in the harem system in Egypt. The central objective of Shaʿrawi's childhood memoirs is to talk about present-day issues facing women.

Marilyn Booth's study of women's biography in modern Egypt argues that biographies in twentieth-century Egypt were a way in which women and men could collectively propose and debate their ideas on women's emancipation.[59] Autobiographies of girlhood served as a similar tool in the feminist movement. Childhood is useful in the expression of feminist reforms because children have symbolic importance. As Stefan Tanaka theorizes, "The child [...] serves as the embodied site for the future of the nation; it reminds adults of what is wrong with the present and provides the possibility for reform."[60] Girlhood is particularly symbolic because girls are seen as the future reproducers of society. Girls' lives in early twentieth-century Egypt were under the regulation of adults more so than boys. Giving voice to the girl through autobiography is a form of resistance. Even though the adult author is crafting the girl's voice, there is symbolic meaning in allowing the girl to be the microphone. The act is empowering for girls because it allows them to speak for themselves and to express concerns relating to their lives. As opposed to prioritizing the polemics of male intellectuals debating women's status, autobiography permits the girl to be at the center of the debate.

A common concern in autobiographies written by women was the early and non-consensual marriage of girls. Feminist demands from 1923 to 1952 prioritized women's education, followed by new work opportunities and the reform of personal status laws. The minimum age of marriage was raised for both sexes in 1923 and 1924, but in the 1930s no further changes were made to personal status laws. Arranged marriage was commonly practiced in all classes, among the elite in order to secure political alliances between households and consolidate land. For example, Shaʿrawi's mother arranged for her

13-year-old daughter to marry a cousin who already had children older than Sha'rawi herself. When Sha'rawi overheard this news, she recalls feeling as if "the room was spinning."[61] She refused the marriage, saying that her proposed partner could be as old as her father. To assuage Sha'rawi's discomfort, her mother lied that preparations in the garden were related to another girl's wedding. The mother temporarily relocated Sha'rawi to a neighboring suburb. Relatives laid guilt on Sha'rawi by warning that refusal to marry would make her mother ill and bedridden. Sha'rawi writes that the cutting down of the trees in the garden (her playground) for the marriage celebration was indicative of the ending of her childhood.

Sha'rawi documented her experience with forced marriage to help to improve conditions for all Egyptian women. One way in which she did this was by showing the context that she liberated herself from. This served as an example for other women. Additionally, Sha'rawi's critique of early marriage was a way of saying that her body, and that of other women, could not be subsumed into a cult of domesticity. Her stance against early marriage was also a response to some nationalist leaders' use of the family in order to build the Egyptian nation.[62] Companionate marriage was a fundamental aspect of the changes called for by feminists such as Sha'rawi. The issue of marriage, and women's rights generally, was contentious in Egyptian political and cultural life because it touched upon splits in nationalist camps. As Beth Baron writes, "Religious and secularly-oriented nationalists used the 'Woman Question' as the field upon which they pitched their battles over the cultural content of Egyptian nationalism."[63] Sha'rawi's stance against early marriage was a marker of her feminist ideals as well as her support for national liberalism. In her younger years she was on the Wafd's Women's Central Committee, but resigned when they would not go far enough in meeting her nationalist and feminist demands. Later she headed the Egyptian Feminist Union (EFU), which was secular. Sha'rawi's adult battles for feminism reverberated in her autobiography, most particularly through the powerful symbol of girlhood.

Ahmad Amin

Of urban middle-class background, Ahmad Amin (1886–1954) was a journalist, social affairs commentator, and professor. Amin's vision for Egypt came at the intersection of West and East. He criticized colonialism, but thought there were some western ideas and ways, such as secularism, that were of value for Egypt. Known for his eight-volume series on Islamic history, which used western scholarship, Amin thought that Muslims could learn from non-Muslims without losing the unique aspects of Islamic civilization. Amin published his autobiography in 1950, four years before his death. Dotted with Freudian terms such as consciousness and unconsciousness, it seeks to show the childhood influences that shaped his adult self. It is also replete with comparisons between the time of his childhood and the time at which he was writing. Through his memories of childhood, Amin defines his vision of the present through the past. Frederic Jameson describes this style of autobiographical writing as "nostalgia for the present." Authors no longer experience their history as they did when it occurred, and instead project current situations onto the past. Historicity, or a sense of history, is not a representation of the past but "a process of reification whereby we draw back from our immersion in the here and now (not yet identified as a present) and grasp it as a kind of thing."[64] Amin uses his childhood memories to lament the passing of traditional forms of societal and family structures and also to laud the arrival of new forms of education. Through these examples, Amin articulates a vision of Egypt as a society that should at once embrace stability and change.

There is a strong critique in Amin's autobiography of certain aspects of Egyptian heritage that have disappeared. He regrets that individualism reigns supreme in society and in the family. He notes that in his childhood the neighborhood used to be the basic unit of the city, with relations between people based on cooperation. The neighborhood coalesced around storytellers and collective meeting points: seuks, baths, and coffee shops, for example. If a person was sick everyone from the area knew and came to visit. Amin identifies collectivity with Egyptian heritage by juxtaposing the way he lived as a child with the way the European occupiers lived. He remembers that the Europeans did not even know one another in their own neighborhoods.

Amin laments that European individualism has taken hold of the Egyptian family. The father used to be the basic unit around which everyone coalesced, and he praises patriarchal rule through the example of his upbringing. Amin's father ate, slept, and studied alone in the upper part of the house, and the children came to see him only to practice reading. The father controlled everything that went on below: for example, mother and children did not go out of the house without asking permission. Amin writes that the one time his father shared his power with the children, organization of the house gave way to chaos.[65] When reading Amin's autobiography against the backdrop of essays he published throughout his life, this praise of patriarchy becomes all the more evident. In 1938, he wrote an essay entitled "Power of the Fathers" in which he discusses changes in the family since the time of his father. Patriarchal rule, he argues, has given way to individualism and self-assertion.[66] Amin uses autobiography to document an awareness of and concern for new ways of organizing society and the family around the individual. He writes that if his deceased grandmother came back and saw all the changes, she would go crazy.[67]

Amin's autobiography demands a return to certain ways of his childhood but a divergence from others, most notably traditional forms of pedagogy. The main stress in his childhood came from his father's decision about schooling. Amin recalls the he did not want to attend religious school, but instead the new government-run secular school. The latter was in his eyes beautiful and clean.[68] For a while his father let him attend both, but this busy schedule left no time for play. Sometimes Amin lied that he was sick so that he could have a break from school. Despite his son's wishes, Amin's father withdrew him from government school altogether at ten years of age. Amin detested the religious school and writes that it made him become a man prematurely. Peers teased him for wearing religious garb, and shaykhs hit him if he did not rock back and forth while reading in the *kuttāb*. Sometimes the shaykh tied the legs of a student together so he could not move, and then hit him with a cane. Amin also recalls other suffering in the religious schools, as well as in his home, which his father imbued with religious education: he wrote that the scent of religion was all one could smell when one opened the doors to the house.[69] His father prohibited laughter and instilled fear of the afterlife, while reading the Qur'an aloud every day.

When Amin wrote his autobiography, he stated that schools had better pedagogical methods than when he was growing up, and that they motivated children to learn; studying had become a fun game for children. Amin writes that he used to be bored in the *kuttāb* because the focus was on memorization and not understanding.

No matter with which shaykh a child studied, "be it a tender one or a strict one; a blind one or a sighted one," Amin says learning was always undertaken using the same useless method of sitting in a circle, rocking back and forth and reading aloud. He attended various *kuttāb* as a child and recalls that the only difference between them was "the size of the rooms."[70] He also claims that schools have become more hygienic, with doctors visiting and children not allowed to come to school when they are sick. He compares his education to his son's, saying that his son's is happier and not welded to poverty and struggle.

In his retrospective look at his childhood, Amin depicts enormous stress that was caused by a traditional father who did not let him attend government school. Yet at the same time, Amin uses his memories of childhood to praise patriarchy. This seemingly contradictory message is less opaque when considering Amin's role as a public intellectual who sought to shape Egypt's course. Autobiography is a tool with which intellectuals can identify society's present through representations of the past. For Amin, it was clear that Egyptian society needed to embrace secular education and avoid a full onslaught of European individualism. This message chimed with nationalist sentiments of his era. His book was published two years before the death knell of colonialism, whereupon Egypt witnessed the establishment of a socialist state that brought religious schools under secular control. It is clear that expressing societal identity through childhood has symbolic weight. Childhood is a period of transition in which a person evolves from one stage to another. It is also a period that remains forever fixed because of its timeless nature. By speaking of societal change through the lens of childhood, Amin conveys once more his push for change alongside stability.

ʿAʾisha ʿAbd al-Rahman (Bint al-Shatiʾ)

ʿAʾisha ʿAbd al-Rahman was born in 1913 and grew up in a rural area that was considered the backwater of Egypt. She struggled to obtain an education, as her father belonged to a generation that did not like women to leave the sanctuary of the home. ʿAbd al-Rahman obtained a PhD, and broke ground as one of the first women to engage in Islamic scholarship. In addition to teaching Arabic literature at university level, she wrote extensively on issues relating to

women and social justice. Published in 1966, her memoir of childhood contributed to the building of a post-colonial national identity.
A fundamental problem in any post-colonial state is the rebuilding
of economic and political institutions, as well as national identity.
The question of where women should fit in the post-colonial state
was central to reconstruction. Debates circulated about the degree to
which the East should copy the West in advancing women's rights.
There was a tension between feminism and cultural authenticity
because feminists often came from the upper classes and adopted
elements of western dress and languages.[71] ʿAbd al-Rahman believed
progress for women could come within an Islamic context, as she
conveys in her writing about her educational journey. The obstacles she faced were caused by patriarchy, and the British occupiers,
symbols of the West, only served as further obstacle.

ʿAbd al-Rahman depicts herself as devout from an early age and
firmly embedded in the social fabric. A childhood dream in which
she received a Qurʾan set her on the life path to become an Islamic
scholar; and the young ʿAbd al-Rahman quietly corrected to herself her father's misinterpretations of Qurʾanic verses that related to
women. She was from a large Egyptian family whose lineage could
be traced back many generations. She creates a metaphorical image
of this in describing her family home: it belonged to her great-
grandmother, and it was so old that its foundations were under the
Nile.[72] ʿAbd al-Rahman opens her autobiography by linking her existence to that of her ancestors: "When I began to understand my steps
on the earth, I was in the childhood playground on the shore of the
Nile in the city of Dumyat where my great-grandmother lived."[73] The
reader has the sense that ʿAbd al-Rahman's connections to Egypt are
so solid that they are embedded in Egypt's natural environment.

ʿAbd al-Rahman's autobiography includes numerous humiliating
childhood experiences with westerners. The message she internalized
as a child was that her Egyptian ways and customs were inferior to
those of the West. British school officials told her that her clothes
were provincial and that she did not know how to eat properly.[74]
She writes that she was fearful at her first eye exam because her
entrance to school depended upon passing, and because the person
who administered the exam was a foreigner, Miss Jarfus. Before ʿAbd
al-Rahman entered the appointment at the Ministry of Information
she asked to borrow her mother's glasses, hoping they would help her

pass. Not knowing that glasses are assigned by prescription, she failed the exam. This is a detail that she seems to mention not so much for its importance to her life (she retook the exam another day, passed and entered school), but more for the feelings the exam with a foreigner evoked in her. She writes: "I was never calm with this foreign lady, in the dryness of her expressions, the coarseness of her features, and what appeared in her movements and tone of voice as signs of power and prestige."[75] Interactions with foreigners had a debilitating impact on ʿAbd al-Rahman's educational pursuits.

Negative accounts of the British serve as rejection of the idea that models for female identity in the post-colonial state must come from the outside (the West). ʿAbd al-Rahman depicts herself as a model: a deeply religious person who overcame patriarchal blocks to her education through hard work and tenacity. Writing about examples of strong Muslim women was a common literary practice for some activists. There was a twentieth-century literary genre in which female Egyptian writers produced abundant biographies of famous women (mother, wives, and daughters of the Prophet), to convey the idea that progressive practices concerning women's status could be found in Muslim and/or Arab heritage. As a delegate at a 1962 conference to discuss socialism in Egypt, ʿAbd al-Rahman declared on the radio that equality for women would not damage Islam.[76] Her autobiography is a testament to her belief. The book is structured chronologically around her relationship with her husband, as indicated by the chapter titles: "Before We Met," "On the Road to Him," and so on. Her marriage embodied new gender roles in the context of Islam: the marriage was consensual and her husband was one of the most renowned religious scholars in Egypt. ʿAbd al-Rahman published her autobiography one year after her husband's death. Tetz Rooke observes: "The frame of this story is the narrator's elegy for her newly deceased husband, a traditional feminine genre in classical Arabic literature, but the discourse is dominated by the modern demands of women's personal freedom and social equality with men from an Islamic standpoint."[77] ʿAbd al-Rahman used autobiography to articulate a vision for women's rights that was grounded in Islam. The child, normally thought of as weak in the face of patriarchy and colonialism, emerges as a powerful symbol for reformers who were seeking to reshape gender norms in post-colonial Egypt.

Conclusion

In using the discourse and consciousness of the adult to write about the child, these authors employ memory as a tool to shape mid-twentieth-century Egyptian national identity and project aspirations for its future. Ideas expressed in autobiographies belong not just to the time of childhood but also to the time of writing. Authors use the voice of the child because its innocence creates a sense of believability and authority. Children speak back to the empire that treated them as less than human. Recounting a different version of the past is tied to the activism in the authors' adulthood. Autobiographers share how they broke away from the repressive aspects of a society that they are seeking to reform. Their personal struggles parallel the struggles of the nation. The emotional experiences of childhood linger in the subjects and impact their present day movements. Emotions are intangible and hard to quantify or pinpoint; but the writers show that building the Egyptian nation is not an institutional, economic, and political process inseparable from childhood sensibilities. Some of the crucial debates going on in Egypt about the identity and future of the nation during the twentieth century played out through the politics of memory.

Conclusion

Historians are often motivated to write about the past as a result of problems facing the contemporary world. The field of the history of childhood in the West came to form in the late twentieth century in large part because of an explosion in the public's anxieties about how to bring up children, the nature of children, and their rights and responsibilities. Historian Hugh Cunningham articulates this phenomenon: "More, perhaps, than any other branch of history, the history of childhood has been shaped by the concerns of the world in which its historians live."[1] Historians of childhood desire to find roots and guidance for contemporary forces (such as commercialization) that face their own children. They also hope that a historical perspective of western children (once predominantly entrenched in poverty) can contribute to the understanding of the circumstances of poverty in which most of the rest of world's children exist today.

The history of childhood in the Middle East as a field of study is still in its infancy. This book on the role of children in Egyptian state-building opens the door for further development of this field, which can come at no more critical time. An estimated 40 percent of Egyptians are under the age of 18. As in many "developing" countries, the statistics regarding the conditions of children in Egypt are staggering. An estimated 9.3 percent of Egyptian children work as child laborers; 28.9 percent have stunted growth due to malnutrition; 90.7 percent are exposed to violent discipline; and 69.5 percent of females participate in secondary school.[2] Considerable debate has arisen regarding why implementation of international treaties for children's rights is not working in countries such as Egypt, focusing not just on institutional and economic obstacles, but also on challenges arising from different cultural conceptions of childhood.

The modern history of Egypt reveals a distinct evolution and change in the cultural conception of childhood. When Egypt entered the twentieth century, children spent most of their time either working and playing in the fields or attending the *kuttāb* for a few hours of the day. Households were autocratic and parents did not listen to their children when making decisions. Adults used physical punishment and fear of evil spirits to discipline children. Intellectuals and nationalists played an important role in presenting new ideas about childhood for the sake of reforming the nation, calling for an increased role of the state in the lives of children, as well as moving children away from total subservience to adults. They grounded their calls for change in Arab, Egyptian, and Islamic heritage, thus showing that in a century that was moving toward a uniform conception of childhood, Egyptians were actively engaged in defining their own child-rearing techniques. Children's literature was a site and locus in which these transformations played out. The British and landed elite kept children in the workforce, preventing many from taking part in the changes in conception of childhood experienced in elite families. Children experienced increasing contact with the state and colonial officials with fear and humiliation, and at the same time longed to take part in all that modernity had to offer. Children were an integral part of Egypt's nation-building process.

The changes in childhood at the turn of the twentieth century led to the country moving toward what has become today's international children's rights framework (as defined in the 1989 Convention on the Rights of the Child and ensuing protocols/conventions). Egyptian intellectuals and nationalists of the era rarely used the word "rights" in the context of children.[3] By adopting this international framework, Egypt began to adopt at a political and cultural level some of the framework's cornerstone concepts, such as viewing children as a uniquely vulnerable group different from adults; as requiring government/legal attention and concern; and capable of playing some role in decision-making.[4] During the first half of the twentieth century, Egypt witnessed increased interest in state care for children, through such institutions as schools, and increased chances for children to develop independent voices, through such means as children's literature. This does not mean that notions of childhood care, dependency, and choice appeared in Egyptian culture during the first half of the twentieth century, but that these notions underwent a significant change (at least among the literate elite).[5]

There are two key insights into present-day conditions of children's rights in Egypt that the country's changing conception of childhood communicates to us. First, there is an ethnocentric tendency to focus on the spread of western trends as related to childhood in other parts of the world, but this assumes that non-western countries copied western tenets of childhood without engaging in their own process of change. Egyptians actively engaged in the creation of their own model of modern childhood, and did not import their ideas directly from the West. This is particularly relevant when we seek to understand individual rights versus group rights. Modern western notions of children's rights, as embodied in the 1989 Convention on the Rights of the Child and ensuing protocols, hold that the nation is a mechanism that allows the child to exist and not that the child exists for the nation. Human rights scholars and activists who advocate the latter point of view favor group rights over individual rights. When western scholars and children's rights activists talk about contemporary Egypt's preponderance of group rights, they often wrongly attribute this to Islam and its inherent lack of space for the individual, ignoring the fact that children's rights in Egypt emerged in large part out of the nationalist movement and resistance to colonialism – not Islam. The context in which a children's rights framework emerged in Egypt was vastly different from that in the West, where norms, values, and ideals of a safe, happy, and protected childhood are historically bound to the priorities of capitalism, the evolution of human rights, philanthropy/child-saving efforts, Romanticism/Enlightenment ideas, and late eighteenth-century state movements to educate children in order to compete with other industrializing countries.

In large part the nationalist movement in Egypt sought to save the child for the sake of the nation. This means that when we theorize about conceptions of children's rights today in Egypt and their implementation we must recognize that their origin is not the same as in the West. As such, divergent (i.e. group rights oriented) institutional forms of family, school, nursery, and hospital that may have emerged in Egypt to foster children's rights must not be disqualified. A look at the history of children's rights in the second half of the twentieth century is necessary to better understand the long-term implications of the origin of children's rights in Egypt. To a certain extent, Egypt today continues to value the worth of the child in terms of worth to the nation. World historian of childhood Peter Stearns says that the conventional focus on western childhood as a model for the world leads to a devaluation of alternatives.[6]

Second, the emergence of a children's rights framework in Egypt during the first half of the twentieth century took place in the context of racialized and gentrified structures regarding who deserved rights. The British and landed elites sent clear messages that children were not universally equal in Egypt, since the Egyptian child him/herself was viewed as essentially different from the western child. Although Swedish sociologist Ellen Key wrote in 1900 that this was going to be the "century of the child," such was not the case for many children around the world. The British occupiers did not export their model of childhood to Egypt in the early twentieth century, but instead took actions that sent Egyptian children in the opposite direction of British children back home. The occupiers and Egyptian landed elite spent little public money on schools,[7] and Egyptian children worked to provide raw cotton for British mills. While the British made protecting childhood a priority at home (with new child labor laws and universal, free schooling, for example), they did not prioritize it in Egypt, but actively kept Egyptian children impoverished and without means for recourse. The British propagated the idea that there was a fundamental racial difference between western children and Egyptian children. For example, British administrators in the cotton industry claimed that Egyptian children went through puberty earlier than western children, thus justifying why Egyptians should work at ages that were legally unacceptable in the West. The administrators also denigrated indigenous child-rearing practices. British imperialism functioned through subordination of the local populations' children. While elites paid lip service to the impoverished conditions of the peasantry, they kept them submissive in order to consolidate their own privileged place in society.

The hierarchical climate in which conceptions of children's rights emerged in Egypt during the first half of the twentieth century set in place a pattern of inequality that continued to shape children's rights culture in Egypt during the second half of the twentieth century. The perpetuation at international and national levels of the notion that the average Egyptian child is different from the average western or elite Egyptian child, and hence undeserving of the same rights, has continued to impair human rights laws. The imposition of, and resentment of, a western model of childhood on Egypt, as well as the resulting confusion, has also continued to impede human rights laws.[8] As sociologist of childhood Sharon Stephens cautions, "Within high modernity, 'deviant childhood' of third world childhoods could be interpreted as local particularities and instances of backwardness and underdevelopment, thus justifying expanded efforts to export modern childhood around the world."[9]

To better understand modern Egyptian conceptions of childhood, research must be done on such topics as when and how the Islamic movement (for example, *al-Ikhwān al-Muslimūn*) entered the fray on childhood; the Nasser era socialist policies in the 1950s and if they heralded a change in conditions for children; the Sadat era's neo-liberalism and its possible impact on prioritizing the sovereignty of an individual child (or family) over the sovereignty of the nation; and Suzanne Mubarak's groundbreaking foundation of the National Council on Womanhood and Childhood, and its role in connecting Egypt to the international children's rights movement.

Study of the history of childhood in Egypt, and the Middle East more generally, has a long way to go. The smallest voices are calling out for attention.

Glossary

ʿālim, pl. *ʿulamāʾ*	learned, erudite, scholar, expert in the religious sciences
awlād	children
bābā	father
bulūgh	puberty
effendī, pl. *effendīya*	educated Egyptian elite, middle-class, middle class, from *afandī* (gentleman)
fallāḥ, pl. *fallāḥūn*	peasant, peasantry, fellaheen
gallābīya	long gown worn by peasants, also *galabia*
ʿĪd alAḍḥā	Feast of the sacrifice, religious festival celebrated by Muslims 70 days after the end of Ramadan
ʿifrīt, pl. *ʿafārīt*	evil spirit, a type of *jinn*
imama	traditional head wrap
jāhilī	pagan, pre-Islamic
jinn (coll.)	demons, spirits that can be good or bad
kuttāb, pl. *katātib*	traditional Qurʾanic elementary school
magzūb (*majdhūb*)	possessed, mad, sometimes believed to have divine healing powers
qarīna	jinn-like companion
Miṣr/Miṣriyya	Egypt/Egyptian
zajal, pl. *azjāl*	popular Arabic poem in strophic form
shaykh	Islamic scholar, tribal chieftain, respected elder
tamyīz	age of discernment
tarboosh	felt, cone-shaped hat worn by Egyptian, upper-class, educated elite
tilmīdh	student
waladī	my son
waqf, pl. *awqāf*	pious religious endowment, inalienable property

Notes

Introduction

1. In Bint al-Shati᾽'s autobiography, ῾Ala al-jisr (Cairo: Maktabat al-Usra, 1999 [1966]), p. 22, she recalls many times joyfully swimming in the canal, only to be told to get out of the water by her mother anxiously shouting about underwater jinn. As a child, she had a recurring nightmare of a mermaid, whose upper body was in the form of a human, lured children toward her before grabbing them and taking them down to underwater caves.
2. Ibid., p. 38.
3. Elizabeth Warnock Fernea (Ed.), *Remembering Childhood in the Middle East: Memoirs from a Century of Change* (Austin, TX: University of Texas Press, 2002).
4. For a history of schooling in Egypt during the nineteenth century, see Linda Ann Herrera, "The Sanctity of the School: New Islamic Education and Modern Egypt" (PhD dissertation, Columbia University, New York, 2000), pp. 43–68.
5. Ibid., p. 67.
6. Khaled Fahmy, *All the Pasha's Men: Mehmed Ali, His Army, and the Making of Modern Egypt* (Cairo and New York: American University in Cairo Press, 2002).
7. This evolution can be seen in the historiography of women in the history of the Middle East. Margot Badran's *Feminists, Islam, and the Nation* (Princeton, NJ: Princeton University Press, 1996) inserts women in the history of nationalism by showing that they were players in the nationalist movement. Beth Baron's *Egypt as a Woman: Nationalism, Gender, and Politics* (Berkeley, CA: University of California Press, 2005) explores how the nationalist movement used maternal imagery. Mona L. Russell's *Creating the New Egyptian Woman: Consumerism, Education and National Identity, 1863–1922* (New York: Palgrave Macmillan, 2004) looks at how nationalists recast women as consumers; and Lisa Pollard's *Nurturing the Nation: The Family Politics of Modernizing, Colonizing, and Liberating Egypt 1805–1923* (Berkeley, CA: University of California Press, 2005) explores how nationalists recast women in the domicile.
8. Philippe Ariès, *Centuries of Childhood: A Social History of Family Life*, trans. by Robert Baldick (New York: Vintage Books, 1962).
9. Shulamith Shahar, *Childhood in the Middle Ages* (London and New York: Routledge, 1990).
10. Colin Heywood, *A History of Childhood: Children and Childhood in the West from Medieval to Modern Times* (Cambridge: Polity, and Malden, MA: Blackwell, 2001).

11. Chris Jenks, *Childhood* (London and New York: Routledge, 2005), p. 69.
12. Paula S. Fass, *Kidnapped: Child Abduction in America* (New York: Oxford University Press, 1997).
13. Nara B. Milanich, *Children of Fate: Childhood, Class and the State in Chile, 1850–1930* (Durham, NC: Duke University Press, 2009).
14. Jane Humphries, *Childhood and Child Labour in the Industrial Revolution* (Cambridge: Cambridge University Press, 2010).
15. Of course, there are also indications that this shift is slow in coming. The way that the world allocates its resources and conducts its wars evidences a devaluation of the child. Some children grow up in conditions of grinding poverty, while other children are born into privilege, with dietary regimes and toys waiting for them. Furthermore, sociologist Daniel Thomas Cook argues that children become largely aware of what it means to be a child in a language acquired from parents and school, that is to say in a world where adults do the thinking for them. Daniel Thomas Cook, "Introduction: Interrogating Symbolic Childhood," in Daniel Thomas Cook (Ed.), *Symbolic Childhood* (New York: Peter Lang Publishing, 2002), p. 3.
16. Jenks, *Childhood*, p. 19.
17. Sociological studies show that children's peer groups can play an important role in a child's socialization, emotional development, and linguistic ability and communication. See Frances Chaput Waksler (Ed.), *Studying the Social Worlds of Children* (London: Routledge, 1991).
18. Catriona Kelly, "Thank You for the Wonderful Book: Soviet Child Readers and the Management of Children's Reading, 1950–75," *Kritika: Explorations in Russian and Eurasian History*, 6 (4) (2005), pp. 717–753.
19. Heidi Morrison, *Global History of Childhood Reader* (London and New York: Routledge, 2012).
20. Scholarship on the legal standing of children during the early Islamic and medieval periods usually comes as a tangential aspect of scholarship on women and gender (Jonathan P. Berkey, "Circumcision Circumscribed: Female Excision and Cultural Accommodation in the Medieval Near East," *International Journal of Middle East Studies*, 28 (1) (1996), pp. 19–38; Margaret L. Meriwether, "Rights of Children and the Responsibilities of Women: Women as Wasis in Ottoman Aleppo, 1170–1840," in Amira El Azhary Sonbol (Ed.), *Women, the Family, and Divorce Laws in Islamic History*, 1st edn., Contemporary Issues in the Middle East (Syracuse, NY: Syracuse University Press, 1996); and Kristina Richardson, "Singing Slave Girls (Qiyan) of the ʿAbbasid Court in the Ninth and Tenth Centuries," in Gwyn Campbell, Suzanne Miers and Joseph C. Miller (Eds.), *Children in Slavery through the Ages* (Athens, OH: Ohio University Press, 2009).
21. Benjamin C. Fortna, *Imperial Classroom: Islam, the State, and Education in the Late Ottoman Empire* (Oxford: Oxford University Press, 2002). Other works on the topic during the Ottoman period include Selçuk Akşin Somel's *The Modernization of Public Education in the Ottoman Empire* (Leiden: Brill Academic Publishers, 2001); and Hale Yılmaz's "Learning to Read (Again): The Social Experiences of Turkey's 1928 Alphabet Reform,"

International Journal of Middle East Studies, 43 (4) (2011), pp. 677–697. Monica Ringer's *Education, Religion, and the Discourse of Multiple Reforms in Qajar Iran* (Costa Mesa, CA: Mazda, 2001) discusses education reform in nineteenth-century Iran. Ela Greenberg's "Educating Muslim Girls in Mandatory Jerusalem," *International Journal of Middle East Studies*, 36 (1) (2004), pp. 1–19 argues that the education of elementary school-aged Muslim girls in British Mandated Palestine contributed to the creation of generations of nationalists.

22. Ethnographies of childhood, such as Erika Friedl's, *Children of Deh Koh* (Syracuse, NY: Syracuse University Press, 1997), do not place children in a historical context.

23. Peter N. Stearns, *Childhood in World History* (New York and London: Routledge, 2006 and 2011), p. 7.

24. Ellis Goldberg, *Trade, Reputation, and Child Labor in Twentieth-Century Egypt* (New York: Palgrave Macmillan, 2004).

25. "Reports on the Finances, Administration and Condition of Egypt and the Progress of Reforms," House of Commons Parliamentary Papers (London, 1898).

26. Nancy Gallagher, *Egypt's Other Wars: Epidemics and the Politics of Public Health* (Syracuse, NY: Syracuse University Press, 1990), p. 12.

27. Ibid., p. 15.

28. Psychologists label the instilling of respect in parents and submissiveness to adults as the "apprenticeship and obedience" model. For more reading on this topic in contemporary society, see Gary Gregg, *The Middle East: A Cultural Psychology* (New York: Oxford University Press, 2005).

29. In her book, *Creating the New Egyptian Woman, 1863–1922* (New York: Palgrave Macmillan, 2004), Russell makes a similar argument for consumerism in Egyptian society. She says that Egyptian consumerism did not arise only in response to the West. There already had to be a structure in place to allow it to flourish.

30. See Avner Gil'adi, *Children of Islam: Concepts of Childhood in Medieval Muslim Society* (New York: St. Martin's Press, 1992), on medieval Islamic attitudes toward childhood and infancy.

31. Huda Shaʿrawi, *Mudhakkirat Huda Shaʿrawi, raʾidat al-marʾa al-ʾarabiyya al-haditha* (Cairo: Dar al-Hilal, 1981), p. 10.

32. Omnia El Shakry, "Youth as Peril and Promise: The Emergence of Adolescent Psychology in Postwar Egypt," *International Journal of Middle East Studies*, 43 (4) (2011), pp. 591–610. James Jankowski, in *Egypt's Young Rebels: "Young Egypt," 1933–1952* (Stanford, CA: Hoover Institution Press, 1975), argues that intellectuals effectively introduced to Egyptian society the stage of life called "teen-ager" through the expansion of secondary and university enrollment and the education of this group in popular sovereignty and participation in government by way of on-campus movements and periodicals.

33. See the work of Heywood, *A History of Childhood*; and Hugh Cunningham, *Children and Childhood in Western Society since 1500* (Harlow and New York: Pearson Longman, 2005).

34. Muhammad ʿAbduh, *al-Islam wa-l-radd ʿala muntaqidihi* (Cairo: Al-Maktabah al-Tijariyya al-Kubra, 1928), p. 165.
35. Rifaʿa Rafiʿal-Tahtawi, *al-Murshid al-amin li-l-banat wa-l-banin* (Cairo: Majlis al-Aʿla li-l-Thaqafa, 2002), p. 19.
36. Ibrahim al-Mazini, "*al-Saghir wa-l-kubar*," Ibid., *Ibrahim al-Katib* (Cairo: Dar al-Taraqqi, 1931).
37. al-Shatiʾ, ʿ*Ala al-jisr*, p. 81.
38. Barbara Rosenwein, *Emotional Communities in the Early Middle Ages* (New York: Cornell University Press, 2007), p. 2.
39. Joanna Bourke, *Fear: A Cultural History* (Emeryville, CA: Shoemaker Hoard, 2006), p. 6.
40. M. OConner, "A History of Fear: Professor Joanna Bourke in Interview," *TMO Magazine*, 1 May 2005, available at: http://www.threemon keysonline.com/a-history-of-fear-professor-joanna-bourke-in-interview/ (accessed 25 May 2014).
41. Robert Darnton, *The Great Cat Massacre and Other Episodes in French Cultural History* (New York: Basic Books, 2009), p. 4. According to Darnton (Ibid.), if a historian is doing his or her job accurately, then he or she will be constantly facing culture shock in the archives about the lives of past people. He says that historians often fall in to a false sense of familiarity with the past, assuming that people in the past felt and thought as we do today, "allowing for the wigs and wooden shoes."
42. The following two examples help illustrate this idea. First, in Kathleen S. Uno's book, *Passages to Modernity: Motherhood, Childhood, and Social Reform in Early Twentieth-Century Japan* (Honolulu, HI: University of Hawaiʻi Press, 1999), she shows that the Japanese had a delicate balance between the traditional practice of children spending their childhoods with kin and the new phenomenon of children spending time away from non-kin in age-graded schools and day-care institutions. Second, Benjamin C. Fortna, in "Emphasizing the Islamic: Modifying the Curriculum of Late Ottoman State Schools," in François Georgeon and Klaus Kreiser (Eds.), *Enfance et jeunesse dans l'islam* (Paris: Maisonneuve et Larose, 2007), pp. 193–209, argues that western ideas about education were integrated into late Ottoman society while still preserving aspects of Islamic traditions.
43. Stearns, *Childhood in World History*.
44. Acceptable treatment of children in the West varied by race, class, gender, and ability. See, for example, the work of Joseph Illick, *American Childhoods* (Philadelphia, PA: University of Pennsylvania Press, 2002); and Philip Safford and Elizabeth Safford, *A History of Childhood and Disability* (New York: Teacher's College Press, 1996).
45. ʿAbduh, *al-Islam*.
46. For more information on the Boy Scouts in Egypt, see Wilson C. Jacob, *Working Out Egypt: Effendi Masculinity and Subject Formation in Colonial Modernity, 1870–1940* (Durham, NC: Duke University Press, 2011); and Aaron Jakes, "Extracurricular Nationalism: Youth Culture in the Age of Egypt's Parliamentary Monarchy" (MPhil dissertation, Oxford University, 2005).

1 Reforming Childhood in the Context of Colonialism

1. Born in Constantinople in 1883 and of Armenian descent, Alban emigrated to Egypt with his family at an early age. In the 1940s and 1950s, he became one of Cairo's most popular society photographers and often used his studio to transform ordinary Egyptian people to look like Hollywood film stars.

2. For a discussion on the link between dress and Egyptian middle-class masculine identity, see Jacob's *Working out Egypt* (Durham, NC: Duke University Press, 2011), pp. 214–224.

3. Keith David Watenpaugh, *Being Modern in the Middle East: Revolution, Nationalism, Colonialism, and the Arab Middle Class* (Princeton, NJ, and Oxford: Princeton University Press, 2006).

4. Ashis Nandy, *The Intimate Enemy: Loss and Recovery of Self under Colonialism* (New Delhi: Oxford University Press, 2011), p. 116.

5. Joel Beinin and Zachary Lockman, *Workers on the Nile: Nationalism, Communism, Islam, and the Egyptian Working Class, 1882–1954* (Cairo: The American University in Cairo Press, 1998).

6. Humphries, *Childhood and Child Labour*; Anna Davin, *Growing up Poor: Home, School and Street in London 1870–1914* (London: Rivers Oram Press, 1996); Ning de Coninck-Smith et al., *Industrious Children: Work and Childhood in the Nordic Countries, 1850–1990* (Odense: Odense University Press, 1997).

7. Beinin and Lockman, *Workers on the Nile*.

8. International Labour Organization (ILO), *Labour Survey of North Africa* (Geneva: International Labour Organization, 1960).

9. Beinin and Lockman, *Workers on the Nile*; and Elinor Burns, *British Imperialism in Egypt* (London: Labour Research Department, 1928). Furthermore, starting in 1912, birth certificates were required by law, but this law was not enforced by the government. Badran, *Feminists, Islam, and the Nation*, p. 128. In his autobiography, *Fi al-khamsin ʿaraftu tariqi: Sira dhatiyya* (Cairo: Dar Gharib, 2000), p. 19, Egyptian intellectual Mahmud Rabiʿi illustrates the lack of precise birth records during the first half of the twentieth century:

   > My mother told me I was born in the early morning on a cold night in one of the field cow-enclosures [ghaiṭ abū mulaysa], that I described in the last chapter...On my birth certificate I am born the 15th of January 1932 but it was not necessary that this date be exact. It is possible that the wet nurse [ḥalīmat al-dāya] who noted my birth and sent it to the birth records was late in sending it by a day or two, but it is not possible that she was late by a month or months.

   When a government organization tried to determine age levels, it usually did so by height. Sayyid Qutb, *A Child from the Village*, translated by John Calvert and William Shepard (New York: Syracuse University Press, 2004), pp. 23 and 37.

10. Burns, *British Imperialism in Egypt*.

11. H. B. Butler, *Report on Labour Conditions in Egypt with Suggestions for Future Social Legislation* (Cairo: Government Press, 1932).

12. Beinin and Lockman, *Workers on the Nile.*

13. Goldberg, *Trade*, p. 38.

14. Peter N. Stearns, "Child Labor in the Industrial Revolution," in Hugh D. Hindman (Ed.), *The World of Child Labor: An Historical and Regional Survey* (New York: M. E. Sharpe, 2009), p. 38.

15. Jacob, *Working Out Egypt.*

16. Pollard, *Nurturing the Nation*, p. 48.

17. Egyptian intellectuals also employed the image of the Egyptian peasant in their nationalist campaigns. For more information on this, see the work of Michael Gasper, *The Power of Representation* (Stanford, CA: Stanford University Press, 2009).

18. Omnia El Shakry, *The Great Social Laboratory: Subjects of Knowledge in Colonial and Postcolonial Egypt* (Stanford, CA: Stanford University Press, 2007), p. 27.

19. Furthermore, these misrepresentations of colonial children were taught to European children. British children, for example, were raised to believe in British superiority. Teachers taught British school children that all subjects of the British Empire welcomed British rule and it was a pleasure for the British to civilize non-westerners (Davin, *Growing Up Poor*), p. 201.

20. Beverly Carolease Grier, *Invisible Hands: Child Labor and the State in Colonial Zimbabwe* (Portsmouth, NH: Heinemann, 2006).

21. A. Dirk Moses (Ed.), *Genocide and Settler Society: Frontier Violence and Stolen Indigenous Children in Australian History* (New York: Berghahn Books, 2004).

22. Humphries, *Childhood and Child Labour*, p. 369.

23. Ibid., p. 9.

24. Harry Hendrick, "Periods of History: Childhood and Child Work, *c.*1800–Present," in Hindman (Ed.), *The World of Child Labor*, p. 37.

25. In his book, *Childhood in World History*, p. 84, Stearns makes this same claim about all peasant colonial children.

26. Goldberg, *Trade*, p. 65.

27. The system employed then was that of the Ottoman Land Code of 1858, which divided land into three categories: *mulk* (lands over which the owner had full control); *mīrī* (lands that were state domains and that could be taxed directly by the occupiers of the country); and *waqf* (lands dedicated to religious or charitable purposes).

28. Butler, *Report on Labour Conditions in Egypt.*

29. Ibid.

30. Within Egypt, the British made distinctions between the physical capabilities of children, based on the different regions of the country. Beinin finds that during the British occupation, the Saʿidis (Egyptians from the south) were reputed to surpass the fellaheen from the Nile Delta region in stamina and physical strength and as such monopolized the more strenuous jobs such as weighing and transporting raw cotton. The British likewise held notions in their own country that the migrant Irish

in nineteenth-century England often performed heavy physical labor because their physique or temperament made them more suitable for this than the English worker. See Beinin and Lockman, *Workers on the Nile.*

31. Henry Habib Ayrout, *The Egyptian Peasant* (Cairo: American University in Cairo Press, 2005), p. 3.
32. Butler, *Report on Labour Conditions in Egypt.*
33. Ibid.
34. "Report by Her Majesty's Agent and Consul-General on the Finances, Administration and Condition of Egypt and the Sudan in 1898," House of Commons Parliamentary Papers (London, 1899).
35. Ibid.
36. "Report on the Finances, Administration and Condition of Egypt and the Progress of Reforms," House of Commons Parliamentary Papers (London, 1895).
37. "Reports by Her Majesty's Agent and Consul-General on the Finances, Administration and Condition of Egypt and the Sudan in 1899," House of Commons Parliamentary Papers (London, 1900).
38. "Report on the Administration and Condition of Egypt and the Progress of Reforms," House of Commons Parliamentary Papers (London, 1891).
39. Ibid.; and "Reports by Mr Villiers Stuart Respecting the Progress of Reorganization in Egypt since the British Occupation in 1882," House of Commons Parliamentary Papers (London, 1895).
40. "Reports on the Finances, Administration and Condition of Egypt" (1898).
41. When westerners represented Egyptian children in photographs, they were most often portrayed in the context of upper-class harems or in photographic "reconstructions" of supposed Egyptian families. In attempting to recreate the private space of the harem, westerners did not represent women and girls but, rather, the western man's phantasm of the Oriental female. Ingres' *The Turkish Bath* (1862), a painting containing numerous lounging naked women, is a quintessential example of this Orientalist tendency. Women and girls became objects of exotic sexual fantasy for western men, as well as objects of disapproval and disgust since western men perceived the culture as one that sanctioned females to live in brothels. The sexualized depictions of female private spaces ignored the fact that these spaces were places where mothers and children created a culture of songs and stories; as was the fact that mothers took their children out of the harem in groups to parks, where the children played, ran around, and picnicked.
42. Sarah Graham-Brown, *Images of Women: The Portrayal of Women in the Photography of the Middle East* (New York: Columbia University Press, 1988).
43. Nandy, *The Intimate Enemy*, p. 116.
44. Jacob, *Working Out Egypt*, p. 90.
45. Nandy, *The Intimate Enemy*, p. 35.
46. In "Schooled Mothers and Structured Play: Child-Rearing in Turn-of-the-Century Egypt," in Lila Abu-Lughod (Ed.), *Remaking Women: Feminism*

and Modernity in the Middle East (Princeton, NJ: Princeton University Press, 1998), p. 151, El Shakry reminds us that Egyptian responses to imperialism should not be viewed only as reactions to the West, but also as part of a long tradition of Islamic reform.

47. Nandy, *The Intimate Enemy*, p. xi.
48. See the work of Ziad Fahmy, *Ordinary Egyptians: Creating the Modern Nation through Popular Culture* (Stanford, CA: Stanford University Press, 2011), for a discussion of everyday non-elite Egyptians' reaction to imperialism.
49. See, for instance, Wilson Jacob, Beth Baron, and Lisa Pollard.
50. For a discussion on Ottoman reforms to educational systems in the context of imperialism, see Fortna's, Emphasizing the Islamic.
51. El Shakry, *The Great Social Laboratory*, p. 4.
52. Russell, *Creating the New Egyptian Woman*, pp. 43–46.
53. Rebecca Kingston, *Public Passion: Rethinking the Grounds for Political Justice* (Montreal: McGill-Queen's University Press, 2011), p. 165.
54. Bourke, *Fear*, p. 4.
55. ʿAbduh, *al-Islam*, p. 137.
56. *al-Ustadh*, 24 August 1892, p. 202.
57. Ibid.
58. ʿAbduh, *al-Islam*, p. 137.
59. Ibid., p. 165.
60. Ibid., pp. 139 and 147.
61. Qasim Amin, *Kalimat* (Cairo: Matbaʿat al-Jarida, 1908), p. 11.
62. Reading Arabic can pose grammatical challenges because the vowelling is often left unmarked.
63. Amin, *Kalimat*, p. 12.
64. Taha Husayn is perhaps remembered less for his moderate stance between Islam and the West than for his argument that Egypt belonged to the Mediterranean civilization because of its pharaonic past. Nonetheless, a close reading of Husayn's works shows that he did seek to fuse western concepts of secularism and democracy with Islam.
65. Taha Husayn, *Mustaqbal al-thaqafa fi Misr* (Cairo: Matbaʿat al-Maʿarif wa-Maktabatuha, 1938), p. 95.
66. El Shakry, *The Great Social Laboratory*, p. 5.
67. Ibid.
68. al-Tahtawi, *al-Murshid*, p. 6.
69. ʿAbduh, *al-Islam*, p. 165.
70. Amin, *Kalimat*, p. 37. Amin goes on to illustrate the connection between input in childhood and output in adulthood by citing an anecdote from a visit to France: while he was at the Louvre with three Egyptians, one got tired and sat down, the second walked around solely for the exercise, and the third only asked about the prices of the jewellery on display. Amin (*Kalimat*, p. 29) links the behavior of these Egyptians to an improper upbringing: "Love of beauty (reified taste) is an instinctual feeling that grows with education."
71. See Gilʿadi's, *Children of Islam: Concepts of Childhood in Medieval Muslim Society* (New York: St. Martin's Press, 1992), p. 12. According to medieval

Muslim thinkers, character training should start when the child's soul is pure in early childhood and systematic education should begin around the age of six or seven or when the child begins to discern the differences between good and evil (*tamyīz*).

72. Don S. Browning and Marcia J. Bunge (Eds.), *Children and Childhood in World Religions* (New Brunswick, NJ: Rutgers University Press, 2009), p. 155.

73. Rifaʿa Rafiʿ al-Tahtawi, *al-Murshid*, p. 8.

74. Ibid., *Manahij al-albab al-misriyya fi mabahij al-adab al-ʿasriyya* (Cairo: Supreme Council for Culture, 2002 [1912]), p. 59.

75. Jamal al-Din al-Afghani, *al-Aʿmal al-kamila* (Cairo: Dar al-Katib al-ʿArabi, 1968), p. 274.

76. Ibid., p. 367.

77. Ibid., p. 377.

78. The Arabic words Nadim uses for civil rights are *al-ḥuqūq al-madanīya*.

79. *al-Ustadh*, 6 December 1892, p. 364. In this same issue, girls have a lesson on what is expected of them when in the role of a wife, that is to say to obey their husbands and keep a clean house (*al-Ustadh*, p. 369). A common proverb used today that captures the sentiment that even an educated girl belongs in the house is the following: *Maṣīr al-bint li bait-hā* (A girl's destiny is her home).

80. Ibid., p. 361.

81. Salamah Musa, *al-Shakhsiya al-najiʿa: Kitab li-l-shabab* (Cairo: Salamah Musa li-l-Nashr wa-l-Tawziʿ, 1965), p. 33.

82. Ibid., p. 62.

83. Husayn, *Mustaqbal al-thaqafa fi Misr*, p. 108. For many intellectuals, the education of girls is important to prepare them for motherhood. See, for example, Qasim Amin's, *The Liberation of Women*; and, *The New Woman: Two Documents in the History of Egyptian Feminism* (Cairo: American University in Cairo Press, 2000 [1899 and 1900, respectively]); or ʿAbduh, *al-Islam*, p. 149.

84. El Shakry, "Schooled Mothers and Structured Play," p. 153.

85. Cunningham, *Children and Childhood*, p. 59.

86. Suad Joseph, "Introduction: Theories and Dynamics of Gender, Self, and Identity in Arab Families," in Joseph (Ed.), *Intimate Selving in Arab Families: Gender, Self, and Identity* (New York: Syracuse University Press, 1999), p. 11.

87. During this era, numerous non-western countries were engaged in processes of reforming children through meshing local cultural ideas about child-rearing with new ideas. For instance, Uno's *Passages to Modernity* finds that in late nineteenth-century Japan, insecurity toward the industrialized western states spurred Japanese leaders to assume that placing children in day-care centers would shape them for national advancement. Japanese families were not accustomed to mandatory, institutionalized schooling for their children. However, an indigenous widespread practice of nurturing infants by household members other than mothers fostered acceptance of day-care facilities.

88. El Shakry, *The Great Social Laboratory*, p. 153.
89. Ibid.
90. Cunningham (*Children and Childhood*, p. ix) writes, for example, "If the world is in some degree (but by no means wholly) a legatee of Western ideas of childhood, it is because the West exported childhood, and sometimes children, as part and parcel of an age of imperialism."
91. Joseph, "Introduction: Theories and Dynamics," p. 15.

2   Nation-Building and the Redefinition of the Child

1. *al-Musawwar*, 19 July 1935, pp. 16–17. This magazine published only photographs, with little written commentary.
2. Jacob, *Working Out Egypt*.
3. Even the word *tarbiya* (upbringing) changed from referring to how to make anything grow (cotton, cattle, or children) to mean "education." See Timothy Mitchell, *Colonizing Egypt* (Berkeley, CA: University of California Press, 1998), p. 88; and El Shakry, "Schooled Mothers and Structured Play," p. 126.
4. El Shakry, "Schooled Mothers and Structured Play."
5. Children's poet Muhammad al-Harawi, in *al-Tifl al-jadid* (1931), p. 38, writes a poem called "Sports and School" that encourages children to play at specific intervals in between their lessons. In 1905, *al-Tarbiya* (Upbringing) ran an article that defined the two types of sports possible for children, spiritual and physical, the former including visiting old monuments, reading, and listening to music and the latter including walking and swimming. The stated purpose of the article is to show the difference between activities that are for the mind and those that are for the body and ideal activities that combine both, such as billiards. The editor's introduction in the October 1933 issue of the popular children's magazine, *Samir al-Tilmidh*, p. 1, tells children that it hopes that they will grow sound in body and mind through play and thought. Every issue of *Waladi* included a column about exercises with illustrations on how to perform them. This column advises the child to do the exercises ten times each day before school. *Waladi* (18 February 1937, p. 24) also ran a column entitled, "Come, Let's Play," in which examples of children's games were explained, such as one in which children form a circle holding hands and one child is in the middle who must escape. Thus, the idea emerged that experts should play a role in supervising children's play.
6. The scope of this book does not allow for an examination of the discourse and laws of specific political leaders that involved children.
7. During the late nineteenth and early twentieth centuries, several parties in Egypt held contesting visions for schools. The dominant party consisted of the moderate, secular intellectuals who sought to combine modernity with authenticity. Examples of other parties include those that advocated for private foreign schools, missionary schools, religious schools, or Islamic Benevolent Society Schools. For an in-depth discussion of ʿAbduh's ideas on national education, see Albert Hourani, *Arabic*

Thought in the Liberal Age, 1798–1939 (London: Oxford University Press, 1962), Chapter 6.

8. al-Afghani, *al-A'mal al-kamila*, p. 377.
9. Ibid., pp. 274–276.
10. *al-Ustadh*, 9 May 1892, p. 873.
11. Ibid., p. 875.
12. Ibid.
13. Ibid., 24 August 1892, p. 208.
14. Amin, *Kalimat*, p. 27.
15. Ibid., pp. 42–43.
16. Ibid., p. 44.
17. Husayn, *Mustaqbal al-thaqafa fi Misr*, p. 101.
18. This is in addition to the fact that by this point education was compulsory in the constitution.
19. Husayn, *Mustaqbal al-thaqafa fi Misr*, p. 71.
20. Mitchell, *Colonizing Egypt*.
21. Any Egyptian, from doorman to university professor, to whom I mentioned the name Kamil Kilani knew him as a children's author. Egyptians still read to their children reprint editions of Kilani's work as well as those of his now elderly son, who is both a children's author and the owner of the downtown Kamil Kilani Children's Bookshop. (After the Revolution of 1952, official government efforts would be undertaken to promote children's literature by providing training for writers and also establishing libraries, resulting in more diversity in children's authors.)
22. Television programming for children did not become widespread in Egypt until after the 1952 Revolution. As for radio, there were children's shows in the 1920s and they continued to air to a lesser extent after radio stations were nationalized in 1934. Usually the shows took their ideas from children's magazines.
23. The Egyptian children's press was nationalized under the Free Officers' government in 1962. Although there was legislation directed at controlling the children's press, censorship came from the editor-in-chief, who did not permit open criticism of official ideology. There have been many technological and commercial constraints on children's magazines, such as the fact that it has been cheaper to translate foreign-produced material than to create new magazines with local artists and writers.
24. This was perhaps in line with the standardization of education taking place on a national level. In the education section of the annual British parliamentary reports on conditions in Egypt, there is always mention of the progress made in establishing in the country a system of primary and secondary school certificates. Uniform examinations for these certificates were intended to guard against the practice of promoting pupils without due regard to their results ("Report on the Administration, Finances and Condition of Egypt and the Progress of Reforms," London: House of Commons Parliamentary Papers, 1892), p. 30.
25. For a full review of these magazines, see Bertrand Millet, *Samir, Micky, Sindbad et les Autres: Histoire de la presse enfantine en Égypte* (Cairo: Centre

d'études et de documentation économiques, juridiques et sociales (Cairo, CEDEJ, 1987), 1987).

26. Mine Ener, *Managing Egypt's Poor and the Politics of Benevolence, 1800–1952* (Princeton, NJ: Princeton University Press, 2003), p. 124. There was for all people a trend toward more government control over social services. See also Pollard, *Nurturing the Nation*. Regarding the legal institutions and bureaucracies assuming medical responsibility of the body, see Liat Kozma's, "Girls, Labor, and Sex in Precolonial Egypt, 1850–1882," in Jennifer Helgren and Colleen A. Vasconcellos (Eds.), *Girlhood: A Global History*, Rutgers Series in Childhood Studies (New Brunswick, NJ: Rutgers University Press, 2010), p. 348.

27. Gallagher, *Egypt's Other Wars*, p. 12.

28. For information on feminist efforts to create minimum marriage age laws in the personal status code, see Badran, *Feminists, Islam, and the Nation*, pp. 127–128.

29. Governorate du Caire, *Rapport Détaillé sur les Colonies de Vacances de 1933* (Cairo [Bulaq]: Imprimerie Nationale, 1934, in Arabic and French), p. 10.

30. Unlike the conception of childhood, it could be argued that the conception of adolescence was invented at the turn of the last century. The emergence of the category of adolescence is beyond the scope of this book. Its creation was largely a by-product of the nationalist movement. Intellectuals effectively introduced to Egyptian society the stage of life called "teen-ager" through the expansion of secondary and university enrollment, and the education of this group in popular sovereignty and participation in government by way of on-campus movements and periodicals (Jankowski, *Egypt's Young Rebels*).

31. Ahmad Afandi Salih, *Kitab ʿallimu al-atfal ma yafʿalunahu wa-hum rijal* (Cairo: Al-Matbaʿa al-Amira, 1894), p. 22.

32. *Samir al-Tilmidh*, February 1934, p. 1; Kamil Kilani, *al-Malik al-Najjar* (Cairo: Matbaʿat al-Maʿrifa, 1935), p. 1.

33. Muhammad al-Harawi, *Samir al-atfal* (Cairo: Dar al-Kutub, 1924), p. 3.

34. Ibid., p. 10.

35. This is very similar to the ideas of Afghani (*al-Aʿmal al-kamila*, p. 280), who decades earlier wrote, "Every time the student learns something, it must be with a part of his body, such as learning smithing, carpentry, raising animals, herding cows, producing cheese." According to Afghani, the value of the child's mind and body can be measured in its potential contributions to the nation. The teaching of morals was one part of Afghani's two-part plan for repairing the fissures in society caused by colonization. He also says that young people should learn trades as this will allow them to have skills as adults and to be hard-working.

36. In Egyptian magazines and newspapers of the late 1920s, there was widespread discussion around clothing, particularly with regard the *imama* (traditional head wrap) versus the tarboosh (felt, cone-shaped hat worn by the educated upper-class Egyptian elite). For women, Qasim Amin and Huda Shaʾrawi led a movement in the 1930s and 1940s regarding the wearing of the veil (referred to in modern Egyptian memory as *al-sufūr wa-l-ḥijāb* [unveiling and the veil]).

37. The attempt to underplay sectarian differences was a common theme in Egyptian cinema as well during the first half of the twentieth century. Film roles did not distinguish between Muslims and Christians, playing instead a normative role in asserting the conviction that "religion is for God and the homeland is for all" (Viola Shafik, *Popular Egyptian Cinema*, Cairo: American University in Cairo Press, 2006, p. 44). Representations of the woman in nationalist movements also obscured religious difference. Baron writes in *Egypt as a Woman* (2005, p. 39):

> Muslims and Christians could not literally join in one family, but they could figuratively. Here the familial metaphors produced by male and female nationalists helped the two communities – and other minorities – to combine lineages. This gave Egyptians a myth of continuity from antiquity to the present. Female activists became "Mothers of the Nation," with special nurturing and protection mission.

38. During this time, there were efforts by Egyptian reformers to create secular non-religious citizenship. For example, after the 1919 unrest, politically marginalized segments in society, such as women and Copts, joined forces under the Wafd Party to protest British occupation.
39. Cunningham, *Children and Childhood*, p. 102.
40. Similarly, Paula Fass (*Children of a New World: Society, Culture, and Globalization*, New York: New York University Press, 2007), pp. 208–209 finds that in early twentieth-century America, some immigrants regretted coming to the country because they thought that mandatory schooling was a waste of their children's time.
41. Sayyid Qutb, *Tifl min al-qarya* (Cairo: Maktabat Misr, 1945), p. 36.
42. Fahmy, *All the Pasha's Men*, p. 225.
43. Qutb, *A Child from the Village*, p. 18.
44. Although not addressed in this book, orphans and street children raise further doubts about the homogeneity of children's experiences in Egypt. In what ways were children who did not have identifiable kin or an identifiable home legally excluded from receiving aid from the government? For readings on orphans in Egyptian history, see Beth Baron, *The Orphan Scandal: Christian Missionaries and the Rise of the Muslim Brotherhood* (Stanford, CA: Stanford University Press, 2014).

3   Child-Rearing and Class

1. The significance of this new form of interaction could be compared to today's interaction between children from different corners of the world through Internet chat rooms.
2. For an in-depth description of elite Egyptian society, see C. Soliman Hamamsy, *Zamalek: The Changing Life of a Cairo Elite, 1850–1945* (Cairo: American University in Cairo Press, 2005).
3. Jacques Berque, *Egypt: Imperialism and Revolution*, translated by Jean Stewart (Glasgow: Glasgow University Press, 1972), p. 484.

4. Winifred S. Blackman, *The Fellahin of Upper Egypt* (Cairo: American University in Cairo Press, 2000), p. 25.
5. Magda Baraka, *The Egyptian Upper Class between Revolutions 1912–1952* (Beirut: Garnet Publishing Limited, 1998), p. 58.
6. Psychologists label the instilling of respect for parents and submissiveness to adults as the "apprenticeship and obedience" model. For more reading on this topic, see Gregg, *The Middle East*.
7. Raja al-Naqqash, *Najib Mahfuz: Safahat min mudhakkiratihi wa-adwaʾ jadida ʿala adabihi wa-hayatihi* (Cairo: Al-Ahram Center, 1998), p. 16.
8. Rabiʿi, *Fi al-khamsin*, p. 16; and Taha Husayn, *al-Ayyam* (Cairo: Al-Ahram Center, 2004), p. 15.
9. Ahmad Amin, *Hayati* (Cairo: Maktabat al-Usra, 2003 [1950]), p. 43.
10. Ibid., p. 51.
11. Yahya Haqqi, *Khalliha ʿala Allah* (Cairo: Nahdat Misr, 2008), pp. 27 and 33.
12. Salamah Musa, *Tarbiyat Salamah Musa* (Cairo: Muʿassasat al-Khanji, 1958), p. 24.
13. Taha Husayn, *The Days*, translated by E. H. Paxton, Hilary Wayment and Kenneth Cragg (Cairo: American University in Cairo Press, 1997), p. 11.
14. al-Naqqash, *Najib Mahfuz*, p. 20. Another example of children's obedience extending into adulthood was the custom of adult children not smoking in front of their fathers, even if they smoked. Smoking would give the impression that the child thought himself as mature as his father. Edward Lane, *An Account of the Manner and Customs of the Modern Egyptians* (London: Darf Publishers, 1986), p. 70.
15. Latifa Zayyat, *The Search: Personal Papers* (London: Quartet Books, 1996), p. 7.
16. One of the few memories that Shaʿrawi has of her father when he was alive is of going every morning to his room to kiss his hand. Sitting on the ground praying, he would hand her chocolate before she departed. See Shaʿrawi, *Mudhakkirat*, p. 11.
17. Husayn, *al-Ayyam*, p. 19.
18. Ayrout, *The Egyptian Peasant*, p. 123. There is a famous scene in *Palace Walk*, the first book of Naguib Mahfouz's trilogy set in the 1920s, in which the mother and daughters sit down and eat after the sons finish eating with their father. This points to the idea that sometimes children did eat with their parents, and also to the idea that there was a hierarchical distinction between boys and girls.
19. Lane, *Modern Egyptians*, p. 70. For a more nuanced look at how patriarchy in families was socially constructed in the early part of the twentieth century, see Soraya Altorki, "Patriarchy and Imperialism: Father–Son and British–Egyptian Relations in Najib Mahfouz's Trilogy," in Joseph (Ed.), *Intimate Selving in Arab Families*, pp. 214–234.
20. Shaʿrawi, *Mudhakkirat*, pp. 52–53.
21. al-Naqqash, *Najib Mahfuz*, p. 32; and al-Shatiʾ, *ʿAla al-jisr*, p. 22.
22. Amin, *Hayati*, p. 21.

23. Sometimes, however, it seems that the writers' emphasis on describing the lack of individuality in their childhood environments comes down to desire for reform in contemporary Egyptian society, that is to say, drawing attention to the conformity and complacency of the masses in the time period in which they are writing. An example of this use of collectivity can be found in Haykal's description of how the children in his school formed groups out of peer pressure. Haykal writes that the "spirit of the masses" is a phenomenon that still existed at the time that he was writing. See Muhammad Husayn Haykal, *Fi awqat al-faragh* (Cairo: Maktabat al-Nahda al-Misriyya, 1968), p. 328.

24. Amin, *Hayati*, p. 39.

25. Rabiʿi, *Fi al-khamsin*, p. 7.

26. Qutb, *A Child from the Village*, pp. 150–153.

27. Lucie Ryzvoa, "Egyptianizing Modernity through the 'New Effendiya': Social and Cultural Constructions of the Middle Class in Egypt under the Monarchy," in Arthur Goldschmidt, Amy J. Johnson, and Barak A. Salmoni (Eds.), *Re-Envisioning Egypt, 1919–1952* (Cairo and New York: American University in Cairo Press, 2005), p. 125.

28. El Shakry, *The Great Social Laboratory*, pp. 16–18. Another example is Taha Husayn serving as Minister of Education.

29. Ryzvoa, "Egyptianizing Modernity," p. 131.

30. Watenpaugh, *Being Modern in the Middle East*, p. 10.

31. Gasper, *The Power of Representation*, p. 51.

32. Jacob, *Working Out Egypt*, p. 77.

33. Watenpaugh, *Being Modern in the Middle East*, p. 11.

34. Russell, *Creating the New Egyptian Woman*, p. 40.

35. Relli Shechter (Ed.), *Transitions in Domestic Consumption and Family Life in the Modern Middle East: Houses in Motion* (New York: Palgrave Macmillan, 2003).

36. Watenpaugh, *Being Modern in the Middle East*, p. 9.

37. Russell, *Creating the New Egyptian Woman*, p. 6.

38. Relli Shechter, "Introduction," in Relli Shechter (Ed.), *Transitions in Domestic Consumption*, p. 4.

39. Jacob, *Working Out Egypt*, p. 94.

40. Mark A. Jones, *Children as Treasures: Childhood and the Middle Class in Early Twentieth-Century Japan* (Cambridge, MA, and London: Harvard University Press, 2010).

41. Carol Summers, *Colonial Lessons: Africans' Education in Southern Rhodesia, 1918–1940* (Portsmouth, NH: Heinemann, 2002), p. xiii.

42. Jones, *Children as Treasures*, p. 3.

43. In a similar way that Egyptians educated children about new middle-class values through literature, so, too, did this process happen in Europe with the re-elaboration of a mythical corpus of fables, such as those of Jean de La Fontaine.

44. *Samir al-Tilmidh*, May 1933 and January 1934.

45. For an example of "Around the World" focusing on China, see *Waladi*, 18 February 1937.

46. This is particularly true for girls who, because of the physical restrictions placed on them to stay at home, expanded their world by expanding their cultural space. Women also used reading as a way to expand their social opportunities because literacy sometimes gave secluded women a chance to speak to men (Badran, *Feminists, Islam, and the Nation*, p. 15).

47. National Center for the Culture of the Child, *al-Mukhtarat min ash'ar Muhammad al-Harawi* (Giza: High Council for Culture), p. 20. A similar appeal to the value in reading is found in Kamil Kilani's Introduction to his selected translated works of Shakespeare for children *Qisas Shiksbir li-l-atfal* (Cairo: Matba'at al-Ma'rifa, 1937): "This story [Julius Caesar] explains some of the intricacies of life and the secrets of the soul to you, what you most need to know in order to brighten your future and proceed on the right path."

48. Badran, *Feminists, Islam, and the Nation*, p. 140.

49. *al-Atfal*, 14 May 1936, p. 12.

50. *Waladi*, 24 February 1936, p. 11.

51. *al-Atfal*, 14 May 1936, p. 12.

52. Ibid.

53. Ibid., 21 and 28 May 1936.

54. Precise descriptions of how to make the figures were included. For example, the caption below one picture reads:

> The body of this bird consists of a banana and its beak and legs of almonds. It is on a stand made of half of an apple. Next to it is a nest consisting of thin slices of apple, four grape seeds as the eggs, and the wings and tail are made of feathers.
>
> (*Samir al-Tilmidh*, February 1934, p. 3)

55. Even some storybooks introduced this theme of working on one's own. Kamil Kilani often started his books with a letter to the reader, encouraging the child to read the story on his or her own if his or her mother, father or grandparents are too busy. These letters are written in the first person and in them Kilani tells the children that the stories are written in language that is easy enough for them to read on their own so that they can then tell the story to others. See, for example, the Introduction to *Baba 'Abdallah* (Cairo: Matba'at al-Ma'rifa, 1942).

56. *Samir al-Tilmidh*, November 1933, p. 15.

57. The following are summaries of other stories by Kilani with the same theme. In *Shanth wa Sidh* (Cairo: Matba'at Kilani, n.d.), two brothers, Shanth and Sidh, divide up the land that their deceased father has left them, but when Sidh fails to reap a good harvest on his half he blames his brother for taking the better section. Even after they exchange fields, Shanth's land still yields a better crop, which Sidh steals and runs away with. Eventually he meets a shaykh, who tells him that he can unleash his luck by climbing to the peak of a certain mountain. On his ascent, Sidh helps several people with their problems and eventually learns that success comes from hard work. This story conveys the idea that each child can seek and find his or her own solutions in life, resulting in success.

The story also conveys the idea that children are responsible for the consequences of their behavior, regardless of their conditions.

Kilani emphasizes this message in stories that convey the idea that having good morals is a question of individual choice. In *Safrut al-Hattab* (Cairo: Matbaʿat Kilani, n.d.), the main character, a boy attempting to take care of himself after his father's death, earns money by collecting wood, and one day he finds a bag of gold secretly left by a witch to test his trust and honesty. He returns the gold, and at the end of the story is rewarded by the sultan, who offers him his daughter in marriage. This story conveys the idea that a child can make good choices on his own.

In *Dimna al-makar* (Cairo: Matbaʿat Kilani, n.d.), a fox becomes jealous when a lion becomes best friends with one of his own friends (a bull). The fox sabotages the new friendship between the lion and the bull, and as a result the lion kills the bull. The judge of the forest sentences the fox to ten years in prison. The moral of the story is that the fox is punished because he chose to act on his envy, conveying the idea that the individual is responsible for the decisions that he or she makes in life.

In *ʿAduw al-maʿiz* (Cairo: Matbaʿat Kilani, n.d.), three goats each build their own house out of different material. A fox wants to eat the goats, but has trouble getting into the house made of bricks because it is too strong to knock down. The goat in this house places a pot of boiling water at the bottom of the chimney, into which the fox drops when trying to enter the house from above. The goat lives in peace thereafter, conveying the idea that brains trump physical strength and also that a person can choose to live on his own as an individual separate from his family.

Al-Dik al-zarif (Cairo: Matbaʿat Kilani, n.d.) is about a rooster who is conned by a wolf who wants to eat him; but the rooster cons the wolf back and escapes with the help of three animal friends. When the rooster returns, he resumes his morning crow, and his animal friends say that the rooster's successful escape is a victory for all the animals, because now they have his singing to enjoy again. In this story, the rooster takes action to protect himself and his future, and the results are successful not only for him, but for the society in which he lives.

58. al-Tahtawi, *al-Murshid*, p. 19.
59. Ibid., p. 18. Tahtawi cites the example of a woman named Khansaʾ who never became angry at the fact that her four children died in war. Caliph Omar rewarded her for this with money.
60. Musa, *al-Shakhsiya al-najiʿa*, pp. 35–36.
61. *Samir al-Tilmidh,* October 1933, p. 5.
62. al-Harawi, *al-Tifl al-jadid*, pp. 12–21.
63. *Waladi,* 18 February 1937.
64. Russell, *Creating the New Egyptian Woman*, p. 7.
65. al-Tahtawi, *Manahij*, p. 60.
66. Ibid., *al-Murshid*, p. 20.
67. Ibid., *Manahij*, p. 50.
68. Ibid., p. 70.
69. Ibid., *al-Murshid*, p. 17.

70. Ibid., p. 11.
71. al-Afghani, *al-Aʿmal al-kamila*, p. 178.
72. Ibid., p. 188.
73. By freedom, Amin means freedom of the self, which he says allows for tolerance of others. By freedom of the self, Amin (*Kalimat*, pp. 4 and 16) means a person is forgiving of his own sins, accepts his desires and admits to the struggle in each of us.
74. Ibid., p. 14.
75. El Shakry, *The Great Social Laboratory*, p. 115.
76. Ibid., p. 90.
77. Ibid., p. 114; and Gasper, *The Power of Representation*, pp. 6 and 10.
78. Ener, *Managing Egypt's Poor*, p. 117.
79. See the work of El Shakry, "Schooled Mothers and Structured Play"; Pollard, *Nurturing the Nation*; and Russell, *Creating the New Egyptian Woman*.
80. The poem could also be read as a praise song for the peasants in the national resistance movement. There was armed struggle against the British amongst the fellaheen in the countryside and, in the early twentieth century, Egyptian nationalists glorified the peasants, who made up the majority of the population.
81. Marilyn Booth, *May Her Likes Be Multiplied: Biography and Gender Politics in Egypt* (Berkeley and Los Angeles, LA, and London: University of California Press, 2001), p. xx.
82. Fahmy, *Ordinary Egyptians*.
83. Some work exists by El Shakry (*The Great Social Laboratory*) and Ener (*Managing Egypt's Poor*) on how charities sought to educate lower-class mothers on proper hygiene, discipline, and cooking for their children.
84. Allison James and Alan Prout (Eds.), *Constructing and Reconstructing Childhood: Contemporary Issues in the Sociological Study of Childhood* (London: Routledge, 1997).
85. The use of children to define class status happened globally. Milanich's work, *Children of Fate*, shows how post-independence Chile reconfigured family rights and entitlements such that children reared in non-kin networks became locked for generations into dependence on charity and handouts. Davin's work on the poor in London, *Growing up Poor*, p. 3, argues that the introduction of compulsory schooling in the 1870s made the struggle for daily life for poor families all the more difficult since it limited the children's ability to help out.
86. Gasper, *The Power of Representation*, p. 6.
87. This idea builds on the work of feminist theorists Maxine Baca Zinn and Bonnie Thornton Dill, "Theorizing Difference from Multiracial Feminism," *Feminist Studies*, 22 (2) (1996), pp. 321–331, who say that we must go beyond simply recognizing differences between women to understanding structures of domination.

4 Girls and the Building of Modern Egypt

1. Harawi, *Samir al-atfal*, p. 22.
2. Ibid., p. 24.
3. Hanan Kholoussy, *For Better, For Worse: The Marriage Crisis that Made Modern Egypt* (Cario: American University in Cairo Press, 2010), p. 51. For more information about the Jews in Egypt during his time, see Dario Miccoli, "The Jews of Modern Egypt: Schools, Family, and the Making of an Imagined Bourgeoisie, 1880s–1950s" (PhD dissertation, European University Institute, 2012).
4. Mona L. Russell, "Education: Colonial: Egypt," in Suad Joseph (Ed.), *Encyclopedia of Women and Islamic Cultures, Vol. 4: Economics, Education, Mobility and Space* (Leiden: Koninklijke Brill NV, 2007), p. 274.
5. Gil'adi, *Children of Islam*, p. 19.
6. Kozma, "Girls, Labor, and Sex," p. 347.
7. Ibid., pp. 347–348.
8. al-Shati', *'Ala al-jisr*, p. 34.
9. Leila Ahmed, *A Border Passage: From Cairo to America – A Woman's Journey* (New York: Farrar, Straus and Giroux, 1999), pp. 78–81.
10. In Ayrout's observations of village life, he claims that boys could choose when they wanted to get married but the family decided whom they married. For information on bride-prices, see Ayrout, *The Egyptian Peasant*, pp. 118–119.
11. Cynthia Nelson and Doria Shafik, *Egyptian Feminist: A Woman Apart* (Cairo: American University in Cairo Press, 1996), p. 20.
12. Husayn, *al-Ayyam*, p. 98.
13. Russell, *Creating the New Egyptian Woman*.
14. The seminal work on this is Amin, *The Liberation of Women*, originally published in 1899, in which he argued that children are ignorant because mothers are ignorant. For more information on the role of mothers in early twentieth-century Egyptian society, see El Shakry, "Schooled Mothers and Structured Play."
15. *al-Tarbiya*, 1 March 1905, p. 10.
16. For a complete history of schooling in Egypt during the nineteenth century, see Herrera, "The Sanctity of the School," pp. 43–68.
17. For a more detailed account of the process of bringing education under state control in the nineteenth century, see Pollard, *Nurturing the Nation*, pp. 101–106.
18. Ibid., p. 64.
19. Goldberg, *Trade*, p. 157.
20. Herrera, "The Sanctity of the School," p. 67.
21. Russell, "Education: Colonial: Egypt," p. 275.
22. Goldberg, *Trade*, pp. 66 and 157.
23. ILO, *Labour Survey of North Africa*, p. 25.
24. Baron finds that one reason that female activists placed a value on domestic work was because women who worked outside the home would be viewed as disturbing the social order or being labelled by some as "a third

sex" (neither male nor female). See Beth Baron, *The Women's Awakening in Egypt: Culture, Society, and the Press* (New Haven, CT: Yale University Press, 1994).

25. Russell, *Creating the New Egyptian Woman*, p. 2.
26. al-Tahtawi, *al-Murshid*, p. 67.
27. Musa, *al-Shakhsiya al-naji'a*, p. 37. He develops this idea when he goes on to claim that removing the veil is not enough to make a girl independent as she could still be wearing a "spiritual veil" (Musa, *al-Shakhsiya al-naji'a*, p. 60).
28. Kholoussy, *For Better, For Worse*, p. 50.
29. Ibid.
30. Ibid., p. 67.
31. *al-Ustadh*, 24 August 1892, p. 246. Other housekeeping skills that a girl must learn include as follows:

> Look my girl, the first thing that a lady must know is how to organize her pantry, putting oil in a well-closed clean container ... and placing a towel over the lid so that flies don't come ... You must put the honey, sugar, jams and sweets in a clean closet and lay a paper under them ... close the closet well so that flies, geckos, mice and cockroaches don't enter.

> (*al-Ustadh*, 24 August 1892, p. 298)

32. For example, in one of Nadim's columns, a mother tells her daughter that an upper-class girl must learn how to supervise her servants (*al-Ustadh*, 24 August 1892). There were also some who criticized teaching girls how to supervise, saying that reliance on nannies would create lazy children (El Shakry, "Schooled Mothers and Structured Play").
33. The counterpoint to creating the new Egyptian woman was creating the new Egyptian man. The changing characteristics of childhood discussed in Chapters 1–3 here are indicative of new male gender roles. For more analysis of masculinity during this period, see Hoda Elsadda, "Imaging the 'New Man': Gender and Nation in Arab Literary Narratives in the Early Twentieth Century," *Journal of Middle East Women's Studies*, 3 (2) (2007), pp. 31–55; and Wilson, *Working Out Egypt*.
34. In 1937, the magazine *Waladi*, run by a female editor, published a piece on Joan of Arc, but the female heroine did not reappear and the name of the magazine itself means "My Boy."
35. Kamil Kilani, *Bisat al-rih* (Cairo: Matba'at al-'Asriya, 1936), p. 81.
36. Russell, *Creating the New Egyptian Woman*, p. 1.
37. This was the case not only in Egypt, but globally as well. There were "circuits of exchange" between local elements and those drawn from elsewhere: see The Modern Girl Around the World Research Group (Eds.), *The Modern Girl Around the World: Consumption, Modernity, and Globalization* (Durham, NC: Duke University Press, 2008), p. 4. This reference is also useful for a discussion of the changing role of girls around the world in the early twentieth century.
38. As an exception, Pollard, in *Nurturing the Nation*, p. 131, notes that children participated in the birth of the nation by acting out the roles for the new nation that they were taught in school and in magazines.

39. Nawal al-Saʿdawi, *Awraqi: Hayati* (Cairo: Maktabat Madbouly, 2005), p. 58.
40. Ibid., p. 35.
41. Ibid., p. 77.
42. Ibid., p. 34.
43. Nabawiya Musa, *Tarikhi bi-qalami* (Cairo: Multaqa al-Marʾa wa-l-Dhakira, 1999), p. 45.
44. Ibid., p. 32.
45. Qutb, *Tifl min al-qarya*, p. 31.
46. al-Saʿdawi, *Awraqi*, p. 87.
47. Here I am relying heavily on the theoretical framework for selfhood articulated in Joseph (Ed.), *Intimate Selving in Arab Families*.
48. Because Taymuriyya's mother did not encourage education for her daughter, this does not mean that she did not offer other forms of learning, such as learning rules of conduct, sources of temptation and taboos. See Mervat Hatem, "The Microdynamics of Patriarchal Change in Egypt and the Development of an Alternative Discourse on Mother–Daughter Relations: The Case of ʿAʾisha Taymur," in Joseph (Ed.), *Intimate Selving in Arab Families*, pp. 191–209. Additionally, the mother's contribution to the daughter's ability to study must not be devalued. The mother was ultimately willing to go along with the father's request for her to study with him (*Mervat Hatem* "ʿAʾisha Taymur's Tears and the Critique of the Modernist and the Feminist Discourses on Nineteenth-Century Egypt," in Abu-Lughod (Ed.), *Remaking Women*), pp. 73–86.
49. ʿAʾisha Ismat Taymuriyya, *Nataʾij al-ahwal fi al-aqwal wa-l-afʿal* (Cairo: Matbaʿat Muhammad Afandi Mustafa, 1888), p. 3.
50. Ibid.
51. Taymuriyya would resume her intellectual pursuits much later in life when she was able to have her own daughter take over her household role. See Hatem, "ʿAʾisha Taymur's Tears."
52. Ibid., pp. 79–80.
53. al-Shatiʾ, ʿAla al-jisr, pp. 61–72.
54. Baron, *Egypt as a Woman*, p. 2.
55. Ibid., p. 3.
56. Tucker Judith, *Women in Nineteenth-Century Egypt*, Cambridge and New York: Cambridge University Press, 1985.
57. Baron, Beth, *The Women's Awakening in Egypt: Culture, Society, and the Press*, New Haven, CT: Yale University Press, 1994.
58. Hatem, "ʿAʾisha Taymur's Tears," p. 82.
59. Ibid.

5 Constructing National Identity through Autobiographical Memory of Childhood

1. Peasant studies was an early twentieth-century literary genre that used representation of the peasant to build the Egyptian nation. The *effendiya* wrote about the peasants in the countryside to distinguish themselves

as the more civilized (Gasper, *The Power of Representation*). The role of children in peasant studies was explored in Chapter 3 of this book.

2. Sometimes authors write their autobiographies in the third person but the reader understands that this is the author's technique for representing himself or herself.

3. Booth, *May Her Likes Be Multiplied*, p. xviii.

4. Tetz Rooke claims that Arabic autobiographers generally place an extended narrative focus on childhood, one that is out of proportion to the temporal guidelines of "real life." He calls this variant of the Arabic autobiography the "autobiography of childhood." See *Tetz Rooke* "The Arabic Autobiography of Childhood," in Robin Ostle et al., *Writing the Self: Autobiographical Writing in Modern Arabic Literature* (London: Saqi Press, 1998), pp. 100–114.

5. Charles D. Smith, *Islam and the Search for Social Order in Modern Egypt: A Biography of Muhammad Husayn Haykal* (Albany, NY: State University of New York Press, 1983).

6. Muhammad Husayn Haykal's *Fi awqat al-faragh* (Cairo: Maktabat al-Nahda al-Misriyya, 1968) is actually a collection of essays and letters rather than an autobiography *per se*.

7. Ibid., p. 328.

8. For an in-depth discussion of how Haykal's thoughts fit into historical theories of the period, see Israel Gershoni and James Jankowski, *Egypt, Islam and the Arabs* (New York: Oxford University Press, 1987), p. 36.

9. Ibid., p. 37.

10. Many intellectuals claimed that the mentality and culture of Egyptian peasants came from geography. See, for example, the works of El Shakry, *The Great Social Laboratory*; and Gasper, *The Power of Representation*.

11. Haykal, *Fi awqat al-faragh*, p. 330.

12. Ibid., Haykal writes that when the foreign inspector of the school showed contempt for its Egyptian director, the director in turn showed contempt for the Egyptian teacher, who in his turn treated the Egyptian children with disdain. In many senses, children were at the bottom of the colonial hierarchy, taking the brunt not only of the westerners' racism but of the frustration of adult Egyptians who suffered from it as well. For a deeper analysis of how colonized people can have the tendency to inflict violence against themselves, see Frantz Fanon, *The Wretched of the Earth* (London: Penguin Classics, 2001).

13. Gershoni and Jankowski, *Egypt, Islam and the Arabs*.

14. Stephen Guth, "Why Novels – Not Autobiographies? An Essay in the Analysis of a Historical Development," in Ostle et al. (Eds.), *Writing the Self*, p. 144.

15. Ibid.

16. Gasper, *The Power of Representation*, p. 192.

17. Gershoni and Jankowski, *Egypt, Islam and the Arabs*.

18. Ibid., p. 95.

19. With the dissolution of the Ottoman Empire, Egyptian-ness was also formulated in opposition to Ottoman-ness.

20. Some Muslims consider the period prior to the revelation of the Qur'an to Muhammad as a period of ignorance and paganism.
21. Sidonie Smith and Julia Watson, *Reading Autobiography: A Guide for Interpreting Life Narratives* (Minneapolis, MN: University of Minnesota Press, 2010), p. 103.
22. As if to emphasize further how adult-imposed he felt the honorific of "shaykh" to be, he adds in this section of his autobiography the adjective "small" to his usual literary reference to himself as "our friend" (Husayn, *The Days*, p. 38).
23. Ibid., *al-Ayyam*, pp. 89–90.
24. Husayn explains that a completely religious education is not good because it is only concerned with religion, but a completely European-style secular education is also not good because it ignores Egyptian identity. See Husayn, *Mustaqbal al-thaqafa fi Misr*, p. 76.
25. Ibid., p. 91.
26. Husayn, *The Days*, p. 20.
27. Ibid., p. 18.
28. Ibid., *al-Ayyam*, pp. 69 and 73. Similarly, autobiographer Jalila Rida recalls that one of the big scandals at her school involved the shaykh from whose pocket the students saw fall a picture of a pretty female. See Jalila Rida, *Safahat min hayati* (Cairo: Dar al-Hilal, 1986).
29. Fedwa Malti-Douglas, *Blindness and Autobiography:* Al-Ayyam *of Taha Husayn* (Princeton, NJ: Princeton University Press, 1988).
30. Husayn, *The Days*, p. 48.
31. Ibid., *al-Ayyam*, p. 117.
32. Hoda Elsadda, "Egypt," in Radwa Ashour, Ferial J. Ghazoul, and Hasna Reda-Mekdashi (Eds.), *Arab Women Writers: A Critical Reference Guide, 1873–1999*, trans. by Mandy McClure (Cairo and New York: American University in Cairo Press, 2008), p. 112.
33. The first and second editions of Musa' memoirs are undated, but the third was published in 1999 (Nabawiya Musa), p. 157.
34. Gillian Whitlock, *The Intimate Empire: Reading Women's Autobiography* (London: Cassell, 2000), p. 203.
35. Musa, *Tarikhi bi-qalami*, p. 31.
36. Ibid., pp. 54–55.
37. Margot Badran, "Competing Agenda: Feminists, Islam and the State in 19th- and 20th-Century Egypt," in Deniz Kandiyoti (Ed.), *Women, Islam, and the State* (Philadelphia, PA: Temple University Press, 1991), p. 213.
38. Ibid., p. 214.
39. Stefan Tanaka, *New Times in Modern Japan* (Princeton, NJ: Princeton University Press, 2006), p. 180.
40. Qutb, *A Child from the Village*, p. 156.
41. Ibid., pp. 150–153.
42. Ibid., p. 68.
43. In cases where Egyptians became aware of vaccines and microbes, concepts were often combined in that people believed that microbes caused diseases but evil spirits made them enter the body.

44. Qutb, *A Child from the Village*, p. 59.
45. Qutb, *A Child from the Village*, p. 70. To convince the students, the teacher took them at midnight to the alley in which they all believed that *'afārīt* (evil spirits) appeared in the form of rabbits. In the face of the glowing red and blue eyes of the rabbits, the teacher caught one of them and brought it back to the schoolhouse, and when it was still a rabbit the next morning (and had not transformed into another animal), the children's belief in *'afārīt* was shaken.
46. Israel Gershoni and James Jankowski, *Redefining the Egyptian Nation, 1930–1945* (London: Cambridge University Press, 1995), p. 37.
47. Ibid., p. 41.
48. The ideology of the Muslim Brotherhood places stress on preserving the patriarchal family with traditional gender roles. The mother as child-rearer is one of these roles. Qutb lauds his mother for her refusal to buy into all aspects of religious folklore, and holds her up as an example of how women should raise their children in Islam. The anecdote that he recalls is as follows: The common practice in the village to remedy a child's malady was to leave the child for a night with Shaykh Naqib, a man believed to have divine healing powers (*magzūb*, i.e. *majdhūb*) and who went around the village with matted hair and a perpetually unclothed body. Despite a problem that Qutb had with his back, his mother announced that she would not send her son to spend the night with the shaykh but would leave the matter to God, p. 6. Qutb recalls that the decision came as a relief because he feared the shaykh and thought he was crazy and strange.
49. Qutb also depicts solidarity with the village in his memories of the injustice suffered by peasants. He says that he discovered this at a very young age. The peasants lived so poorly that even though they lived on nothing but bread, water, salt, and *mulūkhīya* (green-leaf soup), they preferred to receive donations in the form of money rather than not food. Qutb also remembers observing as a child the hard life of the farm animals, specifically those used to turn the wheel of the grinder. Gasper, *The Power of Representation*, an authority on the use of representation by literate intelligentsia in early twentieth-century Egypt, argues that the desire of intellectuals to depict a unitary identity was often linked with their own personal political and social aspirations.
50. El Shakry, *The Great Social Laboratory*, p. 63.
51. Nandy, *The Intimate Enemy*, p. 115. For an analysis of how Egyptian historiography was taught in the state-run school curricula during the early twentieth century, see Barak A. Salmoni, "Historical Consciousness for Modern Citizenship: Egyptian Schooling and the Lessons of History during the Constitutional Monarchy," in Arthur Goldschmidt, Amy J. Johnson, and Barak A. Salmoni (Eds.), *Re-Envisioning Egypt*, pp. 164–193.
52. Musa, *Tarbiyat Salamah Musa*, p. 18. This book was first published in 1947.
53. Ibid., p. 40.
54. Ibid., p. 34.
55. Ibid., p. 21.

56. Ibid., p. 38.
57. Smith and Watson, *Reading Autobiography*, p. 103.
58. Philippe Lejeune, *On Autobiography* translated by Katherine M. Leary (Minneapolis, MN: University of Minnesota Press, 1989), p. ix, defined this as follows:

> *Le pacte autobiographique* is a form of contract between author and reader in which the autobiographer explicitly commits himself or herself not to some impossible historical exactitude but rather to the sincere effort to come to terms with and to understand his or her own life.

59. Booth, *May Her Likes Be Multiplied*.
60. Tanaka, *New Times in Modern Japan*, p. 180.
61. Shaʿrawi, *Mudhakkirat*, p. 71.
62. See the work of Pollard, *Nurturing the Nation*, for more on how family politics figured in the liberation of Egypt.
63. Baron, *Egypt as a Woman*, p. 34.
64. Frederic Jameson, *Postmodernism or the Cultural Logic of Late Capitalism* (Durham, NC: Duke University Press, 2005).
65. Ibid., p. 28.
66. Kenneth Cragg, "Then and Now in Egypt: The Reflections of Ahmad Amin, 1886–1954," *Middle East Journal*, 9 (1) (1955), p. 31. Many early twentieth-century Egyptians blamed an increasing incidence of bachelorhood on factors such as male emasculation which were perceived to be caused by increasingly active women (see Kholoussy, *For Better, For Worse*).
67. Amin, *Hayati*, p. 29.
68. Ibid., pp. 55–56.
69. Ibid., p. 28.
70. Ibid., p. 51.
71. Badran, "Competing Agenda," in Kandiyoti (Ed.), *Women, Islam, and the State*, p. 209.
72. al-Shatiʾ, *ʿAla al-jisr*, p. 20.
73. Ibid.
74. Ibid., pp. 79 and 81.
75. Ibid., p. 58.
76. Ruth Roded, "Bint al-Shati's *Wives of the Prophet*: Feminist or Feminine?," *British Journal of Middle Eastern Studies*, 33 (1) (2006), p. 57.
77. Rooke, "The Arabic Autobiography of Childhood," p. 104.

Conclusion

1. Hugh Cunningham, "Review Essay: Histories of Childhood," *American Historical Review*, 103 (4) (1998), p. 1195.
2. UNICEF website: http://www.unicef.org/infobycountry/egypt_statistics.html#117, (Accessed September 1, 2015).

3. In rare cases where the word "rights" was employed in Egypt in the context of children, conditions were attached to those rights. This is drastically different from the situation today, where we are assured that children have rights on the sole condition of being children. Tahtawi writes, for example, that children have rights, but that these rights go hand in hand with obligations. For example, children have the right to be educated in a style that involves science (this is the parents' obligation), and likewise children have the obligation to pray for their parents. Children are also obliged to publish the work of their father if he dies before he is able to do so. According to Tahtawi, after the death of their parents, children are obliged to give money to the poor and the disabled on their behalf. He also claims that boys and girls have the right to decide what they want to study, as long as boys learn swimming, archery, and horseback-riding and girls learn reading, knitting, and religion (Tahtawi, *Manahij*, pp. 60, 61, and 65). In advice manuals for children, the word "rights" does not exist, although the word "duty" often appears. These manuals claim that children's duties include obeying their parents and helping in the house. Examples of such manuals include Salih, *Kitab ʿallimu al-atfal* (1894) and al-Shaykh Husn Afandi Tawfiq, *Kitab hidayat al-atfal* (Cairo: Ministry of Information, 1924).

4. At that time children's rights as we know them today did not exist in Egypt, or globally. My approach to accessing children's rights in Egyptian history through the lens of concepts is similar to that taken by historians of human rights in tracing the origins of human rights. The idea of human rights itself has ancient origins associated with religion and morality, as well as with the practice of government. It was articulated most dramatically as the prime goal of the French Revolution, and also the American Revolution. Yet it took another 150 years or so for human rights to be acknowledged on an international level. See Stephen James, "The Origins of Universal Human Rights: An Evaluation" (PhD dissertation, Princeton University, 2005); and Lynn Hunt, *Inventing Human Rights: A History* (New York: W. W. Norton & Company, 2007).

5. The first historians of childhood in the West presented the idea that western children had been invisible in the past (that is to say, the concept of childhood did not always exist), and that society progressed toward an enlightened present in which children obtained their rights. In this version of history, a horrific past (characterized by child labor, for example) is presented as a counterpoint to the large amount of attention paid by twentieth-century society to vulnerable and disadvantaged groups, such as children. Historians of childhood in the West no longer subscribe to this vision of the past, and instead claim that the concept of childhood has always existed, but in different forms and with different ideologies of care and dependency, which were caused in large part by poverty. As the first historical account of childhood in modern Egypt, this book attempts to avoid making the mistake that the first historians of childhood in the West made, and does not claim that the concept of childhood develops in stages toward an enlightened end.

6. Stearns, *Childhood in World History*, p. 71.
7. In 1910, about 3.4 percent of the state budget was spent on public education and 90 percent of pupils in elementary schools were boys (Goldberg, *Trade*, p. 157). Public expenditure on education was dismally low under the British, and even after independence most Egyptian children only attended school for two to three years and only for half a day at a time, to leave them available for work (Goldberg, *Trade*, pp. 66 and 157). By 1955, only 9 percent of the total child population were in school (ILO, *Labour Survey of North Africa*, p. 25).
8. It could also be speculated that fear of western concepts of modern childhood, yet longing to have all that the West has to offer in terms of opportunities for children, continues to influence decisions made about children's rights today.
9. Sharon Stephens, "Introduction: Children and the Politics of Culture in 'Late Capitalism'," in Sharon Stephens (Ed.), *Children and the Politics of Culture* (Princeton, NJ: Princeton University Press, 1995), p. 18.

Bibliography

Primary sources

Autobiographies

Aflatun, Inji, *Mudhakkirat Inji Aflatun*, Kuwait: Dar Suʿad al-Sabah, 1993.

Ahmed, Leila, *A Border Passage: From Cairo to America – A Woman's Journey*, New York: Farrar, Straus and Giroux, 1999.

Amin, Ahmad, *Hayati*, Cairo: Maktabat al-Usra, 2003 (1950).

Anis, ʿAbd al-Azim, *Dhikrayat min Hayati*, Cairo: Dar al-Hilal, 2002.

Fathy, Hassan, *Architecture for the Poor*, Cairo: American University in Cairo Press, 1989.

al-Hakim, Tawfiq, *The Prison of Life: An Autobiographical Essay*, trans. by Pierre Cachia, Cairo: American University in Cairo Press, 1997.

al-Hakim, Tawfiq, *Sijn al-ʿumr*, Cairo: Dar al-Shuruq, 2003.

Haqqi, Yahya, *Khalliha ʿala Allah*, Cairo: Nahdat Misr, 2008.

Haykal, Muhammad Husayn, *Fi awqat al-faragh*, Cairo: Maktabat al-Nahda al-Misriyya, 1968.

Husayn, Taha, *The Days*, trans. by E. H. Paxton, Hilary Wayment, and Kenneth Cragg, Cairo: American University in Cairo Press, 1997.

Husayn, Taha, *al-Ayyam*, Cairo: Al-Ahram Center, 2004.

Idris, Yusuf, *Jabarti al-sittinat*, Cairo: Maktabat Misr, 1983.

Mahfuz, Najib, *Asdaʾ al-sira al-dhatiyya*, Cairo: Maktabat Misr, 1995.

Musa, Nabawiya, *Tarikhi bi-qalami*, Cairo: Multaqa al-Marʾa wa-l-Dhakira, 1999.

Musa, Salamah, *Tarbiyat Salamah Musa*, Cairo: Muʾassasat al-Khanji, 1958.

al-Naqqash, Raja, *Najib Mahfuz: Safahat min mudhakkiratihi wa-adwaʾ jadida ʿala adabihi wa-hayatihi*, Cairo: Al-Ahram Center, 1998.

Qutb, Sayyid, *Tifl min al-qarya*, Cairo: Maktabat Misr, 1945.

Qutb, Sayyid, *A Child from the Village*, trans. by John Calvert and William Shepard, New York: Syracuse University Press, 2004.

Rabiʿi, Mahmud, *Fi al-khamsin ʿaraftu tariqi: Sira dhatiyya*, Cairo: Dar Gharib, 2000.

Rida, Jalila, *Safahat min hayati*, Cairo: Dar al-Hilal, 1986.

Rushdi, Fatima, *Fatima Rushdi baina al-hubb wa-l-fann*, Cairo: Matbaʿat Saʿdi wa Shandi, 1971.

al-Saʿdawi, Nawal, *Awraqi: Hayati*, Cairo: Maktabat Madbouly, 2005.

Shaʿrawi, Huda, *Mudhakkirat Huda Shaʿrawi, raʾidat al-marʾa al-ʿarabiyya al-haditha*, Cairo: Dar al-Hilal, 1981.

al-Shatiʾ, Bint (ʿAʾisha ʿAbd al-Rahman), *ʿAla al-jisr baina al-haya wa-l-maut: Sira dhatiyya*, Cairo: Maktabat al-Usra, 1999 (1966).

Tanahi, Tahir, *Mudhakkirat al-Imam Muhammad ʿAbdu*, Cairo: Dar al-Hilal, n.d.

Taymuriyya, ʿAʾisha Ismat, *Nata ʿij al-ahwal fi al-aqwal wa-l-afʿal*, Cairo: Matbaʿat Muhammad Afandi Mustafa, 1888.

Zayyat, Latifa, *Hamlat taftish: Awraq shakhsiyya*, Cairo: Dar al-Hilal, 1992.

Zayyat, Latifa, *The Search: Personal Papers*, London: Quartet Books, 1996.

Children's magazines

al-Atfal, 13 April–4 July 1936.

al-Hadiqa wa-l-manzil, 10 May 1937.

al-Musawwar, 19 July 1935.

al-Tarbiya, 1 February–1 July 1905.

al-Ustadh, 24 August–9 May 1892.

Baba Sadiq, 18 October 1934–December 1935.

Bulbul, 19 December 1943.

Samir al-Talib, 13 November 1924.

Samir al-Tilmidh, May 1933–May 1934 and January 1936–February 1938.

Waladi, 18 February–11 March 1937.

Children's books

al-Harawi, Muhammad, *al-Tifl al-jadid*, 1924 and 1931.

al-Harawi, Muhammad, *Samir al-atfal*, Cairo: Dar al-Kutub, 1924.

Kilani, Kamil, *Baba ʿAbdallah*, Cairo: Matbaʿat al-Maʿrifa, 1942.

Kilani, Kamil, *Bisat al-rih*, Cairo: Matbaʿat al-ʿAsriya, 1936.

Kilani, Kamil, *al-Malik Madas*, Cairo: Matbaʿat al-Maʿrifa, 1935.

Kilani, Kamil, *al-Malik al-Najjar*, Cairo: Matbaʿat al-Maʿrifa, 1935.

ʿKilani, Kamil, *Qisas Shiksbir li-l-atfal*, Cairo: Matbaʿat al-Maʿrifa, 1937.

Kilani, Kamil, *al-ʿUlba al-mashur*, Cairo: Matbaʿat al-Maʿrifa, 1935.

I purchased the following undated reprints of books by Kamil Kilani in the Kamil Kilani Bookshop in downtown Cairo, which is now run by his son (who is also a children's book author).

Kilani, Kamil, *Abu Kharbush*, Cairo: Matbaʿat Kilani.

Kilani, Kamil, *ʿAduw al-maʿiz*, Cairo: Matbaʿat Kilani.

Kilani, Kamil, *Ahlam Besbesa*, Cairo: Matbaʿat Kilani.

Kilani, Kamil, *al-Amir Mishmish*, Cairo: Matbaʿat Kilani.

Kilani, Kamil, *al-Arnab wa-l-sayyad*, Cairo: Matbaʿat Kilani.

Kilani, Kamil, *al-Dik al-zarif*, Cairo: Matbaʿat Kilani.

Kilani, Kamil, *Dimna al-makar*, Cairo: Matbaʿat Kilani.

Kilani, Kamil, *Narada*, Cairo: Matbaʿat Kilani.

Kilani, Kamil, *Safrut al-Hattab*, Cairo: Matbaʿat Kilani.

Kilani, Kamil, *Shamsun al-Jabbar*, Cairo: Matbaʿat Kilani.

Kilani, Kamil, *Shanth wa Sidh*, Cairo: Matbaʿat Kilani.

Kilani, Kamil, *al-Tajir Marmar*, Cairo: Matbaʿat Kilani.

Salih, Ahmad Afandi, *Kitab ʿallimu al-atfal ma yafʿalunahu wa-hum rijal*, Cairo: Al-Matbaʿa al-Amira, 1894.

Tawfiq, al-Shaykh Husn Afandi, *Kitab hidayat al-atfal*, Cairo: Ministry of Information, 1924.

Intellectual discourse

ʿAbduh, Muhammad, *al-Islam wa-l-radd ʿala muntaqidihi*, Cairo: Al-Maktaba al-Tijariyya al-Kubra, 1928.

ʿAbduh, Muhammad, *al-Islam wa-l-marʾa*, Cairo: Al-Qahira li-l-Thaqafa al-ʿArabiyya, 1975.

al-Afghani, Jamal al-Din, *al-Aʿmal al-kamila*, Cairo: Dar al-Katib al-ʿArabi, 1968.

Amin, Qasim, *Kalimat*, Cairo: Matbaʿat al-Jarida, 1908.

Amin, Qasim, *The Liberation of Women; and, The New Woman: Two Documents in the History of Egyptian Feminism*, trans. by Samiha Sidhom Peterson, Cairo: American University in Cairo Press, 2000 [1899 and 1900, respectively].

al-Hadidi, ʿAli, *ʿAbdallah al-Nadim: Khatib al-wataniya*, Cairo: Maktabat Misr, 1961.

Husayn, Taha, *Mustaqbal al-thaqafa fi Misr*, Cairo: Matbaʿat al-Maʿarif wa-Maktabatuha, 1938.

Musa, Salamah, *al-Shakhsiya al-najiʿa: Kitab li-l-shabab*, Cairo: Salamah Musa li-l-Nashr wa-l-Tawziʿ, 1965.

al-Shatiʾ, Bint (ʿAʾisha ʿAbd al-Rahman), *Qadiyat al-fallah*, Maktabat al-Nahda al-Misriyya, 1939.

al-Tahtawi, Rifaʿa Rafiʿ, *Manahij al-albab al-misriyya fi mabahij al-adab al-ʿasriyya*, Cairo: Supreme Council for Culture, 2002 (1912).

al-Tahtawi, Rifaʿa Rafiʿ, *al-Murshid al-amin li-l-banat wa-l-banin*, Cairo: Majlis al-Aʿla li-l-Thaqafa, 2002.

Archives and reports

House of Commons Parliamentary Papers, London

"Reports by Sir H. Drummond Wolff on the Administration of Egypt," 1887.

"Copy of a Dispatch from Sir E. Baring, Enclosing a Report on the Condition of the Agricultural Population in Egypt," 1888.

"Report on the Administration and Condition of Egypt and the Progress of Reforms," 1891.

"Report on the Administration, Finances and Condition of Egypt and the Progress of Reforms," 1892.

"Report on the Finances, Administration and Condition of Egypt and the Progress of Reforms," 1894.

"Report on the Finances, Administration and Condition of Egypt and the Progress of Reforms," 1895.

"Reports by Mr Villiers Stuart Respecting the Progress of Reorganization in Egypt since the British Occupation in 1882," 1895.

"Report on the Finances, Administration and Condition of Egypt and the Progress of Reforms," 1897.

"Reports on the Finances, Administration and Condition of Egypt and the Progress of Reforms," 1898.

"Report by Her Majesty's Agent and Consul-General on the Finances, Administration and Condition of Egypt and the Sudan in 1898," 1899.

"'Reports by Her Majesty's Agent and Consul-General on the Finances, Administration and Condition of Egypt and the Sudan in 1899," 1900.

Other

Dar al-Watha'iq, Cairo, Box 9(4) *Ministry of Foreign Affairs*, File: Muʿtamarat Duwaliyya li-l-Tarbiya al-Riyadiyya.

International Labour Organization (ILO), *Act No. 14 of 1909* (Egypt), *Legislative Series*, 1926, pp. 586–588.

International Labour Organization (ILO), *Act No. 48 of 1933* (Egypt), *Legislative Series*, 1933, pp. 505–509.

International Federation of Master Cotton Spinners' and Manufacturers' Association, *Official Report of the International Cotton Congress Held in Egypt, 1927*, T. G. Evans & Co. Ltd, 1927.

Dissertations

Herrera, Linda Ann, "The Sanctity of the School: New Islamic Education and Modern Egypt," PhD dissertation, Columbia University, New York, 2000.

Jacob, Wilson C., "Working Out Egypt: Masculinity and Subject Formation between Colonial Modernity and Nationalism, 1870–1940," PhD dissertation, New York University, 2005.

Jakes, Aaron, "Extracurricular Nationalism: Youth Culture in the Age of Egypt's Parliamentary Monarchy," MPhil dissertation, Oxford University, 2005.

James, Stephen, "The Origins of Universal Human Rights: An Evaluation," PhD dissertation, Princeton University, 2005.

Miccoli, Dario, "The Jews of Modern Egypt: Schools, Family, and the Making of an Imagined Bourgeoisie, 1880s–1950s," PhD dissertation, European University Institute, Bologna, 2012.

Rooke, Tetz, "In My Childhood: A Study of Arabic Autobiography," PhD dissertation, Stockholm University, 1997.

Secondary Sources

Abdalla, Ahmed, *The Student Movement and National Politics in Egypt 1923–1973*, Cairo: American University in Cairo Press, 2008.

Abu-Lughod, Lila (Ed.), *Remaking Women: Feminism and Modernity in the Middle East*, Princeton, NJ: Princeton University Press, 1998.

Ahmed, Leila, *Women and Gender in Islam: Historical Debates of a Modern Debate*, New Haven, CT: Yale University Press, 1992.

Ali, Kamran Asdar, *Planning the Family in Egypt: New Bodies, New Selves*, Austin: University of Texas Press, 2002.

Allen, Ann Taylor, *Feminism and Motherhood in Western Europe, 1890–1970*, New York: Palgrave Macmillan, 2005.

Alloula, Malek, *The Colonial Harem*, trans. by Myrna Godzich and Wald Godzich, Minneapolis: University of Minnesota Press, 1986.

Alston, Philip (Ed.), *The Best Interests of the Child: Reconciling Culture and Human Rights*, Oxford: Clarendon Press, 1994.

Alston, Philip, Stephen Parker and John Seymour (Eds.), *Children, Rights, and the Law*, Oxford: Clarendon Press, 1992.

Altorki, Soraya, "Patriarchy and Imperialism: Father–Son and British–Egyptian Relations in Najib Mahfouz's Trilogy," in Suad Joseph (Ed.), *Intimate Selving in Arab Families: Gender, Self, and Identity*, New York: Syracuse University Press, 1999, pp. 214–234.

Alwan, Yasser, *Imagining Egypt: The Photographs of Lehnert & Landrock*, Cairo: Lehnert & Landrock, 2007.

Ammar, Hamed, *Growing Up in an Egyptian Village: Silwa, Province of Aswan*, London: Routledge & Kegan Paul Ltd, 1954.

Anderson, Benedict, *Imagined Communities*, New York: Verso, 2000.

Ariès, Philippe, *Centuries of Childhood: A Social History of Family Life*, trans. by Robert Baldick, New York: Vintage Books, 1962.

Ashour, Radwa, Ferial J. Ghazoul, and Hasna Reda-Mekdashi (Eds.), *Arab Women Writers: A Critical Reference Guide, 1873–1999*, trans. by Mandy McClure, Cairo and New York: American University in Cairo Press, 2008.

Awad, Louis, *The Literature of Ideas in Egypt, Part I*, Atlanta, GA: Scholars Press, 1986.

Ayrout, Henry Habib, *The Egyptian Peasant*, Cairo: American University in Cairo Press, 2005.

Badran, Margot, "Competing Agenda: Feminists, Islam and the State in 19th- and 20th-Century Egypt," in Deniz Kandiyoti (Ed.), *Women, Islam, and the State*, Philadelphia, PA: Temple University Press, 1991, pp. 201–236.

Badran, Margot, *Feminists, Islam, and the Nation: Gender and the Making of Modern Egypt*, Princeton, NJ: Princeton University Press, 1996.

Badran, Margot (Ed.), *Harem Years: The Memoirs of an Egyptian Feminist (1879–1924)*, New York: Feminist Press at the City University of New York, 1987.

Baena, Rosalia, "Of *Misses* and *Tuan Kechils*: Colonial Childhood Memoirs as Cultural Mediation in British Malaya," in Marlene Kadar, Linda Warley, and Jeanne Perreault (Eds.), *Ariel: A Review of International English Literature, Special Issue on Life Writing*, 39 (1–2) (2008), pp. 89–112.

Baraka, Magda, *The Egyptian Upper Class between Revolutions 1912–1952*, Beirut: Garnet Publishing Limited, 1998.

Bargach, Jamila, *Orphans of Islam: Family Abandonment and Secret Adoption in Morroco*, Lanham, MD: Rowman and Littlefield Publishers, 2002.

Baron, Beth, *Egypt as a Woman: Nationalism, Gender, and Politics*, Berkeley, CA: University of California Press, 2005.

Baron, Beth, "Orphans and Abandoned Children in Modern Egypt," in Nefissa Naguib and Inger Marie Okkenhaug (Eds.), *Interpreting Welfare in the Middle East*, Leiden and Boston, MA: Brill, 2008.

Baron, Beth, *The Orphan Scandal: Christian Missionaries and the Rise of the Muslim Brotherhood*, Stanford, CA: Stanford University Press, 2014, pp. 13–34.

Baron, Beth, *The Women's Awakening in Egypt: Culture, Society, and the Press*, New Haven, CT: Yale University Press, 1994.

Bassil, Karl, Zeina Maasri, and Akram Zaatari, *Mapping Sitting: On Portraiture and Photography*, Beirut: Arab Image Foundation, 2002.

Beinin, Joel and Zachary Lockman, *Workers on the Nile: Nationalism, Communism, Islam, and the Egyptian Working Class, 1882–1954*, Cairo: American University in Cairo Press, 1998.

Bender, Daniel, *Sweated Work, Weak Bodies: Anti-Sweatshop Campaigns and Languages of Labor*, New Brunswick, NJ: Rutgers University Press, 2004.

Berkey, Jonathan P., "Circumcision Circumscribed: Female Excision and Cultural Accommodation in the Medieval Near East," *International Journal of Middle East Studies*, 28 (1) (1996), pp. 19–38.

Berque, Jacques, *Egypt: Imperialism and Revolution*, trans. by Jean Stewart, Glasgow: Glasgow University Press, 1972.

Black, Antony, *The History of Islamic Political Thought*, New York: Routledge, 2001.

Blackman, Winifred S., *The Fellahin of Upper Egypt*, Cairo: American University in Cairo Press, 2000.

Booth, Marilyn, *May Her Likes Be Multiplied: Biography and Gender Politics in Egypt*, Berkeley and Los Angeles, CA, and London: University of California Press, 2001.

Boris, Eileen and S. J. Kleinberg, "Mothers and Other Workers: (Re)Conceiving Labor, Maternalism, and the State," *Journal of Women's History*, 15 (3) (2003), pp. 90–117.

Bourke, Joanna, *Fear: A Cultural History*, Emeryville, CA: Shoemaker Hoard, 2006.

Browning, Don S. and Marcia J. Bunge (Eds.), *Children and Childhood in World Religions*, New Brunswick, NJ: Rutgers University Press, 2009.

Burns, Elinor, *British Imperialism in Egypt*, London: Labour Research Department, 1928.

Burns, Weston, *Child Labor and Human Rights: Making Children Matter*, Boulder, CO: Lynne Rienner Publishers, 2005.

Butler, H. B., *Report on Labour Conditions in Egypt with Suggestions for Future Social Legislation*, Cairo: Government Press, 1932.

Butler, Judith and Joan W. Scott, *Feminists Theorize the Political*, New York: Routledge, 1992.

Calvert, Karin, *Children in the House*, Boston, MA: Northeastern University Press, 1993.

Chatterjee, Partha, *The Nation and its Fragments: Colonial and Post-Colonial Histories*, Princeton, NJ: Princeton University Press, 1993.

Cheah, Pheng and Jonathan Culler, *Grounds of Comparison Around the Work of Benedict Anderson*, London: Routledge, 2003.

Chevedden, Paul E., *The Photographic Heritage of the Middle East*, Malibu, CA: Undena Publications, 1981.

Clancy-Smith, Julia (Ed.), *Domesticating the Empire: Race, Gender, and Family Life in French and Dutch Colonialism*, Charlottesville: University of Virginia Press, 1998.

Coe, Richard, *When the Grass Was Taller: Autobiography and the Experience of Childhood*, New Haven, CT: Yale University Press, 1984.

Coles, Robert, *The Political Life of Children*, New York: Atlantic Monthly Press, 1986.

Cook, Daniel Thomas, "Introduction: Interrogating Symbolic Childhood," in ibid. (Ed.), *Symbolic Childhood*, New York: Peter Lang Publishing, 2002.

Cook, Daniel Thomas (Ed.), *Symbolic Childhood*, New York: Peter Lang Publishing, 2002.

Cooper, Frederick and Ann Stoler, *Tensions of Empire: Colonial Cultures in a Bourgeois World*, Berkeley: University of California Press, 1997.

Cragg, Kenneth, "Then and Now in Egypt: The Reflections of Ahmad Amin, 1886–1954," *Middle East Journal*, 9 (1) (1955), pp. 28–40.

Cunningham, Hugh, *Children and Childhood in Western Society since 1500*, Harlow and New York: Pearson Longman, 2005.

Cunningham, Hugh, "Review Essay: Histories of Childhood," *American Historical Review*, 103 (4) (1998), pp. 1195–1208.

Danielson, Virginia, *The Voice of Egypt: Umm Kulthum, Arabic Song, and Egyptian Society in the Twentieth-Century*, Chicago, IL: University of Chicago Press, 1997.

Darnton, Robert, *The Great Cat Massacre and Other Episodes in French Cultural History*, New York: Basic Books, 2009.

Davin, Anna, *Growing up Poor: Home, School and Street in London 1870–1914*, London: Rivers Oram Press, 1996.

de Coninck-Smith, Ning, Bengt Sandin, and Ellen Schrumpf, *Industrious Children: Work and Childhood in the Nordic Countries, 1850–1990*, Odense: Odense University Press, 1997.

Doumani, Beshara (Ed.), *Family History in the Middle East: Household, Property, and Gender*, New York: State University of New York Press, 2003.

Elsadda, Hoda, "Egypt," in Radwa Ashour, Ferial J. Ghazoul, and Hasna Reda-Mekdashi (Eds.), *Arab Women Writers: A Critical Reference Guide, 1873–1999*, trans. by Mandy McClure, Cairo and New York: American University in Cairo Press, 2008, pp. 98–161.

Elsadda, Hoda, "Imaging the 'New Man': Gender and Nation in Arab Literary Narratives in the Early Twentieth Century," *Journal of Middle East Women's Studies*, 3 (2) (2007), pp. 31–55.

Ener, Mine, *Managing Egypt's Poor and the Politics of Benevolence, 1800–1952*, Princeton, NJ: Princeton University Press, 2003.

Ensalaco, Mark, and Linda C. Majka (Eds.), *Children's Human Rights: Progress and Challenges for Children Worldwide*, New York: Rowman & Littlefield Publishers, 2005.

Evered, Emine, *Empire and Education under the Ottomans: Politics, Reform and Resistance from the Tanzimat to the Young Turks*, London: I. B. Tauris, 2012.

Evered, Emine Ö., "An Educational Prescription for the Sultan: Hüseyin Hilmi Paşa's Advice for the Maladies of Empire," *Middle Eastern Studies*, 43 (3) (2007), pp. 439–459.

Fahmi, Kamal, *Beyond the Victim: The Politics and Ethics of Empowering Cairo's Street Children*, Cairo: American University in Cairo Press, 2007.

Fahmy, Khaled, *All the Pasha's Men: Mehmed Ali, His Army, and the Making of Modern Egypt*, Cairo and New York: American University in Cairo Press, 2002.

Fahmy, Ziad, *Ordinary Egyptians: Creating the Modern Nation through Popular Culture*, Stanford, CA: Stanford University Press, 2011.

Fanon, Frantz, *The Wretched of the Earth*, London: Penguin Classics, 2001.

Fargues, Philippe, *Générations Arabes*, Paris: Fayard, 2001.

Fass, Paula S., *Children of a New World: Society, Culture, and Globalization*, New York: New York University Press, 2007.

Fass, Paula S., *Kidnapped: Child Abduction in America*, New York: Oxford University Press, 1997.

Faust, Drew, *The Republic of Suffering: Death and the American Civil War*, New York: Vintage Books, 2009.

Fernea, Elizabeth Warnock (Ed.), *Children in the Muslim Middle East*, Austin: University of Texas Press, 1995.

Fernea, Elizabeth Warnock (Ed.), *Remembering Childhood in the Middle East: Memoirs from a Century of Change*, Austin: University of Texas Press, 2002.

Formanek-Brunell, Miriam, *Made to Play House: Dolls and the Commercialization of American Girlhood, 1830–1930*, New Haven, CT: Yale University Press, 1993.

Fortna, Benjamin C., "Emphasizing the Islamic: Modifying the Curriculum of Late Ottoman State Schools," in François Georgeon and Klaus Kreiser (Eds.), *Enfance et jeunesse dans l'islam = Childhood and Youth in the Muslim World*, Paris: Maisonneuve et Larose, 2007.

Fortna, Benjamin C., *Imperial Classroom: Islam, the State, and Education in the Late Ottoman Empire*, Oxford: Oxford University Press, 2002, pp. 193–209.

Fortna, Benjamin C., *Learning to Read in the Late Ottoman Empire and the Early Turkish Republic*, Basingstoke and New York: Palgrave Macmillan, 2011.

Friedl, Erika, *Children of Deh Koh*, Syracuse, NY: Syracuse University Press, 1997.

Gallagher, Nancy, *Egypt's Other Wars: Epidemics and the Politics of Public Health*, Syracuse, NY: Syracuse University Press, 1990.

Gasper, Michael, *The Power of Representation*, Stanford, CA: Stanford University Press, 2009.

Gay, Peter, *Cultivation of Hatred*, New York: W. W. Norton & Company, 1993.

Gellner, Ernest, *Nations and Nationalism*, New York: Cornell University Press, 1983.

Georgeon, François and Klaus Kreiser (Eds.), *Enfance et jeunesse dans l'islam = Childhood and Youth in the Muslim World*, Paris: Maisonneuve et Larose.

Gershoni, Israel and James Jankowski, *Egypt, Islam and the Arabs*, New York: Oxford University Press, 1987.

Gershoni, Israel and James Jankowski, *Redefining the Egyptian Nation, 1930–1945*, London: Cambridge University Press, 1995.

Gil'adi, Avner, *Children of Islam: Concepts of Childhood in Medieval Muslim Society*, New York: St. Martin's Press, 1992.

Goldberg, Ellis, *Trade, Reputation, and Child Labor in Twentieth-Century Egypt*, New York: Palgrave Macmillan, 2004.

Goldschmidt, Arthur, Amy J. Johnson, and Barak A. Salmoni (Eds.), *Re-Envisioning Egypt 1919–1952*, Cairo and New York: American University in Cairo Press, 2005.

Governorate du Caire, *Rapport Détaillé sur les Colonies de Vacances de 1933*, Cairo (Bulaq): Imprimerie Nationale, 1934 (in Arabic and French).

Graham-Brown, Sarah, *Images of Women: The Portrayal of Women in the Photography of the Middle East*, New York: Columbia University Press, 1988.

Granqvist, Hilma, *Birth and Childhood among the Arabs: Studies in a Muhammadan Village in Palestine*, Finland: Ekenas, 1947.

Granqvist, Hilma, *Child Problems among the Arabs: Studies in a Muhammadan Village in Palestine*, Finland: Ekenas, 1950.

Greenberg, Ela, "Educating Muslim Girls in Mandatory Jerusalem," *International Journal of Middle East Studies*, 36 (1) (2004), pp. 1–19.

Gregg, Gary, *The Middle East: A Cultural Psychology*, New York: Oxford University Press, 2005.

Grier, Beverly Carolease, *Invisible Hands: Child Labor and the State in Colonial Zimbabwe*, Portsmouth, NH: Heinemann, 2006.

Grigsby, Darcy Grimaldo, "Rumor, Contagion, and Colonization in Gros's Plague-Stricken of Jaffa (1804)," *Representations*, 51 (Summer) (1995), pp. 1–46.

Guha, Ranajit and Gayatri Chakravorty Spivak, *Selected Subaltern Studies*, London: Oxford University Press, 1988.

Gupta, Akhil, "Reliving Childhood? The Temporality of Childhood and Narratives of Reincarnation," *Ethos*, 67 (1) 2002, pp. 33–55.

Guth, Stephen, "Why Novels – Not Autobiographies? An Essay in the Analysis of a Historical Development," in Robin Ostle, Ed de Moor, and Stefan Wild (Eds.), *Writing the Self: Autobiographical Writing in Modern Arabic Literature*, London: Saqi Press, 1998, pp. 139–147.

Gutman, Marta and Ning de Coninck-Smith (Ed.), *Designing Modern Childhoods: History, Space, and the Material Culture of Children*, New Brunswick, NJ: Rutgers University Press, 2008.

Hamamsy, C. Soliman, *Zamalek: The Changing Life of a Cairo Elite, 1850–1945*, Cairo: American University in Cairo Press, 2005.

Hamdan, Jamal, *Shakhsiyat Misr: Dirasa fi ʿAbqariyat al-Makan*, Vol. 4, Cairo: Dar al-Hilal, 1995.

Hatem, Mervat, "ʿAʾisha Taymur's Tears and the Critique of the Modernist and the Feminist Discourses on Nineteenth-Century Egypt," in Lila Abu-Lughod (Ed.), *Remaking Women: Feminism and Modernity in the Middle East*, Princeton, NJ: Princeton University Press, 1998, pp. 73–87.

Hatem, Mervat F., "The Microdynamics of Patriarchal Change in Egypt and the Development of an Alternative Discourse on Mother–Daughter Relations:

The Case of ʿAʾisha Taymur," in Suad Joseph (Ed.), *Intimate Selving in Arab Families: Gender, Self, and Identity*, New York: Syracuse University Press, 1999, pp. 101–208.

Haykal, Muhammad Husayn, *The Life of Muhammad*, trans. by Ismaʿil Ragi al-Faruqi, Indianapolis, IN: North American Trust Publications, *c.*1976.

Hecht, Tobias (Ed.), *Minor Omissions: Children in Latin American History and Society*, Madison: University of Wisconsin Press, 2002.

Helgren, Jennifer and Colleen Vasconcellos (Eds.), *Girlhood: A Global History*, New Brunswick, NJ, and London: Rutgers University Press, 2010.

Hendrick, Harry, "Periods of History: Childhood and Child Work, *c.*1800– Present," in Hugh Hindman (Ed.), *The World of Child Labor: An Historical and Regional Survey*, New York: M. E. Sharpe, 2009.

Herrera, Linda Ann, "'The Soul of a Nation': ʿAbdallah Nadim and Educational Reform in Egypt (1845–1896)," *Mediterranean Journal of Educational Studies*, 7 (1) (2002), pp. 1–24.

Heywood, Colin, *A History of Childhood: Children and Childhood in the West from Medieval to Modern Times*, Cambridge: Polity, and Malden, MA: Blackwell, 2001.

Hindman, Hugh D. (Ed.), *The World of Child Labor: An Historical and Regional Survey*, New York: M. E. Sharpe, 2009.

Hobsbawm, E. J., *Nations and Nationalism since 1780*, Cambridge: Cambridge University Press, 1993.

Hourani, Albert, *Arabic Thought in the Liberal Age, 1798–1939*, London: Oxford University Press, 1962.

Howard, Martin, *Napoleon's Doctors*, Stroud: Spellmount, 2006.

Humphries, Jane, *Childhood and Child Labour in the British Industrial Revolution*, Cambridge: Cambridge University Press, 2010.

Hunt, Lynn, *Inventing Human Rights: A History*, New York: W. W. Norton & Co., 2007.

Illick, Joseph, *American Childhoods*, Philadelphia: University of Pennsylvania Press, 2002.

International Labour Organization (ILO), *Labour Survey of North Africa*, Geneva: International Labour Organization, 1960.

Jacob, Wilson Chacko, *Working Out Egypt: Effendi Masculinity and Subject Formation in Colonial Modernity, 1870–1940*, Durham, NC: Duke University Press, 2011.

James, Allison and Alan Prout (Eds.), *Constructing and Reconstructing Childhood: Contemporary Issues in the Sociological Study of Childhood*, London: Routledge, 1997.

James, Allison, Chris Jenks, and Alan Prout (Eds.), *Theorizing Childhood*, New York: Teacher's College Press, 1998.

Jameson, Frederic, *Postmodernism or the Cultural Logic of Late Capitalism*, Durham, NC: Duke University Press, 2005.

Jankowski, James, *Egypt's Young Rebels: 'Young Egypt', 1933–1952*, Stanford, CA: Hoover Institution Press, 1975.

Jenks, Chris, *Childhood*, London and New York: Routledge, 2005.

Jones, Mark A., *Children as Treasures: Childhood and the Middle Class in Early Twentieth-Century Japan*, Cambridge, MA, and London: Harvard University Press, 2010.

Joseph, Suad (Ed.), *Encyclopedia of Women and Islamic Cultures, Vol. 4: Economics, Education, Mobility and Space*, Leiden: Koninklijke Brill NV, 2007.

Joseph, Suad (Ed.), *Intimate Selving in Arab Families: Gender, Self, and Identity*, New York: Syracuse University Press, 1999.

Joseph, Suad, "Introduction: Theories and Dynamics of Gender, Self, and Identity in Arab Families," in ibid. (Ed.), *Intimate Selving in Arab Families: Gender, Self, and Identity*, New York: Syracuse University Press, 1999 , pp.1–17.

Kandiyoti, Deniz, *Women, Islam, and the State*, Philadelphia, PA: Temple University Press, 1991.

Kashani-Sabet, Firoozeh, *Conceiving Citizens: Women and the Politics of Motherhood in Iran*, Oxford: Oxford University Press, 2011.

Keddie, Nikki R., "Women in the Limelight: Some Recent Books on Middle Eastern Women's History since 1800," *International Journal of Middle East Studies*, 34 (3) (2002), pp. 553–573.

Kelly, Catriona, "Thank You for the Wonderful Book: Soviet Child Readers and the Management of Children's Reading, 1950–75," *Kritika: Explorations in Russian and Eurasian History*, 6 (4) (2005), pp. 717–753.

Kessler-Harris, Alice, *In Pursuit of Equity: Women, Men, and the Quest for Economic Citizenship in 20th-Century America*, Oxford: Oxford University Press, 2001.

Kholoussy, Hanan, *For Better, For Worse: The Marriage Crisis that Made Modern Egypt*, Cairo: American University in Cairo Press, 2010.

Kingston, Rebecca, *Public Passion: Rethinking the Grounds for Political Justice*, Montreal: McGill-Queen's University Press, 2011.

Kinney, Anne Behnke, *Chinese Views of Childhood*, Honolulu, HI: University of Hawaii Press, 1995.

Kozma, Liat, "Girls, Labor, and Sex in Precolonial Egypt, 1850–1882," in Jennifer Helgren and Colleen A. Vasconcellos (Eds.), *Girlhood: A Global History*, Rutgers Series in Childhood Studies, New Brunswick, NJ: Rutgers University Press, 2010 , pp. 344–362.

Kupferschmidt, Uri M., "The Social History of the Sewing Machine in the Middle East," *Die Welt des Islams*, New Series, 44 (2) (2004), pp. 195–213.

Kupferschmidt, Uri M., "Who Needed Department Stores in Egypt? From Orosdi-Back to Omar Effendi," *Middle Eastern Studies*, 43 (2) (2007), pp. 175–192.

Lane, Edward, *An Account of the Manners and Customs of the Modern Egyptians*, London: Darf Publishers, 1986.

Langhamer, Claire, *Women's Leisure in England, 1920–60*, Manchester: Manchester University Press, 2000.

Le Feuvre, Lisa and Akram Zaatari (Eds.), *Hashem El Madani: Studio Practices*, Beirut: Arab Image Foundation, 2004.

Lejeune, Philippe, *On Autobiography*, trans. by Katherine M. Leary, Minneapolis: University of Minnesota Press, 1989.

Libal, Kathryn, "The Children's Protection Society: Nationalizing Child Welfare in Early Republican Turkey," *New Perspectives on Turkey*, 23 (2000), pp. 53–78.

Libal, Kathryn, "The Robust Child: Discourses on Childhood and Modernity in Early Republican Turkey," in D. T. Cook (Ed.), *Symbolic Childhood*, New York: Peter Lang, 2002.

Long, Taylor, "Political Parenting in Colonial Lebanon," *Journal of the History of Childhood and Youth*, 4 (2) (2011), pp. 257–281.

Lopez, Shaun, "Football as National Allegory: *Al-Ahram* and the Olympics in 1920s Egypt," *History Compass*, 7 (1) (2009), pp. 282–305.

Lüdtke, Alf, *The History of Everyday Life: Reconstructing Historical Experiences and Ways of Life*, trans. by William Templer, Princeton, NJ: Princeton University Press, 1993.

Maghraoui, Abdeslam M., *Liberalism without Democracy: Nationhood and Citizenship in Egypt, 1922–1936*, Durham, NC: Duke University Press, 2006.

Makdisi, Ussama, "Ottoman Orientalism," *American Historical Review*, 107 (3) (2002), pp. 768–796.

Malti-Douglas, Fedwa, *Blindness and Autobiography:* Al-Ayyam *of Taha Husayn*, Princeton, NJ: Princeton University Press, 1988.

Marcus, Leonard, *Minders of Make-Believe: Idealists, Entrepreneurs, and the Shaping of American Children's Literature*, New York: Houghton Mifflin, 2009.

Marshal, Dominique, "The Construction of Children as an Object of International Relations: The Declaration of Children's Rights and the Child Welfare Committee of the League of Nations, 1900–1924," *International Journal of Children's Rights*, 7 (1999), pp. 103–147.

Maynes, Mary J., Jennifer L. Pierce, and Barbara Laslett, *Telling Stories: The Use of Personal Narratives in the Social Sciences and History*, Ithaca, NY: Cornell University Press, 2008.

Maynes, Mary Jo, Brigitte Soland, and Christina Benninghaus (Eds.), *Secret Gardens, Satanic Mills*, Bloomington: Indiana University Press, 2005.

al-Mazini, Ibrahim, '*al-Saghir wa-l-kubar*', in ibid., *Ibrahim al-Katib*, Cairo: Dar al-Taraqqi, 1931.

Meriwether, Margaret L., "Rights of Children and the Responsibilities of Women: Women as Wasis in Ottoman Aleppo, 1170–1840," in Amira El Azhary Sonbol (Ed.), *Women, the Family, and Divorce Laws in Islamic History*, 1st edn., Contemporary Issues in the Middle East, Syracuse, NY: Syracuse University Press, 1996 , pp. 219–235.

El-Messiri, Sawsan, *Ibn Al-Balad: A Concept of Egyptian Identity*, Leiden: E. J. Brill, 1978.

Milanich, Nara B., *Children of Fate: Childhood, Class and the State in Chile, 1850–1930*, Durham, NC: Duke University Press, 2009.

Millet, Bertrand, *Samir, Micky, Sindbad et les Autres: Histoire de la presse enfantine en Égypte*, Cairo: Centre d'études et de documentation économiques, juridiques et sociales (CEDEJ), 1987.

Mintz, Steven, *Huck's Raft: A History of American Childhood*, Cambridge, MA: Belknap Press of Harvard University Press, 2004.

Mitchell, Timothy, *Colonizing Egypt*, Berkeley: University of California Press, 1998.

Mitchell, Timothy, *Rule of Experts*, Berkeley: University of California Press, 2002.

Mitchell, Timothy, 'The Invention and Reinvention of the Egyptian Peasant', *International Journal of Middle East Studies*, 22 (2) (1990), pp. 129–150.

Morrison, Heidi, *Global History of Childhood Reader*, London and New York: Routledge, 2012.

Moses, A. Dirk (Ed.), *Genocide and Settler Society: Frontier Violence and Stolen Indigenous Children in Australian History*, New York: Berghahn Books, 2004.

Mower, Glenn, *The Convention on the Rights of the Child: International Law Support for Children*, Westport, CT: Greenwood Press, 1997.

Murdoch, Lydia, *Imagined Orphans: Poor Families, Child Welfare, and Contested Citizenship in London*, New Brunswick, NJ: Rutgers University Press, 2006.

Nandy, Ashis, *The Intimate Enemy: Loss and Recovery of Self under Colonialism*, New Delhi: Oxford University Press, 2011.

National Center for the Culture of the Child, *al-Mukhtarat min ashʿar Muhammad al-Harawi*, Giza: High Council for Culture, n.d.

National Center for the Culture of the Child, *Surat al-antaʿfi qisas al-atfal*, Giza: High Council for Culture, n.d.

Nelson, Cynthia and Doria Shafik, *Egyptian Feminist: A Woman Apart*, Cairo: American University in Cairo Press, 1996.

Novick, Peter, *That Noble Dream*, New York: Cambridge University Press, 1988.

al-Nowaihi, Magda M., "Resisting Silence in Arab Women's Autobiographies," *International Journal of Middle East Studies*, 33 (4) (2001), pp. 477–502.

Olney, James (Ed.), *Autobiography: Essays Theoretical and Critical*, Princeton, NJ: Princeton University Press, 1980.

Orme, Nicholas, 'The Culture of Children in Medieval England', *Past and Present*, 148 (1) (1995), pp. 48–88.

Ostle, Robin, Ed de Moor, and Stefan Wild (Eds.), *Writing the Self: Autobiographical Writing in Modern Arabic Literature*, London: Saqi Press, 1998.

Owen, Roger, *The Middle East in the World Economy*, London: I. B. Tauris, 1993.

Owen, Roger and Şevket Pamuk, *A History of Middle East Economies in the Twentieth Century*, Cambridge, MA: Harvard University Press, 1998.

Peterson, Mark Allen, *Connected in Cairo: Growing up Cosmopolitan in the Modern Middle East*, Bloomington: Indiana University Press, 2011.

Pollard, Lisa, *Families of a New World: Gender, Politics and State-Building in Global Perspective*, New York and London: Routledge Press, 2003.

Pollard, Lisa, *Nurturing the Nation: The Family Politics of Modernizing, Colonizing, and Liberating Egypt 1805–1923*, Berkeley: University of California Press, 2005.

Pollard, Lisa, "Learning Gendered Modernity: The Home, The Family and the Schoolroom in the Construction of Century Egyptian National Identity

(1885–1919)," in Amira Sonbol (Ed.), *Beyond the Exotic: Women's Histories in Islamic Societies*, Syracuse, NY: Syracuse University Press, 2005, pp. 249–269.

Pollard, Lisa, "The Habits and Customs of Modernity: State Scholarship, Foreign Travel and the Construction of New Egyptian Nationalism," *Arab Studies Journal*, 2 (Fall) (1999)/(Spring) (2000), pp. 52–74.

Portelli, Alessandro. *The Death of Luigi Trastulli and other Stories: Form and Meaning in Oral History*. Albany, New York: State University of New York Press, 1991.

Poslaniec, Christian, *Des Livres d'enfants à la littérature de jeunesse*, Paris: Gallimard/Bibliothèque nationale de France, 2008.

Pritchett, Henry S., *Observations in Egypt, Palestine, and Greece: A Report*, New York: Carnegie Endowment for International Peace, Division of Intercourse and Education, 1926.

Reddy, William, *The Navigation of Feeling: A Framework for the History of Emotions*, Berkeley, Cambridge: Cambridge University Press, 2001.

Reed, Don, *Whose Pharaohs? Archaeology, Museums, and Egyptian National Identity from Napoleon to World War I*, Berkeley and Los Angeles: University of California Press, 2003.

Reynolds, Dwight (Ed.), *Interpreting the Self: Autobiography in the Arabic Literary Tradition*, Berkeley: University of California Press, 2001.

Richardson, Kristina, "Singing Slave Girls (Qiyan) of the ʿAbbasid Court in the Ninth and Tenth Centuries," in Gwyn Campbell, Suzanne Miers, and Joseph C. Miller (Eds.), *Children in Slavery through the Ages*, Athens: Ohio University Press, 2009 , pp. 105–118.

Ringer, Monica, *Education, Religion, and the Discourse of Multiple Reforms in Qajar Iran*, Costa Mesa, CA: Mazda, 2001.

Roded, Ruth, "Bint al-Shati's *Wives of the Prophet*: Feminist or Feminine?," *British Journal of Middle Eastern Studies*, 33 (1) (2006), pp. 51–66.

Rogan, Eugene, *Outside In: On the Margins of the Modern Middle East*, London and New York: I. B. Tauris, 2002.

Rooke, Tetz, "The Arabic Autobiography of Childhood," in Robin Ostle, Ed de Moor, and Stefan Wild (Eds.), *Writing the Self: Autobiographical Writing in Modern Arabic Literature*, London: Saqi Press, 1998 , pp. 100–114.

Roper, Michael, *The Secret Battle: Emotional Survival in the Great War*, Manchester: Manchester University Press, 2009.

Rosenwein, Barbara, *Emotional Communities in the Early Middle Ages*, New York: Cornell University Press, 2007.

Rugh, Andrea, *The Family in Contemporary Egypt*, New York: Syracuse University Press, 1984.

Russell, Mona L., *Creating the New Egyptian Woman: Consumerism, Education and National Identity, 1863–1922*, New York: Palgrave Macmillan, 2004.

Russell, Mona L., "Education: Colonial: Egypt," in Suad Joseph (Ed.), *Encyclopedia of Women and Islamic Cultures*, Vol. 4: *Economics, Education, Mobility and Space*, Leiden: Koninklijke Brill NV, 2007.

Russell, Mona L., "The Use of Textbooks as a Source of History for Women," in Amira El Azhary Sonbol (Ed.), *Beyond the Exotic: Women's Histories in Islamic Societies*, Syracuse, NY: Syracuse University Press, 2005, pp. 270–294.

Ryzvoa, Lucie, "Egyptianizing Modernity through the 'New Effendiya': Social and Cultural Constructions of the Middle Class in Egypt under the Monarchy," in Arthur Goldschmidt, Amy J. Johnson, and Barak A. Salmoni (Eds.), *Re-Envisioning Egypt, 1919–1952*, Cairo and New York: American University in Cairo Press, 2005 , pp. 124–163.

Sachsenmaier, Dominic and Jens Riedel (Eds.), *Reflections on Multiple Modernities*, London: Brill, 2002.

Safford, Philip and Elizabeth Safford, *A History of Childhood and Disability*, New York: Teacher's College Press, 1996.

Salmoni, Barak A., "Historical Consciousness for Modern Citizenship: Egyptian Schooling and the Lessons of History during the Constitutional Monarchy," in Arthur Goldschmidt, Amy J. Johnson, and Barak A. Salmoni (Eds.), *Re-Envisioning Egypt, 1919–1952*, Cairo and New York: American University in Cairo, 2005 , pp. 164–193.

Scott, James Harry, *The Law Affecting Foreigners in Egypt: As the Result of the Capitulations, with an Account of their Origin and Development*, Edinburgh: W. Green and Sons, 1908.

Seth, Sanjay, *Subject Lessons: The Western Education of Colonial India*, Durham, NC, and London: Duke University Press, 2007.

Shafik, Viola, *Popular Egyptian Cinema*, Cairo: American University in Cairo Press, 2006.

Shahar, Shulamith, *Childhood in the Middle Ages*, London and New York: Routledge, 1990.

El Shakry, Omnia, "Schooled Mothers and Structured Play: Child-Rearing in Turn-of-the-Century Egypt," in Lila Abu-Lughod (Ed.), *Remaking Women: Feminism and Modernity in the Middle East*, Princeton, NJ: Princeton University Press, 1998 , pp. 126–170.

El Shakry, Omnia, *The Great Social Laboratory: Subjects of Knowledge in Colonial and Postcolonial Egypt*, Stanford, CA: Stanford University Press, 2007.

El Shakry, Omnia, "Youth as Peril and Promise: The Emergence of Adolescent Psychology in Postwar Egypt," *International Journal of Middle East Studies*, 43 (4) (2011), pp. 591–610.

Shechter, Relli (Ed.), *Transitions in Domestic Consumption and Family Life in the Modern Middle East: Houses in Motion*, New York: Palgrave Macmillan, 2003.

Shechter, Relli, "Reading Advertisements in a Colonial/Developing Context: Cigarette Advertising and Identity Politics in Egypt, *c.*1919–1939," *Journal of Social History*, 3 (2) (2005), pp. 483–503.

Sheehi, Stephen, "A Social History of Early Arab Photography," *International Journal of Middle East Studies*, 39 (2) (2007), pp. 177–208.

Smith, Charles D., *Islam and the Search for Social Order in Modern Egypt: A Biography of Muhammad Husayn Haykal*, Albany: State University of New York Press, 1983.

Smith, Sidonie and Julia Watson (Eds.), *Women, Autobiography, Theory: A Reader*, Madison: University of Wisconsin Press, 1998.

Smith, Sidonie and Julia Watson, *Reading Autobiography: A Guide for Interpreting Life Narratives*, Minneapolis: University of Minnesota Press, 2010.

Somel, Selçuk Akşin, *The Modernization of Public Education in the Ottoman Empire, 1839–1908*, Leiden: Brill Academic Publishers, 2001.

Stearns, Peter N., *Childhood in World History*, New York and London: Routledge, 2006 and 2011.

Stearns, Peter N., "Child Labor in the Industrial Revolution," in Hugh D. Hindman (Ed.), *The World of Child Labor: An Historical and Regional Survey*, New York: M. E. Sharpe, 2009, pp. 38–44.

Stearns, Peter N., *Growing Up: The History of Childhood in a Global Context*, Waco, TX: Baylor University Press, 2005.

Stearns, Peter N., *Schools and Students in Industrial Society: Japan and the West, 1870–1940*, Boston, MA: Bedford Books, 1998.

Stephens, Sharon (Ed.), *Children and the Politics of Culture*, Princeton, NJ: Princeton University Press, 1995.

Stockdale, Nancy, "Palestinian Girls and the British Missionary Enterprise," in Jennifer Helgren and Colleen A. Vasconcellos (Eds.), *Girlhood: A Global History*, Rutgers Series in Childhood Studies, New Brunswick, NJ: Rutgers University Press, 2010 , pp. 217–233.

Summers, Carol, *Colonial Lessons: Africans' Education in Southern Rhodesia, 1918–1940*, Portsmouth, NH: Heinemann, 2002.

Tanaka, Stefan, *New Times in Modern Japan*, Princeton, NJ: Princeton University Press, 2006.

The Modern Girl Around the World Research Group (Eds.), *The Modern Girl Around the World: Consumption, Modernity, and Globalization*, Durham, NC: Duke University Press, 2008.

Thompson, E. P., *Customs in Common*, New York: New Press, 1991.

Tucker, Judith, *Women in Nineteenth-Century Egypt*, Cambridge and New York: Cambridge University Press, 1985.

Uno, Kathleen S., *Passages to Modernity: Motherhood, Childhood, and Social Reform in Early Twentieth-Century Japan*, Honolulu: University of Hawai'i Press, 1999.

Veeser, Aram H. (Ed.), *The New Historicism*, New York: Routledge, 1989.

Waksler, Frances Chaput (Ed.), *Studying the Social Worlds of Children*, London: Routledge, 1991.

Watenpaugh, Keith David, *Being Modern in the Middle East: Revolution, Nationalism, Colonialism, and the Arab Middle Class*, Princeton, NJ, and Oxford: Princeton University Press, 2006.

Weiner, Myron, *The Child and the State in India and Pakistan: Child Labour and Educational Policies in Comparative Perspective*, Karachi: Oxford University Press, 1995.

Whitlock, Gillian, *The Intimate Empire: Reading Women's Autobiography*, London: Cassell, 2000.

Yılmaz, Hale, "Learning to Read (Again): The Social Experiences of Turkey's 1928 Alphabet Reform," *International Journal of Middle East Studies*, 43 (4) (2011), pp. 677–697.

Zelizer, Viviana, *Pricing the Priceless Child*, Princeton, NJ: Princeton University Press, 1994.

Zinn, Maxine Baca and Bonnie Thornton Dill, "Theorizing Difference from Multiracial Feminism," *Feminist Studies*, 22 (2), (1996), pp. 321–331.

Index

ʿAbd al-Nasser, Gamal, 4
ʿAbd al-Rahman, ʿAʾisha, 1–2, 5, 16,
    18–19, 50, 100–1, 119–21
    see also al-Shatiʾ, Bint
ʿAbd al-Rahman, Muhammad Sadiq,
    50
ʿAbduh, Muhammad, 14, 17, 36, 38
A Child from the Village, 60
adab, 6, 18, 39, 41
ʿafārīt, see evil spirits
Ahmed, Leila, 88
al-Afghani, Jamal al-Din, 34–6, 40,
    45, 80
Ali, Muhammad, 3–4, 6, 25–7, 34,
    60, 90
al-Atfal, 57, 77, 93
al-Awlad, 50
Albania, 3
al-ʿArab, Ibrahim Bek, 49
al-Banna, Hasan, 17
al-Harawi, Muhammad, 49, 53–4,
    71, 76, 79, 81–3, 86
al-Katkut, 49
al-Mazini, Ibrahim, 15
al-Nadim, Abdallah, 36, 40, 46, 92
al-Saghir wa-l-kubar, 15
al-Shatiʾ, Bint, 1–2, 68, 88, 96, 99,
    119–21
    see also ʿAbd al-Rahman, ʿAʾisha
al-Siyasa, 102
al-Tahtawi, Rifaʿa Rafiʿ, 15, 34–40,
    48–9, 78–9, 91
al-Tarbiya, 50, 89
al-ʿUlba al-mashur, 77
al-Ustadh, 40, 46, 92
Amin, Ahmad, 65–8, 101, 116–19
Amin, Qasim, 36–8, 46–7, 80, 89
Anderson, Benedict, 45
Anglo-Egyptian Treaty (1936), 4
Arab sociocultural systems, 41

Ariès, Philippe, 7–8
autobiography, 22, 99–127
    ʿAbd al-Rahman, ʿAʾisha, 119–21
    Amin, Ahmad, 116–19
    Haykal, Muhammad Husayn,
        101–4
    Husayn, Taha, 37
    Musa, Nabawiya, 101, 107–9
    Musa, Salamah, 36, 40
    Qutb, Sayyid, 60
    Shaʿrawi, Huda, 114–16
Ayrout, Henry Habib, 31, 67

Baba Sadiq, 50, 56, 58, 62–3
Baraka, Magda, 64
Baron, Beth, 24, 96–7, 116
Benninghaus, Christina, 9
Berque, Jacques, 63–4
Bint al-Nil, 49
Blackman, Winifred S., 64
Booth, Marilyn, 83, 109, 115
bourgeoisie, 44
Bourke, Joanna, 16–17, 35
Britain, 3–4, 9, 28–30, 33, 35, 113
    female education, 90
British imperial rule, 14

Cairo, 1–3, 12, 23, 50, 52, 65, 81–2,
    99, 102, 104–5, 109, 112
Chatterjee, Partha, 45, 84
childhood
    adult conceptions of, 63
    approaches, through past, 7–11
    and autobiographies, 16, 99–127
    in Britain, 29
    and colonialism, 23–42
    conceptions of, 21, 52–9, 124
    conflicts, 15
    educational opportunities, 18–19
    in Egypt, 23–42

childhood – *continued*
  and Europe, 23–42
  and historians, 16–17
  and imperial gaze, 33, 39, 42
  intellectual discourse, gendered
    analysis of, 21
  memory of, 21–2
  and Middle Ages, 7
  and Middle East, 10, 123
  model of, 17
  modernization, process of, 13–20
  modern model of, 20
  and national identity, 99–127
  nation-building, 45–7
  redefinition of, 43–61
  representations of, 5
  role of empire in, 20
  societal tendency, 9
  twentieth-century Egyptian
    history of, 6
  typical, 11–13
  western model of, 14, 17
  in western societies, 7
child labor, 25–30, 123, 126
child-rearing, 62–84
  decision-making, 67–9
  discipline, 66
  effendi, 69–75
  ethnography, 64
  independent thinking, 76–8
  learning, new ways of, 78–80
  peasant child, 80–3
  play, 64–5
  practices, 14
  teaching methods and styles, 65
children's press, 5, 11, 47–51, 53,
    71–4, 76
classroom-based learning, 46, 62–84
colonialism, reforming childhood,
    23–42
  authenticity, 34–8
  child laborers, 25–33
  and imperialism, 33–4
  morality, 38–41
Convention on the Rights of the
    Child (CRC), 9, 17, 124–5

CRC, *see* Convention on the Rights
    of the Child (CRC)
Cunningham, Hugh, 41, 48, 59, 123

Darnton, Robert, 17
decision-making, 11, 20, 67–9, 124
discipline, 8, 11–12, 64, 66, 69, 84,
    97, 123–4
Dumyat, 1–2, 88, 120

effendi, 4, 18, 21, 24, 34, 69–75,
    80–1, 83–4, 86, 91–2
Egypt
  and British, 15–16
  and childhood, 1–22
  child labor in, 25–8
  colonial domination (Britain), 33
  constructions of childhood, 3
  gender roles, 87–9
  and girls, 85–99
  intellectuals, 34
  modern history of, 124
  modernization, process of, 3–5,
    13–20
  Napoleon's adventure in, 3
  nationalist reformers, 5
  nation-building project, 44
  rental system, 26
Egyptian intelligentsia, 16
Egyptian Ministry of Interior, 31
El Shakry, Omnia, 10, 13, 24, 29,
    34–5, 38, 97
Ener, Mine, 4, 45
enlightenment, 14, 17, 20, 36, 38,
    101, 125
Europe, 4, 6–7, 9, 14–15, 20, 23–6,
    28–31, 33–6, 38, 41–2, 46–7, 59,
    69–72, 74, 78, 81, 86, 90, 108,
    112, 114, 117, 119
  and childhood, 23–42
evil spirits, 12, 64, 66, 106, 110–11,
    124

Fahmy, Khalid, 4, 45, 60, 83
Fahmy, Ziad, 83
farm labor, 31

Fass, Paula S., 8, 35
fear, 1, 12–16, 35, 60, 66, 94, 101,
    103, 106, 109, 113, 118, 120,
    124
Fernea, Elizabeth Warnock, 3, 44
Fortna, Benjamin C., 10
Free Officers' Movement, 4
free-trade treaty, 3

Gasper, Michael, 4, 24, 34, 84
gender roles, 2, 5, 87–9, 92–3, 95–8,
    121
German High Middle Ages, 8
Gershoni, Israel, 34
Gil'adi, Avner, 10
girls, 85–99
    education, 91–3
    and gender roles, 93–7
    puberty, 87
    reform for, 89–93
    schools, 90–1
Goldberg, Ellis, 28, 30
Governorate du Caire, 52

Haykal, Muhammad Husayn, 36,
    101–4, 107
Hendrick, Harry, 29
Heywood, Colin, 7
Hourani, Albert, 34
Humphries, Jane, 9, 29
Husayn, Taha, 36–7, 47, 66–7, 89,
    101, 104–7

ILO reports, 27, 30–1
imperialism, 2, 18, 24–5, 33–4, 42,
    70, 111–12, 126
intellectuals, 6, 11, 13–18, 20–2, 25,
    32, 34–6, 38–9, 41–2, 44–5,
    47–8, 52, 54, 71, 78–9, 81, 91,
    93, 97, 101–4, 106, 109, 111,
    115, 119, 124

Jacob, Wilson Chacko, 4, 24, 28,
    33, 45
Jameson, Frederic, 117
Jankowski, James, 34

Jenks, Chris, 9
jinn, 66, 110
Jones, Mark A., 71
Joseph, Suad, 41

Kelly, Catriona, 10
Key, Ellen, 126
Kholoussy, Hanan, 92
Kilani, Kamil, 48–9, 53–4, 58–9, 77,
    92
Kingston, Rebecca, 35
kuttāb, 12, 60, 65–6, 90, 118–19, 124

Lane, Edward, 67
learning, new ways of, 78–80
Libal, Kathryn, 10
Locke, John, 41
Long, Taylor, 10
Lowenthal, David, 100

madrasa, 60
Mahfouz, Naguib, 50, 67
Malti-Douglas, Fedwa, 107
Maynes, Mary J., 9
Middle Ages, 7–8, 18
middle-class identity, 4, 18, 24, 45,
    49, 63, 69–71, 73–4, 76, 78, 84,
    88, 91–2, 101–2, 107, 116
Middle East, 3, 6, 10–11, 34, 39, 61,
    66, 87, 123, 127
Milanich, Nara B., 8
Mitchell, Timothy, 45, 48
motherhood, 34, 97
Musa, Nabawiya, 94, 101, 107–9
Musa, Salamah, 36, 40, 66, 78, 91,
    101, 112–14

Nandy, Ashis, 24, 33, 113
Napoleon, 3
national identity, 22, 24, 54, 99–27
nation-building, 43–61
    children as a tool for, 45–7
    new institutions for children,
        47–52
    professionalization of childcare,
        52–9
    through the lens of age, 59–61

The New Egyptian Child, 71, 86, 89, 93, 98
The New Woman, 89
the Nile, 1, 26, 28, 63, 68, 78, 102, 112, 120

Ottoman Empire, 3, 10, 26
Ottoman Tanzimat (1839–1871), 35

The Past is a Foreign Country, 100
peasant child, 18, 25–6, 31, 80–4
"The Peasant's Anthem," 82–3
Pollard, Lisa, 4, 10, 24, 28, 33, 45
postmodernism, 8

qarīna, 110
Qur'an, 1, 12, 60, 65, 67, 79–81, 94–5, 100–1, 105–6, 118, 120
Qutb, Sayyid, 60, 65–8, 94, 101, 109–12

Rabiʿi, Mahmud, 65, 68
Rawdat al-Madaris al-Misriyya, 49
Remaking Women, 97
Remembering Childhood in the Middle East (2002), 3
Rooke, Tetz, 121
Rousseau, Jean-Jacques, 14, 41
Russell, Mona L., 35, 70, 93

Salafis, 34–5
Samir al-Tilmidh, 50–1, 53, 74, 77, 82
Satanic Mills, 9
Schultz, James A., 7
Secret Gardens, 9
secular school, 1, 3, 35, 118
Shafik, Doria, 88
Shahar, Shulamith, 7

Shaʿrawi, Huda, 13, 49, 53–4, 67, 71, 76–7, 79, 81–3, 86, 88, 95, 97, 101, 114–16
Shawqi, Ahmad, 49
shaykhs, 46–7, 60, 65–6, 78–9, 105–6, 118–19
Soland, Brigitte, 9
state schooling, 90–1
Stearns, Peter N., 17, 28, 126
Stephens, Sharon, 127
Stockdale, Nancy, 10
Suez Canal, 4
Summers, Carol, 71

Tanaka, Stefan, 115
Tarikhi bi-qalami, 107
Taymuriyya, ʿAʾisha, 96
teaching methods and styles, 65
time-honored methods, 32
trade union organization, 27
Tucker, Judith, 97

Urabi Revolt, 4, 115
urban middle class, 18, 21, 69, 71, 116

Waladi, 50–1, 74
Watenpaugh, Keith David, 70
Watson, Julia, 104, 114
welfare projects, 48, 51–2, 61
western model of childhood, 14, 17, 36, 42, 127
Whitlock, Gillian, 108
The Women's Awakening in Egypt, 97

Zaghlul, Saʿd, 4, 104
Zayyat, Latifa, 67

Printed and bound in the United States of America